Evaluation of Reference Services

Topics in *The Reference Librarian* series:

- Conflicts in Reference Services
- Personnel and Reference Services
- Archives and Reference Services
- The Reference Interview
- Online Reference Services
- The Reference Services User
- Reference Services Reviews & Publishing
- Education for Reference Services

Published:

Reference Services in the 1980s, Numbers 1/2
Reference Services Administration and Management, Number 3
Ethics and Reference Services, Number 4
Video to Online: Reference Services and the New Technology, Numbers 5/6
Reference Services for Children and Young Adults, Numbers 7/8
Reference Services and Technical Services: Interactions in Library Practice, Number 9
Library Instruction and Reference Services, Number 10
Evaluation of Reference Services, Number 11

Evaluation of Reference Services

Edited by
Bill Katz and Ruth A. Fraley
School of Library & Information Science
State University of New York at Albany

The Haworth Press
New York

Evaluation of Reference Services has also been published as *The Reference Librarian,* Number 11, Fall/Winter 1984.

The Haworth Press, Inc., 28 East 22 Street, New York, NY 10010

Library of Congress Cataloging in Publication Data
Main entry under title:

Evaluation of reference services.

    "Has also been published as The reference librarian, number 11, Fall/Winter 1984"—Verso of t.p.
    Includes bibliographical references.
    1. Reference services (Libraries)—Evaluation—Addresses, essays, lectures. I. Katz, William A., 1924-   . II. Fraley, Ruth A.
Z711.E92 1984   025.5   84-12898
ISBN 0-86656-377-6

Evaluation of Reference Services

The Reference Librarian
Number 11

CONTENTS

EVALUATING REFERENCE SOURCES

Evaluation of Reference Services

INTRODUCTION

Why We Need
to Evaluate Reference Services:
Several Answers

Bill Katz

Why a compilation of papers on evaluation of reference services? The answer is easy—evaluation is an ongoing process which requires constant attention. True, it may be the subject of much discussion, some research and considerable lack of action, but it is more and more a pressing issue. Why? Well, as the library becomes a factor in America's will to succeed in everything from business and rockets to culture, the role of the reference librarian increases in importance. One may leap the obvious need of information in foreign policy, in economics, and in the war rooms and get down to the basic needs of individuals. Now, possibly for the first time, the average layperson begins to see the librarian as a *necessary* functionary for the location of valuable information—valuable in the sense it may not just help to turn an extra dollar, or solve a research problem, but may enhance the daily pleasure of life.

The emergence of the truly professional reference librarian owes much to three related facts. First, there simply is too much data (whether it be novels or investment reports) for even the experienced layperson to cope with, much less the individual with only a passing knowledge of the field. Second, the advent of the online search and equal high costs not only demands someone able to find the data, but someone who can do it quickly and efficiently. Finally, with more and more Americans at least passing through a hall of higher education, there is an increasing respect for knowledge. The respect is pretty pragmatic, based on the sudden revelation that a wiser person may not only be wealthier, but even happier. Wed these factors and the library doors assume new, major meaning in the lives of more Americans, and particularly the ones who vote and control budgets.

3

As the librarian does become an important, necessary figure in our society, it is obvious that more than just answers are required—certainly more than a nod to the card catalog or the *Readers' Guide*. And at that point the need for evaluation is not only obvious, but downright necessary. No longer will the librarian be able to get on with a 50% batting average. The optimistic user will expect at least a 99% average, as he or she now does when consulting any professional. It is suggested by the papers in this collection that one reason librarians suffer the ignominy of low salaries and even lower community respect is that they do so badly at their work. The hope and the promise, as found in the papers marshalled here, is that evaluation is changing the librarian's poor image.

INTRODUCTION AND OVERVIEW

The news may be bad, but it is improving. This seems to be the general conclusion of those involved with the present compilation. All agree more analysis, more evaluation is needed. They see the final, desired result as better reference librarians, better use of reference materials (including online services) and certainly better results for the library users. True, there are differences, sometimes strong ones, on various methods of evaluation; but no one is willing to concede it is a useless, time-wasting process. Even the most doubtful admit to the absolute necessity of the reference professional stepping back from time to time to look at self and services.

In her overview of the literature on evaluation, Pierce shows how "critical treatments of evaluative processes have grown." She points out that there are two major approaches to evaluation—"the use of goal based internal evaluations and the application of externally established professional standards." The survey ends with the warning that while there is much that is useful on the evaluation of reference services, it is not always applied wisely and there is need for careful selection of the appropriate evaluative method.

The Masons offer suggestions too often lacking in standard studies. They note that most processes fail because they don't take into consideration the nitty gritty of service. Their article examines a broad range of factors. Moving from the positioning of the reference desks, to arrangement of materials and card catalogs, the experienced librarians then go on to methods of judging the librarians. Much more, too, is considered. Yet it all leads to their fervent conclusion that the only truly good reference section is one which says "in its own way, 'Come In!' "

Rothstein believes there is a need to convince the administration, not only the public, that reference services exists and functions effectively. He outlines several approaches which allow the "reference librarians to muster hard evidence" for those services. Along the way he upsets several accepted notions about reference evaluation, such as putting too much emphasis on measuring questions and not enough on measuring how well the librarian succeeds in "enabling the patrons to help themselves effectively."

Turning Rothstein's point of view around, Zweizig looks at evaluation from the desk of the administrator or manager. He calls for selecting a particular focus or mission, then sets down elements to be measured. He concludes with a plea for precision. He admits the process "is lengthy," but even where compromise is necessary, which is often, "the manager must nevertheless apply measurement to the service in order to inform decisions."

Another plea for precision in evaluation is sounded by Emerson who points out the absolute necessity of mutual appreciation of definitions. The value of the clear definition is shown and primary terms considered and explained. She adds the warning that "evaluation should be understood as a step in the process of planning . . . not as an independent process," and then outlines several examples of evaluative application. Each library demands separate decisions, made possible in no small way by an understanding of the *Standard.*

QUESTION, ANSWER AND LIBRARIAN

In considering how well reference questions are answered, Crowley turns to referral centers and compares the quality of answers by three services, including a commercial one. He finds no winner in his study, but suggests "the advantages of independent multiple approaches to the measurement of reference capacity."

Lancaster asks what factors are "likely to influence the probability that a factual-type question will be answered completely and correctly by a particular library." He analyzes some 10 factors and concludes that "it is little wonder that several studies have indicated that the probability of complete success in [answering questions] may not be much more than .5 to .6."

A fellow explorer in this sensitive area, Weech asks "Who's giving all those wrong answers?'' Exploring the literature, he finds there is a ''lack of a cumulative knowledge base for reference personnel evaluation,'' and then explains the variables one should consider in such evaluation. These range from education and experience to searching styles. There is exploration, too, of ''staff characteristic variables'' and online searching. Weech offers several suggestions for personnel evaluation, and particularly stresses peer evaluation.

Young examines the role of the library user in judging the worth of the reference librarian, and finds it wanting, as he does much of the literature. Like Weech, he believes it absolutely necessary to carry on such evaluation, and points out some methods he has learned from his own experience.

Adams and Judd step back from Weech and Young, suggest ''the process of goal analysis'' as a pragmatic and practical method of reference librarian evaluation. The steps are explored, and the authors conclude with a detailed analysis of how goal analysis can be applied to a particular library, e.g., the State University of New York at Oswego. Concluding remarks are on what should be done with the findings.

Given the questions, the answers and the librarians what will insure continuity, and much quality? Vavrek believes at least one answer is to be found in better education and an appreciation of basic problems which he considers. The ultimate response, though, is to accredit libraries. He concludes with a discussion of the elements which should be measured and evaluated for accreditation. Parenthetically, it should be noted that Vavrek is speaking to a larger audience than his first paragraph would suggest.

THOSE WHO ARE SERVED

Bundy and Bridgman warn about the narrowness of some ''current evaluation focus'' and point out that the first consideration is ''who is being served in terms of community elements and with regard to what kinds of information are being provided.'' They note the failure of reference-answer quality shown in numerous studies (including their own), and then turn a careful look at who benefits from the reference services. They show how the library may become more directly involved with the community. The study turns to a report of findings about who is served from some 50 public libraries. The conclusion is that there are practical methods of effecting a community change-oriented reference service. Specific steps to this end are explained.

Murfin and Bunge report on a survey instrument "designed to collect reference transaction data on computer scannable sheets." Results of the study confirm the notion that the size of the library is not as important as the services offered. Joseph explains another method which a reference library may use to "evaluate its success in using staff efficiently to serve appropriate patrons." She particularly is interested in improving such services, not to a few, but to the many; and there are precise instructions on procedures for collecting and evaluating patron data.

OTHER APPROACHES

A major question about evaluation concerns how many, if anyone, really are affected by the articles, reports and studies. Using a select group of such work, Schrader sets out to find the "impact of the research . . . on the discipline of library and information science." Using a citation study, he discovers that the impact on researchers, educators, and practitioners varies, but is less than is desirable. He asks if the problem is not one of failure of librarians to meet head on the problem of reference service accuracy. McClure, also concerned about wrong answers, suggests "applications of output measures and unobtrusive testing" to evaluate reference services. Areas where such measures can be targeted are explained, and then unobtrusive testing is considered. Strategies combining both are explained. In conclusion McClure stresses the need for "some regular assessment technique" as all important.

Shavit enters with a plea for more qualitative methods of evaluation, claims there is too much focus on the quantitative approaches. He takes exception to some of the methodology and procedures of other writers in this issue. He offers several basic qualitative techniques, ends with a plea for using both methods, and not necessarily one over the other.

EVALUATING REFERENCE SOURCES

Turning to reference sources, the paper by Pritchard is in tune with the times in that it is a combination of online searching and women's studies. Here she shows how to evaluate database content, and particularly in relation to a subject area. There is a review of the literature of database reviews, ending with a detailed study of criteria for "evaluating databases in women's studies."

Turning to just who does use databases, Kanter examines the attitudes of law librarians and lawyers to LEXIS and WESTLAW. A survey, which may be adopted for other studies, shows offices of attorneys in at least three large cities tend to prefer LEXIS. Still, no matter which system is employed, Kanter concludes law librarians have a new, important role. They are now given "added research responsibilities which significantly heighten their perception of their own professionalism."

Glunz takes a broader view and asks how online searching may be effectively evaluated, particularly when the search is delegated to a librarian. Basic steps are considered, from the interview, to formulating various review methods of the overall program. The "series of complex and intertwined elements" is explained and analyzed.

Turning to more traditional sources, and the year's outstanding reference sources, Rosswurm tells how the winners are separated from the mass of published reference works. The guidelines seem well suited for evaluation of specific reference books in many libraries, not just by the annual jury. Schmidt, too, is interested in defining and explaining reference sources and, using the mnemonic APPARATUS, offers a handy evaluative checklist. She concludes that "much of the skill of evaluation lies in deciding . . . which criteria have the highest priority."

Batt argues that reference collection policies may be of some use in evaluation, and in general reference services operation, but too many are filled with useless detail. He is "inclined to keep it simple," and explains how this may be achieved. Holt and Falk turn to another type of aid, the library skills workbook. Here they explore the various paths open to evaluation of such works, and give a working example of how such a book was written and evaluated. The conclusion: if properly done it can be "an effective teaching tool."

Finally a word of appreciation for all those who agreed to answer the invitation to write the articles in this issue. There may be no definitive answers, but there certainly are some excellent signs to help the reference librarian locate and move confidently along the road of reference service evaluation.

In Pursuit of the Possible:
Evaluating Reference Services

Sydney Pierce

Mounting concern with good management practice in libraries has brought both increased concern with the evaluation of reference services and what seems to be increasing recognition of the difficulties involved in working out valid evaluative techniques. Since Samuel Rothstein's survey of the literature in the early sixties (1964) in which he found few quantitative studies and fewer still attempts at real evaluation, the literature has grown rapidly (see Weech, 1974; Bunge, 1977; Lancaster, 1977; Klassen, 1983). Critical treatments of evaluative processes have grown with the literature. Both proponents and critics of reference evaluations criticize the model of reference services used as all too often restricted to an emphasis on the reference librarian as a processor of user-generated questions, taking an overly narrow view of both reference and library work (e.g., Monroe, 1974; Beasley, 1974; Pings, 1976; Vavrek, 1978).

Various studies note that librarians themselves tend to be resistant to evaluation (e.g., Feldman, 1974: 395; Bunge, 1977: 66; Lancaster, 1977: 106; DuMont & DuMont, 1979: 127). There is no real consensus on evaluative techniques, and much uneasiness over ultimate applications of the results of evaluations (see, for example, Vavrek, 1978, on the substitution of nonprofessional staff for professionals as an ultimate goal, a possibility seriously advanced by Kok & Pierce, 1982, among others). At the root of these problems would seem to lie a basic, and probably inevitable, clash of management and professional perspectives in evaluating services.

To some extent differences in management and professional perspectives in libraries resemble differences to be found in any bureaucratic organization between those who view the organization

---

Ms. Pierce is Research Assistant, Center for Survey Research, Institute of Social Research, Indiana University, Bloomington, IN 47405.

from the top down and those who view it from the bottom up. Managers are required to be concerned with organizational structure and general workflow. Employees' daily working lives are embedded in the everyday give and take of a localized workplace. Their immediate concerns are heavily influenced by local working conditions and by relations with those members of the organization and its clientele with whom they have regular contact. Thus management evaluations take what may seem to be an overly generalized position, and to be heavily concerned with general workflow, a criticism of many of the more quantitative approaches to library evaluation. Those performing the work, on the other hand, may be painfully aware of the conditions under which local operations are performed, but less concerned with the general picture. To some extent, one might be able to explain differences in some of the more common methods of evaluating libraries as reflections of these differing concerns.

BASIC DIFFERENCES

To this must be added basic differences in management and professional values used in the evaluation of services performed. While managers are concerned with the smooth and efficient functioning of the organization, professionals are presumably pursuing ends that lie outside the organization—that is, the welfare of their clients, and the ideals of service prevalent in the profession itself. It is probably not absolutely necessary that these points of view conflict: the sociological literature includes both convincing arguments that professionals working in bureaucratic organizations must experience conflict (e.g., Derber, 1983) and strong arguments to the contrary (see Benson, 1973). But the two value systems do not necessarily mesh harmoniously either. Much of the uneasiness surrounding the evaluation of reference services seem to be attributable to the difficulty of reconciling management and professional perspectives.

The two major approaches to library evaluation, the use of goal-based internal evaluations and the application of externally established professional standards, each stress a different point of view. Goal-based internal evaluations are a product of management theory. Such evaluations usually begin by identifying organization goals, and then seek to define operational measures that can be used in evaluating the library's success in meeting these goals (see

Bunge, 1977, for a fuller discussion of processes involved). From goal-based perspectives, the library functions as a bureaucratic organization, one composed of separate units each of which has its own part to play in furthering the goals of the larger organization. Goals are institutionally defined, set within the individual organization in response to its internal and external situation. Professionalism, based on an appeal to goals and standards established by groups external to the organization, is relevant to such evaluations only insofar as the authority structure of the local institution chooses to support professional over other organizational goals. (Fortunately, most libraries are accustomed to setting goals in professional terms. There is, however, no compelling reason for them to do so.)

Even given professional and management consensus on goals, the emphasis of goal-based evaluations on quantitative operational measures is a further source of potential conflict. Quantitative measures are raw measures of organizational output, and as such they do have their uses. Though sophisticated typologies may be used in record-keeping, quantitative evaluations ultimately reduce reference transactions to simple tallies of instances in which services were performed. Such basic counts treat librarians, users, and services as interchangeable units. This is, of course, not necessarily a bad thing, especially from a management point of view. No organization can be run efficiently without some way of predicting workload. It is as measures of the library's progress toward the achievement of professional goals that quantitative measures show their limitations. Each entry on a reference tally sheet is alike to a manager estimating workload, but represents a quite different experience from the reference librarian's point of view.

PERSPECTIVES

There may be no good way of reconciling management and professional perspectives on quantitative measures. The most commonly mentioned problem in implementing goal-based evaluations is the difficulty of deriving valid operational measures from library goal statements (see, for example, Lancaster, 1977: 4; DuMont & DuMont, 1979: 107, 111-12). Libraries define their purposes broadly, stating their objectives in terms of general contributions made by the profession to society. The resulting statements are exceeding difficult to translate into objective measures of accomplishment applicable to individual institutions. Also, the successful performance of a professional service depends in part on the professional's skill in social interaction with the client. As Pings (1976) and Vavrek (1978) point out, this is not objectively measurable, nor need the resulting benefit to the user simply consist of the provision of an answer to a question, or of any other clearly identifiable and measurable good.

Professional evaluations of service rendered to library users thus should be multi-dimensional and qualitative in nature. Goal-based evaluations seek to measure achievement of the library's service goals by reducing transactions to clear-cut quantitative units. It is perhaps for this reason that even the most positive summaries of progress made with goal-based evaluation (e.g., Bunge, 1977) acknowledge that such evaluations work well in theory, but need more thought given to measurement issues.

The use of professional standards to evaluate library services is, on the other hand, a specifically "professional" approach, offering advantages not to be found in goal-based evaluations, along with a new set of problems. Instead of treating the library as an autonomous institution which sets its own goals, evaluations based on standards treat it as a dispenser of professional services. Professional institutions external to the local organization define the nature and goals of these services and set them forth in standards which ideally represent the consensus of the profession itself. These standards define the services to be furnished to clients and the necessary preconditions (available materials, and so forth) for the provision of services at acceptable levels.

Standards tend to be measures of library "input" (materials and facilities provided) rather than of "output" (actual services performed). This is a distinction found in various treatments of reference evaluations (e.g., Monroe, 1974: 338-40; Bunge, 1977: 42; Vavrek, 1979: 337). The two terms correspond to what DuMont and DuMont (1979: 124) call workload indicators (output) as opposed to physical standards (input). As their terms suggest, goal-based evaluations, with all their flaws, tend to provide output measures, measures of workload. Standards, at least until recently, have been largely confined to input measures. If the purpose of examining reference services is to evaluate service provided to library users, then standards are unsatisfactory because they substitute measuring a library's capacity for service for evaluating of its actual performance. The distinction is an important one, for here is to be found the weakness of "professional" approaches to evaluation.

Professionals have good reason for resisting precise measures of professional work. The very complexity of professional skills (including the skills in social interaction mentioned above) make quantification of professional performance difficult. Librarians directly involved in reference services may well question the relevance of any quantitative measures to their daily working life. This phenomenon is not, of course, restricted to libraries and librarians. Of various sociological studies describing the plight of professionals in bureaucratic organizations, Freidson's *Doctoring Together* (1975) is one of the more illuminating (and entertaining) studies of the conflicts of interests and perspectives involved, well worth the reading by anyone seriously concerned with clashes of management and professional perspectives in the workplace. One of Freidson's central points is that, while professionals may recognize management's authority to impose its control over the internal workings of the organization, they yet need not view as legitimate the intrusion of management into areas touching on the definition and evaluation of professional functions. Just because managers occupy superior positions in the organizational power structure, in other words, is not reason to attribute to them the superiority in the special skills and knowledges necessary to evaluate professional work.

To a professional, only another professional (a more skilled and/or experienced one) really is capable of evaluating professional services. And professionals may resist even evaluation by experts. Only another professional is sufficiently aware of all the complexities that make professional service so difficult to evaluate, and only the professional performing the particular service for the particular client at the time is fully aware of the precise combination of variables that led to the particular choices made in providing service. Professionals therefore tend to accept other duly qualified professionals as competent until proven otherwise, and to be threatened by direct evaluations of their work. From a professional perspective, once standards laying out necessary preconditions for providing service have been met, services performed by qualified professionals must be presumed to be of good quality.

STANDARDS

If this were the most that one could say for professional standards, they would not prove particularly useful in any detailed evaluation of reference services. Indeed, most general library standards have mentioned reference services only briefly, and the recent ALA/RASD "guidelines" (American Library Association, 1979) are far too vague to serve directly as standards for evaluation (though they are a useful starting point for goal-based evaluation, an approach favored by the new RASD Evaluation of Reference and Adult Services Committee [see Bunge, 1983]). What may become a whole new approach to standards has been generating great excitement in the past ten years or so, however, based on the use of standardized definitions for library statistics. The use of such definitions permits the collection of comparable data for the first time, eventually promising libraries an opportunity to match their performance against that of other libraries in similar situations. Instead of settling for standards outlining basic resources necessary to provide adequate service, librarians can use standardized data to measure themselves against what other libraries have actually done.

These standardized measures offer a new approach to a long-standing problem in reference evaluation, deciding what to measure and how. Both the varied nature of reference work (see Rothstein, 1964: 456-67; Bunge, 1977: 41; Lancaster, 1977: 73-74; Bunge, 1983: 252; Klassen, 1983: 421-22; Lynch, 1983: 404) and difficulties in reaching consensus on definitions of what constitutes a unit of measure (see Weech, 1974: 332; Bunge, 1977: 46-47; Emerson, 1977; King, 1983: 452) have been repeatedly identified as major impediments to the successful evaluation of services. In the absence of general agreement, libraries must decide for themselves what aspects of service should be measured and what units of measure are to be used. The results are rarely directly comparable. Without standardization, the library lacks an external source of data against which to measure its own performance. With it, it is possible to make comparisons that have at least some of the advantages of both professional and management approaches.

Comparative statistics not only share some of the "professional" quality of standards, in that they are generalized, extra-library measures of performance, but also are firmly grounded in organizational realities, in that they are definitions of what has been proven to be feasible in comparable libraries. Standardized measures replace trying to set adequate levels by "guesstimate," as it were, instead measuring the library's performance according to what Kaser (1982: 9-10) has termed "the aggregate experience of the profession." They thus provide opportunity for a major advance in setting truly professional standards. They are, however, quantitative measures, and as such they are still flawed from a professional point of view. They still quantify services in overly general terms, failing to deal with the interpersonal and situational complexities involved in the provision of professional services.

To get at the actual quality of service provided in these terms to individual library users, libraries have often turned to measures of patron satisfaction. This approach still has its defenders, who remind would-be evaluators that the social and psychological issues in interpersonal transactions at the reference desk are exceedingly complex, and librarian judgments of what constitutes a satisfactory answer to a question may be based on criteria which are largely irrelevant to the person asking it (D'Elia & Walsh, 1983; Isaacson, 1983; Vathis, 1983). As D'Elia and Walsh (1983: 111) point out, even the public library performance measures include measures of patron satisfaction as a necessary complement to other measures. Here again, there may be some divergence in management and professional perspectives on the degree of emphasis that should be given to patron satisfaction. From a management point of view, client satisfaction is exceedingly important: unsatisfied clients may choose to go elsewhere for service.

QUESTIONABLE

From a professional point of view, however, client satisfaction is a highly questionable indicator of the quality of service. If even managers (including managers with professional qualifications) are not satisfactory evaluators of professional work, untrained laypeople are wholly unacceptable. Critics of patron satisfaction measures frequently point out that library users are not particularly good evaluators of reference services (Weech, 1974: 328; Pings, 1976: 120-21; Bunge, 1977: 54; Kantor, 1981: 50). Though the users may be the best judges of the librarian's skills in interpersonal interaction (even here, question negotiation skills are problematic), they are notoriously poor judges of the quality of information received. As Weech (1974: 328, 331) notes, the high degree of satisfaction users report with the service they receive (sometimes as high as 90%) contrasts sharply with the results of librarians' performances on test questions, which show the user may at times have no better than a 50-50 chance of receiving a correct answer at a library reference desk. While patron satisfaction is undoubtedly important to a manager, and any abnormally high level of dissatisfaction a worrisome point to a professional as well, it does not touch upon what a professional may see as the central issue in judging the quality of service, the correctness and appropriateness of the response given to the client's demand for service.

To measure reference service at this level is to try to determine what actually happens to average library users asking ordinary questions at typical times of day at the reference desk. Obviously, this is difficult for an evaluator to do. The closest approach to it in library evaluation is the evaluation of responses given to predetermined sets of questions asked by evaluators who often, as in the classic studies by Crowley and Childers (1971), present themselves to reference librarians as ordinary library users. (A particularly useful summation of the literature on such tests, including sample questions, is to be found in Lancaster, 1977: 83-109.) When evaluators do indeed pose as library users, the result is probably the closest possible to a measure of services actually provided to users.

From a manager's point of view, these studies may have their limitations. The lists of questions asked are rarely long, and each is asked of only one librarian, and (usually) asked only one time. It is difficult to know whether a failure is a general departmental problem or a problem with the individual librarian's skills. Even if it is the individual, one does not know how typical the failure is. Various critics have noted that such tests require carefully developed lists of test questions representative of a library's real workload, and without this the validity of the testing is questionable (Bunge, 1977: 57; Lancaster, 1977: 108; Kantor, 1981: 44). Bunge (1977: 57) also notes that the judgment of what constitutes a "correct" answer to a test question cannot escape a certain element of subjectivity. In short, such tests may be good for revealing some gaps and unevenness in reference service, as Weech (1974: 329) suggests, but they are not ideal evaluative tools from a management point of view. They may indicate specific problems in the provision of service, but they are so specific in what they deal with that they cannot be generalized to the level of the department as a whole.

PROBLEMS

From a professional point of view the problems are different. Reference librarians question the ethics of having evaluators conduct unannounced evaluations while posing as library users (see

Feldman, 1974: 397; Weech, 1974: 329). While Feldman feels that this type of evaluation is common elsewhere in professional fields (a perhaps questionable assertion) and Weech justifies the approach as legitimate when evaluating public servants on a public service desk, this resistance is not without reason. Underlying it is a general uneasiness with professional evaluation to be found in other professional fields as well. The greater the complexity of the work being done (and professional fields pride themselves on their complexity), the greater the chance for error.

Professionals are painfully aware of the ease with which they themselves can err, and reluctant to find fault (at least publicly) with their colleagues. (Problems getting doctors to support malpractice actions against one another are the examples that come most readily to mind. Freidson's book treats the sources and manifestations of such reluctance in some detail.) On the other hand, there is general recognition that there are genuine problems with the quality of professional services. Lancaster (1977: 106) even suggests that librarians' objections to such evaluations can be overcome by emphasizing these problems, and the helplessness of the library user faced by them. He also presents an alternative to the deceptively presented "unobtrusive" tests of reference service. This is a direct test of reference skills in which librarians are given lists of what they know to be test questions, and evaluated on the accuracy and efficiency with which they deal with them. Though this may not test the librarian's skills in interacting with the user, it seems to be an excellent way to identify skills that need upgrading, particularly in areas (such as bibliographic verification) that lend themselves to coverage by lists of test questions.

As measures of departmental performance, these evaluations may have their limitations, but as indications of areas in which individual professionals need to upgrade their skills, such tests could be highly effective. They require cooperation on the part of those being evaluated, of course, and even then function more as evaluations of individuals than as evaluations of the general level of reference service provided by the library.

Not goal-based evaluations, nor professional standards, nor performance measures, nor tests of reference skills offer the complete answer to problems faced in the evaluation of reference services. Each views the library in a different way, and the result is that each is evaluating a slightly different aspect of library service. Goal-based evaluations treat the library as a bureaucratic organization which sets its own goals according to its own referents. Though it may be influenced by an awareness of other libraries' experiences or of movements afoot in the field as a whole, the evaluation process is essentially intra-library, self-contained.

Professional standards define what is basic to reference service on a very general level, without reference to individual institutions. They are completely external to the individual library, and the library's unique characteristics are largely irrelevant to their application. Performance measures (standardized data collection and comparison) try to bridge the gap between the individual institution and the level at which general standards are set, and perhaps have only the disadvantage of covering a fairly limited range of factors selected by general consensus, along with the usual shortcomings (i.e., excessive generalization) of quantitative measures. They promise a great deal in terms of inter-library comparisons, but may not be the best evaluations of the performance of individual departments. And tests of reference skills really work only as evaluations of the specific skills of specific individuals; they tell little of performance on the departmental level. Any library evaluating its reference services will find any method chosen lacking in some respects. The important thing in reference evaluation therefore appears to be the awareness of one's own purposes in undertaking the evaluation of services. If each approach selected has different advantages and disadvantages, depending on whether it is viewed from a management or a professional point of view, this is because managers and professionals are presumed to approach evaluation with different goals in mind.

COSTS VS. BENEFITS

It is all too simple to suggest that a weighing of costs versus benefits is the ultimate goal of evaluating services. Various studies point out that budgetary pressures and a concern with cost-effectiveness do tend to figure largely in management justifications for undertaking evaluations (see Vavrek, 1978; Lancaster, 1977; Klassen, 1983: 421). When presented as attempts to insure that public funds appropriated for the library are being wisely allocated, reference evaluations have great appeal. Measuring the value of reference service is by no means a simple process, however. The only concrete measure of the value of reference work that currently appears in the literature is the time saved by the library user (Rothstein, 1964: 467; Bunge, 1977: 60-61). Placing a value on this time can be done in special library contexts in perhaps a somewhat crude fashion (using comparative salary costs). The user's time is not so easily measurable in other situations, even if one accepts the underlying assumption that users without reference services would perform the same searches and eventually locate information of comparable usefulness, so that time need be the only variable measured. Clearly, the value of reference services is a complex issue, beginning with how one is to define "value" itself (see Griffiths, 1982, for a good discussion of the dimensions of the concept). Reference questions answered seems to be the most convenient quantitative measure of reference output, but how does one establish the value of a response to a reference question? As Vavrek (1979: 339) points out, no matter what system of cost accounting you use, its worth is a relative question.

Some larger system of values necessarily provides a context for studies of cost-effectiveness, and the tendency to deny such values exist is no way to escape them (see Beasley, 1974: 338; DuMont & DuMont, 1979: 125-26 on this). Certainly the decision to provide reference services at all (not a functional necessity in a library) was not made to reduce costs. Some other concept of value must have been involved, for which the resulting costs were thought justified. Management and professional points of view may differ in philosophical approaches to what this value might have been.

Restatements of such underlying philosophies may vary in ideological content, but the general points of emphasis should be clear. To a manager, the state of the organization is paramount. To the professional, it is the service around the provision of which the profession is organized. The two approaches have complementary failings, the dependence of management evaluations on quantitative measures yielding overly general measures, and the emphasis of professionals on individual interactions being overly specific. Both perspectives are necessary to the provision of reference services, which require both a healthy organizational environment and a commitment to service to function at an optimal level. Librarians recognizing the differences between them should be better able to focus their evaluative efforts and make use of the results. Evaluations from a management point of view, stressing workload and quantitative measures of output, may identify inefficiencies in staffing patterns and perhaps in the use and/or allocation of resources (Kantor's [1981] identification of collection failure as a major cause of unanswered questions comes immediately to mind). Using comparative statistics may also provide some rough measure of the way the organization's workload compares to that of other libraries.

Measurement of general levels of patron satisfaction—and reasons for dissatisfaction—may indicate the need for revisions in policy. All this is important and may be useful in suggesting areas for organizational change. It does not, however, touch upon what professionals would see as the actual quality of service provided. This can perhaps only be approached through the direct testing of performance. Results may identify areas in which individuals need further training, and reference evaluations on this level can be a useful staff development tool.

There is much that is useful in the literature on the evaluation of reference services. Applying it wisely, however, means not hoping for too much from any one approach to evaluation, but rather selecting that which is appropriate for the library's specific purposes, recognizing the inevitably flawed nature of the approach selected, and following through with remedial action appropriate to the character of the result.

REFERENCES

American Library Association. Reference and Adult Services Division. 1979. "A Commitment to Information Services: Developmental Guidelines." RQ 18: 275-78.

Beasley, Kenneth E. 1974. "Commentary." Library Trends 22: 387-93.

Benson, J. Kenneth. 1973. "The Analysis of Bureaucratic-Professional Conflict." The Sociological Quarterly 14: 376-94.

Bunge, Charles A. 1977. "Approaches to the Evaluation of Library Reference Services." Pp. 41-71 in F. W. Lancaster & C. W. Cleverdon (ed.), Evaluation and Scientific Management of Libraries and Information Centres. Leyden: Noordhof.

Bunge, Charles A. 1983. "Current Issues in Reference and Adult Services: Measurement and Evaluation of Reference and Adult Services." RQ 22: 251-54.

Crowley, Terrence and Thomas Childers. 1971. Information Service in Public Libraries: Two Studies. Metuchen, NJ: Scarecrow Press.

D'Elia, George and Sandra Walsh. 1983. "User Satisfaction with Library Service—A Measure of Public Library Performance?" Library Quarterly 53: 109-33.

Derber, Charles. 1982. Professionals as Workers: Mental Labor in Advanced Capitalism. Boston: G. K. Hall.

DuMont, Rosemary Ruhig and Paul F. DuMont. 1979. "Measuring Library Effectiveness: A Review and Assessment." Advances in Librarianship 9: 103-41.

Emerson, Katharine. 1977. "National Reporting on Reference Transactions, 1976-78." RQ 16: 199-207.

Feldman, Nancy C. 1974. "Commentary." Library Trends 22: 395-401.

Freidson, Eliot. 1975. Doctoring Together: A Study of Professional Social Control. New York: Elsevier.

Griffiths, Jose-Marie. 1982. "The Value of Information and Related Systems, Products, and Services." Annual Review of Information Science and Technology 17: 269-84.

Isaacson, David. 1983. "Library Inreach." RQ 23: 65-74.

Kantor, Paul B. 1981. "Quantitative Evaluation of the Reference Process." RQ 21: 43-52.

Kaser, David. 1982. "Standards for College Libraries." Library Trends 31: 7-19.

King, Geraldine B. 1983. "Current Trends in Reference Service in Public Libraries." Library Trends 31: 447-56.

Klassen, Robert. 1983. "Standards for Reference Services." Library Trends 31: 421-28.

Kok, Victoria T. and Anton R. Pierce. 1982. "The Reference Desk Survey: A Management Tool in an Academic Research Library." RQ 22: 181-87.

Lancaster, F. W. 1977. The Measurement and Evaluation of Library Services. Washington, DC: Information Resources Press.

Lynch, Mary Jo. 1983. "Research in Library Reference/Information Service." Library Trends 31: 401-20.

Monroe, Margaret E. 1974. "Evaluation of Public Services for Adults." Library Trends 22: 337-59.

Murfin, Marjorie E. 1983. "National Reference Measurement: What Can It Tell Us About Staffing?" College & Research Libraries 44: 321-333.

Pings, Vernon M. 1976. "Reference Services Accountability and Measurement." RQ 16: 120-23.

Rothstein, Samuel. 1964. "The Measurement and Evaluation of Reference Service." Library Trends 12: 456-72.

Vathis, Alma Christine. 1983. "Reference Transaction and End Product as Viewed by the Patron." RQ 23: 60-64.

Vavrek, Bernard. 1978. "When Reference Librarianship Died: It Began in Detroit." RQ 17: 301-305.

Vavrek, Bernard. 1979. "Reference Evaluation—What the 'Guidelines' Don't Indicate." RQ 18: 335-40.

Weech, Terry L. 1974. "Evaluation of Adult Reference Service." Library Trends 22: 315-35.

OVERVIEW
OF EVALUATION

The Whole Shebang—Comprehensive Evaluation of Reference Operations

Ellsworth Mason
Joan Mason

It is possible to find man somewhere in the contemporary world in every stage of human development, from the most bestial to the most forlornly technologized. In like manner, since 1935 we seem to have encountered in our library careers the whole span of reference history, from no reference service at all (as late as the 1950s) up to *Star Wars'* prediction of the robotic future in R/2 D/2, obviously, by his designation, a one-man double Reference Department. In between have been some strange encounters of another kind. In the 1960s we saw Reference Desks located so far from the library's entrance (and not visible from there) they were almost out of the building, and the fortress Reference Desk surrounded by a wooden moat forfending treasure from the dwarves, and catalogs split into four alphabets in two different classifications, and other horrors designed by central libraries of large population universities to keep users away from reference. By the 1980s we had generated large numbers of "burnt out" reference librarians who collapse physically after two hours at the Reference Desk, who deprecate reference service in favor of reading book reviews or attending (pardon the expression) committee meetings, and who are rather feeble at using the card catalog and even feebler at the reference computer console. When branch subject libraries are often run by low level unprofes-

Ellsworth Mason needs no introduction to our readers. He is now a library consultant and was former director of libraries at Colorado College, Hofstra University, and the University of Colorado . . . and a reference librarian "for ten happy years." Joan is former Acting Librarian, Colorado College and equally is famous and a library consultant. They both may be found at 716 Sixth St., Boulder, CO 80302.

sionals with minimal training, who serve faculty with little bibliographical skills we wonder what era of reference history we are really in now.

One of the strange developments of recent years has been the feverish surge all of a sudden to evaluate reference service. In a way, this is a throwback to the 1930s when we were evaluated in no uncertain terms daily, or sometimes hourly, but recent evaluation has taken the form of structured, mostly statistical measurement of reference librarians' behavior, with little attention to the content of their heads and no consideration at all to the wide range of other factors that can make or break reference service. Many things besides eye contact or body language speak volumes to library users about the reference department's intentions towards them, and we seem to be very good at driving users away before they ever get to us. The number of these factors is limited only by the imagination of the reference staff and their eagerness to reach out and speak caringly and informingly to users. This article will consider the broad range of factors, in addition to the reference librarian, that an evaluator of reference operations must consider to arrive at totally valid conclusions of how the service can be improved.

Reference Desks

Architects and interior designers are right; physical factors in a library are of high importance in carrying out its goals. The most important of these in a reference department are the Reference Desks. We say ''desks'' because we take for granted that building a piece of furniture large enough to be formidable or high enough nearly to conceal the librarians when they are sitting behind it fends off potential users and develops the tendency to hide that lurks in many librarians. If you can't begin to meet your reference demands, this is the kind of desk to build, for it will drive away users in herds. Desks should be pleasant, unobtrusive, and placed so librarians can easily slide away from them quickly on either side. Their location speaks loudly of their importance or unimportance. When we visited Colgate University and Swarthmore College libraries, they were on the same level as the library entrance but diagonally as far away from it as was possible, on a large area floor. Neither was visible from the entrance. Swarthmore's was baffled from view by an 18 " thick fieldstone wall. Like opening the door of your host's house and finding nobody at home. Reference Desks should be near the library entrance, in direct view from it, and loudly labelled. Rotating, dangling lights above, or signs in 8″ high letters on the desks are useful here. Just as important, the Reference Desks should be near the Circulation Desk, especially in smaller libraries, and should command as wide a scope of vision as possible, especially into the card catalog area, to identify users who need help. They should be near the exit from the reference area to prevent the drift of reference books to other parts of the library. So much will say, "Here we are friends; we see you. Look at us and come on in."

The most ingeniously mislocated Reference Desk that comes to mind was in the University of Colorado library in 1972, the result of a completely inflexible 1939 building, a poor addition, and several dislocations. As you entered the library, a vestibule made you turn south at right angles, which pointed you directly away from the reference area. Straight ahead was a large reading room, which trapped most users. Those canny enough to ask at the large circulation desk inside the entrace where reference was located were pointed north toward a huge room in which the ends of card catalog cases could be seen in the distance.

As you walked into it, indeed the card catalog was there, without a living soul in sight of it. Not until you had traversed two thirds of the length of this room did you discover a door on your right that led to the Reference Desk. Total distance from the library entrance was about 180 feet, if you made the four correct right angle turns along the way. This kind of arrangement is designed to breed a cross between a seeing-eye dog and a jogger. If you can sniff us out and your wind holds out until you reach us, we'll consider your needs. This is not an arrangement that endears itself to users.

Appearance

Next in importance is the appearance and general feeling of the reference area. Is it open and inviting, or cluttered? Some reference areas look like a teenager's room that hasn't been shovelled out recently—paper strewn everywhere, drawers piled on top of each other, books slopped all over the shelves and on the floor. The feeling of so-called "professionals" that they should not clean up makes us cringe. A professional does everything necessary to make the enterprise thrive. An open, orderly, and esthetically pleasant reference area will increase use because it feels good to be in and places a high value on your offerings.

Layout

The layout of all the reference elements should minimize the time it takes librarians to move to the tools, to keep users from waiting long. Long waits turn off the trade. For this reason alone, low *reference shelving* which stretches the collection over an acre of space should be avoided in favor of standard (7½ foot) stacks for the reference collection, which greatly diminishes the time it takes to reach a book. For the same reason low *card catalog cases* should be avoided. Instead, high reference tables should be provided for ease in consulting catalog drawers. *Periodical indexes* should be very close to the Reference Desks on tables with enough room (often absent) for easy consultation of the indexes right where you find them. It grieves us to see users crouched on the floor beside stacks with three large indexes in their lap. *Seating* at tables should be provided beyond the reference stacks, where sound and movement will not disturb study. Sufficient single tables should be near the stacks, with large tables nearby and adjacent to materials like maps and atlases that demand them. The *reference stacks* should use 12 " shelving and be arranged in short ranges with wide aisles, with at least one pull-out shelf per range located at consultation height for quick reference to the books.

In short, the layout of furniture and equipment should indicate in every possible way concern for ease and speed in use by the patron, while at the same time assuring him service by the librarians in as little time as possible. Such a layout can be achieved only be librarians who are deeply dedicated to service, and are willing to think carefully about every movement that they and the user make in the course of reference service. They must think continually about how to improve the layout. Consideration for the user should shine in every physical aspect of the reference area.

Arrangement of Materials

While physical things loom large in human affairs and make the largest initial impact on the reference user, what librarians do in the midst of those things is extremely important. The arrangement of materials in the reference area can help or hinder users. We have seen some wild and wooly arrangements in our time. Ideally, materials should be arranged so the user can easily find anything without assistance if he has its call number. Any book removed for any reason from its place in the general flow of call numbers is likely to be consigned to lesser use. There are exceptions, of which the periodical indexes are the most important, since they must be kept as a separate group near the Reference Desks. They must be shelved in call number order, which keeps related indexes reasonably close together, and not in groups dictated by librarians' logic, which drives users up the wall or, more often, out of the library through frustration. Groups of books separated from the general reference collection must be kept to a minimum, and each should be labelled prominently in large letters, and arranged in call number order. Separate groups, such as ready reference books, oversizes, publishers bibliographies, frequently stolen books must still be made easily available. By all means nail to the barn door the hide of anyone who sets up a hidy-hole for "essential" reference books which "everyone knows are there."

Microforms

Microforms pose a special problem when they are located and serviced in the reference area. They surely must be cataloged and shelved in such a way that they will be easier to locate than anything else. People are wary of using them, and if they get any signals of difficulty in their use they will forego them. If shelved in boxes, no more than six films should be in a box (like the Hollinger boxes) since twelve or more films in one box are heavy to move and re-shelve. Microform readers must be immediately adjacent, and instruction in their use must be available nearby.

Reshelving

Once an arrangement of materials is established as convenient for the user as possible, then prompt reshelving becomes a matter of great importance. Neglected, it can undo much of the effectiveness of the arrangement. *Shelfreading* for accuracy, which is almost unknown these days, should be done whenever slack periods at the Reference Desk allow. In sum, the arrangement of materials in a reference area tells whether the service is tailored to the user or to the librarians.

Visual Aids

Many reference services use audio-visual aids on how to use the card catalog, etc. These should be set up at small tables near the Reference Desks. As the computer console enters the reference operation, it should be used as another visual device, and melded carefully with the already existing operation. *Computer catalog consoles* should be within view of the Reference Desks so help can be offered to solve their perversities. If they tend to generate much conversation, they must be located away from reading areas. For the same reason, *bibliographical retrieval consoles* should be located in a separate room in the reference area where extended conversations can take place to establish thesaurus terms to be used in querying the database. Only reference-related computer consoles should be in the reference area.

The most important visual aid in reference should be a huge *directory of call number locations,* accompanied by a large map of the library, located near the entrance to the reference area where the user can consult it on leaving with call numbers in hand. It should be large, clear, and attractive. The *signs* used throughout the reference area should be located where they are most useful (i.e., on the element they describe), and in a large, esthetically pleasant type face, on a pleasant colored background. In addition, the signs must not clutter the reference area. Their careful placement is of prime importance.

Lighting

Finally, in the consideration of major physical factors, the lighting of the entire reference area should be of good quality and about 60-90 footcandles intensity, especially above the card catalog cases.

Card Catalog

We have dealt so far with the physical layout, and then with the arrangement of materials, which begins to show the impact of human skills. We now turn to intellectual factors in the reference area that show in greater degree what librarians are able to contribute to its usefulness. First of all that most maligned of library tools, the card catalog, which is consistently put down by the I-BuMmers for their own self interests. It is flawed, as some days we think humans are. It can be torn, twisted, slacked, ripped off, and in the 1960s burned. It is still a remarkable instrument, and at present, having been totally refurbished and refiled, the New York Public Library dictionary catalog is one of the most valuable information sources in the world. It takes skillful manipulation, but in

Bill Katz's rule of thumb for experienced reference librarians—if you think it should be in the catalog it *is* there; try another approach.

The card catalog is used by all library users, and it therefore says a great deal to everyone about how much we care about users. In twenty years it will tell how much we despise users, because a very large number of talented librarians spent twenty years perfecting a system to frustrate them, called AACR II. Right now, the catalog hoots at users if it contains much misfiling, indicating low-skilled filers and poor supervision, if cards are filed above the rod and not dropped for a month, if ratty guide cards are not replaced, if the follow-block is shoved to the rear of each drawer allowing cards to flop around in free-form inconvenience. If drawers are not labelled with both the beginning and the ending portion of the alphabet it contains (which we still find) it makes them hard to use. It also avoids delightful accidents like the one in the catalog at Colorado College (presided over by a former Army General William H. Gill) where one drawer was labelled "Gill - God." We know that it's convenient to ignore lapses caused by the cataloging department, but since the card catalog is their main tool it is the Reference Department's responsibility to press anything short of mayhem to make sure that the catalog is efficient, respectable, and designed for users as well as for librarians.

Computer Catalogs

When we tuck the catalog into computers, we impose a much larger burden on the public, because they are far harder to use and require instructions of what to do next at many of the sequential steps in the search process where it is not available. Right now we must press hard to get totally simple and clear instructions on how to use them. These instructions should cover every point at which the search process can become tricky. In huge letters we should be informed how to go back to point zero to begin again when we make errors, mostly mistyping errors. In addition, there should be a much larger number of consoles than we have seen anywhere, even at Ohio State University, because it takes much longer to negotiate a simple inquiry at the console than it does at the card catalog. Finally, we must press hard to get the entire catalog into the computer. The necessity for double-searching says clearly, "who cares about the user; we have our own problems." It may well be that, as computer catalogs become larger and more complicated, especially if new twitches are introduced into them for the sake of computerators we may force users to approach the catalog through barred wickets, behind which sit highly trained technicians who alone can manipulate this data. Then we will really have attained high priesthood. But low volume of use will warrant about seventy such specialists for the entire country.

Analytical Labels

In addition to large and clear numbers on the ends of each stack range, with letters to differentiate each side of the range, so librarians can refer easily to Range 8A, the end panels of the bookstacks should contain comprehensive analytical labels wherever appropriate (viz., on all ranges that contain national bibliographies). These are typed guides that supply call numbers in the reference collection for heavily used kinds of materials such as:

> Biographical sets/Who's Whos, by country.
> Language dictionaries, by language.
> History classifications, by country.
> Literature classifications, by country.
> Subject bibliographies, by heading and sub-heading.
> National bibliographies, by country.

Instructional Sheets

Called "Data Grabs" in our library, these helps for library users contribute mightily to the impression that the reference librarians care about them. They must be simple, starkly clear, and no longer than two sides of a sheet of paper. Various colored paper helps to differentiate them. They fall roughly into four categories:

I.   How to Use the Reference Services (examples):

> Glossary of Library Terms.
> How to Find a Book.
> How to Find a Periodical Article.
> Computer Based Reference Services.
> Interlibrary Loan Services.
> ERIC (how to use it).
> L.C. Subject Headings (how to use it).

II. How to Use Categories of Reference Books (examples):

Book Review Indexes.
Dictionaries (general, and subject dictionaries).
Encyclopedias (general, and subject encyclopedias).
Guides to Style and Research.
Newspapers and News Summaries.
Subject Guidebooks.

III. How to Use Periodical Indexes and Abstracts.

Our library describes for 21 of the most used indexes—the reference collection call number, span of dates and volumes in the set, branch library locations of additional sets, the scope and organization of the indexes, how to use them, and sample citations with each component clearly labelled.

IV. Specialized Sheets for Local Interests (examples):

Footnotes & Bibliographical form (Turabian, and MLA).
Selected Library Resources on Chicanos.
on Mass Media.
on Women.

It is extremely important that these Instructional Sheets be kept easily available in obvious places, and that their stock be continually replenished.

Queues

A final mark of consideration for users is a system for dealing fairly with queues of users when they form, including a method of separating out quick reference questions from those requiring longer exploration. The University of Colorado library has been using a take-a-number system for the past two years at high pressure periods.

Evaluation

To this point we have been talking about the range of objects in the reference area which singly are not of major importance, but cumulated in large numbers will enable users to profit from the reference facilities even when they are not staffed. They also will demonstrate a concern for the users that will color their attitude toward all the reference services. They must be evaluated. By whom, and how? We should be generating a cadre of highly intelligent, thoroughly mature reference librarians with a sharp critical eye who would be hired as outside evaluation consultants. They could use a chart listing the kinds of factors discussed above (as appropriate to any specific library), arranged in categories by degree of importance. Opposite each would be measures of achievement— A,B,C,D,F or 4, 3, 2, 1, 0. Each factor examined would be graded, with an average computed for separate categories. The evaluator would do a walk-through, just as the users would move, in performing certain reference searches, and would note what there is to help or hinder them in the process of using things like the Author Catalog, Subject Catalog, Indexes, Reference Books, Microforms, Computer Consoles, etc. Each would be observed to determine if there is some way in which it falls short of total availability, and what could be done to improve it. This part of the evaluation can be done by eye observation.

Management

When we turn to evaluation of the people in the reference operation, the first thing to look at is the management. Is the department managed, or does it float along on a wobbly keel, punted through shallows by various indifferent hands? Ellsworth's first library experience was in a department that was really managed, by an ancient (he thought) woman, about 52, to whom he had a great deal to offer (he thought) since he was just twenty-one. Anne S. Pratt, at Yale, the finest reference librarian he ever knew, saw some of his promise and all of his callowness and proceeded to shake the pants off of him for three solid months. Evaluation was daily, with white gloves run over the dusted table top. It set the foundations of his professional character.

Nowadays most people don't care that much about passing on a tradition of excellence. Many structures to avoid being held responsible are built into organizations, and the idiotic idea that professional librarians should evaluate themselves twines around common sense like a snake around a tree limb. Nevertheless, it is a fact that a reference department of any size and complexity cannot achieve excellence without good and constant management. Some signs of the quality of management follow.

Priorities

Have the competing demands on the reference desk been thought about and reconciled into clearly stated priorities? Where does the telephone inquiry fit in? We first understood the incredible urgency of this instrument when, about twenty years ago, a burglar in New York City was chased into a house, which the police proceeded to shoot up. Somehow an enterprising reporter got the telephone number of that house and called the burglar for an interview. In the midst of exchanging shots with the police, the burglar answered the phone and refused the interview with the words, "Sorry, I can't talk to you now; I'm busy!" There's nothing like standing in line and, when your turn comes, to have the librarian answer the phone just because it's ringing. Yet telephones must be answered. How is this problem solved?

Do we take inquiries as they come, or try to identify quick ones before setting out on longer explorations? If our clientele consists of faculty, students, administrative offices, politicians, and library staff, which get priority in case of overlap, or do any? How does assistance at the computer console, which can be tricky and very time consuming, fit into the priorities, especially if the console is on the Reference Desk? It is not so important how these issues are resolved, but it is extremely important that they have been clearly resolved, and everyone understands what the priorities are and follows them.

Recruitment Interviews

Are candidates for reference positions thoroughly tested on all the basic knowledge and skills required for effective reference service? Are they set at the Reference Desk to conduct reference interviews with users, an experienced staff librarian at their side to lead them to the tools they choose to use (and to take over the wheel in case of accidents). They should be evaluated for this performance by a highly skilled reference librarian, by observation. They also should be tested in the same way for the areas of knowledge recommended below in our discussion of testing reference librarians. Sheer energy level should rank high among the requirements for selecting a reference librarian, and candidates must be tested for it.

Staffing

Are any of the staff displaced from the Catalog Department? We have worked in both reference and cataloging, and have great admiration for the skills required in a cataloger. Only rarely are they combined with the personality and mentality (i.e. the way of thinking) required for reference service. Most reference librarians would not make good catalogers either. Have candidates from the Catalog Department been screened in the same kind of interview process applied to other candidates? Are students used at the Reference Desk? Joan has seen them set up a user in the Bible section of the Subject Catalog to search for a King James version, and at the *Readers' Guide* for complex problems in criminology, and the like. Behind the Reference Desk students are an abomination. If necessary it is better for users to wait or come back for service rather than to be misguided. Does the department use support staff at the Reference Desk? If so, they should have educational and intellectual attainments nearly at the level of the professionals, plus walloping amounts of training in all aspects of reference work continually.

Communications

Are communications to the reference staff and communications among them both structured and encouraged? Is there an up-to-date reference manual available and used? Are there both formal information meetings and informal gathering places to make sure that information circulates among the staff? Are the librarians who staff the Reference Desk in shifts keenly aware of the importance of passing on to their relief information about today's reference dynamics—the repeated reference inquiry, the long term search that ought to be passed on from hand to hand, rather than allowed to marinate in one librarian's unfinished pile for a week? Do the librarians query each other in their fields of special subject strength? Is information circulated immediately about changes in reference policy and changes in location of reference material, or are these items saved for the weekly or bi-weekly meeting? Everything possible should be done to make sure that the librarians at the Reference Desk are totally informed at all times about anything affecting their reference service. This seldom is done these days except in small reference staffs.

In academic libraries constant communication with the teaching departments must be maintained on as broad a span as possible as often as possible. How is this managed by the department head? The larger the university is, and therefore the more important it is to communicate with the faculty, the less it is done. Yet it must be done, by a carefully planned program that uses most effectively the amount of time available for it.

Academic libraries should have a wide range of communications with students in the form of instructional programs developed to fit anyone from the most naive beginner to graduate students about to begin doctoral dissertation research. Instruction for beginners should be offered whenever a number of new students enter the university, at different times of the day or evening to fit students' available time. Programs should be offered to anticipate shifts in library emphasis in the various departments' teaching—term papers, beginning of major studies, thesis writing. Instruction in resources available for specific fields of study and how to use them, and programs tailored for students of a specific course taught by a specific instructor should be available upon request, given reasonable advance notice. Formal credit or non-credit courses should be offered in the teaching departments whenever it is needed and acceptable. The availability of all these programs should be disseminated by all possible means—student newspapers, radio, faculty and department memos, bulletin boards, kiosks, as well as at every appropriate location in the library building. An examination of the range and adequacy of these programs, how they are viewed by the teaching faculty, and the suitability of librarians who instruct the students should be made by anyone evaluating a reference operation.

The management of the reference operation must be reviewed by an evaluation consultant, who would list factors similar to those discussed above pertinent to the library being assessed. A skillful set of questions designed to produce information on how these factors are managed would be presented orally to every staff member who works at the Reference Desk, and after that to the department head. Any disparity of information between these levels should be noted. A skilled evaluation consultant can summarize the general condition of each factor, and recommend how they can be improved if they fall short of perfection.

The Reference Librarian

Reference librarians are made by strenuous lifetime effort, not sprung fully armed from Minerva's head. Therefore, a young reference librarian is almost a contradiction in terms. We once interviewed a candidate for a position as a Reference Librarian at Hofstra University who became incensed during the interview to realize that she was not being considered for head of the department for, she said, she had *three years* experience. It takes about ten years of avid reading in a broad range of fields, after a good liberal education, to equip anyone to perceive clearly into precisely which subject field a reference inquiry fits, the first thing you must know to develop a reference strategy. Properly performed, reference is the most demanding specialty in the entire range of librarianship, the highest calling of all, one dedicated to limitless expansion of skills and knowledge without pause. Fine reference librarians develop fans who will accept reference work only from their favorite, though this requires coming back to the desk when she is on duty.

The reference librarians stand at the most vulnerable spot in the library operation, having to produce right now. They are expected to cover the greatest expanse of ground, infinite knowledge. Reference librarians are in an awesome position of authority; users are likely to believe what you tell them. They require the largest number of personal and intellectual skills, seldom combined in one person, yet all needed. They are continually dealing with users who are uneasy for a number of reasons, but mostly because of the nature of libraries themselves, which are not user-oriented but process-oriented. Consequently, as was argued in 1969,[1] many of the things we consider highly professional achievements appear to users as wildly irrational and frightening, concerted attempts to defy order.

Reference librarians must be able to relate immediately to people, to make them feel comfortable in their inquiry and lead them deeper into the collection than they had expected to go (but not too deeply). They must have keen, perceptive intellects, which must be kept sharply honed. They must have imagination to develop effective reference strategies. They must know languages, the larger the library the more languages.[2] They must have great skill at using card catalogs, requiring broad knowledge of subject headings, yet know the limitations of the catalog so they do not give up before exhausting all approaches to a problem. They must have thorough knowledge of the books in the reference collection, what they contain and how to use them. They must have knowledge of strengths in the library's collection; and individual books in it.[3] They must know the emphases of the teaching program (in academic libraries). They must have mechanical skills to operate microform readers and computer consoles. They must know thoroughly how to use the systems of inquiry programmed into computer catalog or retrieval systems.

It should not be necessary to state that these skills cannot be measured by taping heartbeats at the Reference Desk or by adding up statistics of reference questions answered, broken into seventeen different categories, or by counting eye-contacts or footsies. The basic skills can be accurately measured if we give up the ridiculous idea of self-sufficient professional librarians, and put them through some demanding testing, as follows:

The reference interview. A fine, highly experienced reference consultant could evaluate without difficulty the librarians' skills at the interview point by working right beside them and observing a series of interviews. Skillfully performed, the interview with the user is a beautiful process to watch, but it takes a practiced eye to see what is going on in it. I am always appalled when youngsters in the reference department cannot see it, and think they are doing the same thing as their mature colleagues are.

Reference strategy. Pose a pre-tested reference problem, to get all the available information on a set topic.

Subject headings/filing rules knowledge. Give written tests. When was this last done in librarianship?

Knowledge of reference books. Give a written test.

Computer console/microform skills. Watch their ease in using them.

Language skills. Have them translate from an encyclopedia before someone who knows the language.

The only reference skill in contemporary practice that is hard to evaluate is performance in computer-based retrieval. This can be done effectively only by someone who had mastered all of the thesauruses of all the databases on-line to your terminal.

In addition to testing individual librarians, the reference evaluator must determine how slack time at the Reference Desk is used, and how time not at the desk is used, because reference skills require continual honing. Skills at the card catalog require continual study of the subject heading books and filing rules, neither of which can be completely mastered, but both of which must be frequently studied by librarians who would grow in skill. The card catalog must be frequently probed in random spots to learn its quirks (the older the catalog the more this is necessary). Reference books must be studied one by one until (ideally) they are all mastered and inside of the reference librarians' heads. Those infrequently used must be studied over and over. Unless the librarian can relate them instantly to a reference inquiry, they might as well be in China. Database thesauruses must be studied repeatedly in like manner by those librarians that use them. Daily practice on the computer consoles should be required, since the process of using them in a reference search must be quick and effortless, with no see-sawing or backtracking, to encourage users to try them. Faltering at this point will reinforce the prevalent feeling that they are impossible to use, one more roadblock invented by librarians to keep the user from getting what he needs. All librarians should practice use of the microform readers weekly to maintain the ability to instruct users on setting up the materials right-side up, without repeating and rewinding and reverse flopping of the microforms. Librarians with low mechanical skills must practice harder and more often on these machines than others. Into all of these activities the reference librarians' slack time must go.

"But we don't have time to do all these things; we're too busy all day." Every day? This seldom is an accurate statement, but if it is, come in nights and weekends to do them; come in a half-hour early and leave a half-hour late every day. For librarianship is a profession, something we profess, a dedication, and dedication, in addition to talent, is really needed to make a fine reference librarian. Nothing else will do it.

The bottom line of this balance sheet should be—everything and everybody in a reference operation should say in its own way, "Come in! Trust us; we like you and want to help you. We *can* help you." This message comes straight from the Christian gospel tradition of loving and helping and sharing as a way of life. Reference librarians should be recruited for these attitudes, as well as for their personal qualities and their skills.

REFERENCES

1. "Unnatural Places and Practices," *Library Journal,* October 1, 1969, pp. 3399-3402.

2. The new trend to require languages for college entrance students will put greater pressure on librarians to attain more language skills within a decade. Andrew Osborn, better known for other contributions to librarianship, wrote an excellent little booklet, *Languages for Librarians,* Pittsburgh, [University of Pittsburgh] Graduate School of Library and Information Science, 1965, which demonstrates how the knowledge of a few languages allows us to manipulate for reference purposes a range of cognate languages, merely by adding a little knowledge of the systematic differences between allied languages.

3. One of the highlights of Ellsworth's career came when a student came into the Colorado College library one night asking for a resume of Ben Jonson's *Volpone.* He produced

one, then proceeded to convince the student that he simply shouldn't deprive himself of the sheer delight of reading the entire play. The student abandoned the resume and checked out the play.

APPENDIX: INSTRUCTIONAL SHEETS
GENERAL AND SUBJECT DICTIONARIES

Dictionaries are useful in research for: defining a topic and key terms; synonyms and suggestions for subject headings; identification and brief information on people, places, and things; and assisting in the communication of research results in clear and correct written form.

General dictionaries typically include most or all of the following: spelling, syllabication (word division), pronunciation, etymology (origins), meaning, synonyms, antonyms, word forms, syntax, usage, abbreviations, slang, foreign terms and phrases, new words, biographical and geographical information, tables, signs, symbols, illustrations, and other supplementary material.

General dictionaries are located in Reference in the Library of Congress "P" classification for language and literature. Following is a partial listing of some of the various types of English language dictionaries:

> PE1580 . . . etymological
> PE1591 . . . synonyms
> PE1625 . . . English language dictionaries
> PE1628 . . . college dictionaries
> PE1670 . . . foreign words and phrases
> PE1693 . . . abbreviations (and acronyms)
> PE3721 . . . slang

Subject dictionaries, often technical in nature, define terms within the context of the particular field. They are shelved in Reference in the LC class covering the particular subject area. Ask a reference librarian for assistance in locating subject dictionaries.

Examples of unabridged dictionaries

WEBSTER'S SECOND (i.e., WEBSTER'S NEW INTERNATIONAL DICTIONARY OF THE ENGLISH LANGUAGE. 2nd ed.) PE1625 W3 1941, 1957, 1959, & PE1625 W4 1966. Prescriptive—critic of language, tells how language *should* be used.

WEBSTER'S THIRD (i.e., WEBSTER'S THIRD NEW INTERNATIONAL DICTIONARY OF THE ENGLISH LANGUAGE. 3rd ed.) PE1625 W36 1961. Descriptive—recorder of language, tells how language *is* used.

THE OED (i.e., THE OXFORD ENGLISH DICTIONARY BEING A CORRECTED REISSUE OF A NEW ENGLISH DICTIONARY ON HISTORICAL PRINCIPLES. 13 vols. Oxford, 1933.) Supplements—vol. 1, A-G, 1972; vol. II, H-N, 1976. (Southeast corner of Reference Department). Traces the etymology, i.e., history, of words with quotations.

Representative list of subject dictionaries

PHILOSOPHICAL DICTIONARY   B43 B713 (1972)
DICTIONARY OF SYMBOLS   BF 1623 S9C513 1971
DICTIONARY OF COMPARATIVE RELIGION   BL31 D54 1970

NEW SMITH'S BIBLE DICTIONARY   BS440 S67 1966
OXFORD DICTIONARY OF ENGLISH CHRISTIAN NAMES   CS2375 G7W5 1977
DICTIONARY OF BATTLES   D25 A2H2 1971
DICTIONARY OF MODERN HISTORY   D299 P32 (1962)
DICTIONARY OF THE AMERICAN INDIAN   E77 S84 (1960)
HISTORICAL DICTIONARY OF GUATEMALA   F1462 M6 1973
A CONCISE GLOSSARY OF GEOGRAPHICAL TERMS   G108 A2S9 1968
DICTIONARY OF ANTHROPOLOGY   GN11 D38 1972b
DICTIONARY OF MYTHOLOGY, FOLKLORE, AND SYMBOLS   GR35 J6 (1961)
DICTIONARY OF COSTUME   GT507 W5 (1969)
DICTIONARY OF THE DANCE   GV1585 R3 1965
DICTIONARY OF THE SOCIAL SCIENCES   H41 G6 (1964)
DICTIONARY OF BUSINESS AND ECONOMICS   HB61 A53 (1977)
DICTIONARY OF SOCIOLOGY   HM17 M56 1968b
VOCABULARY OF COMMUNISM   HX17 D4 (1964)
SAFIRE'S POLITICAL DICTIONARY   JK9 S2 1978
BLACK'S LAW DICTIONARY   KF156 B53 1977
DICTIONARY OF EDUCATION   LB15 G6 1973
HARVARD DICTIONARY OF MUSIC   ML100 A64 (1960)
ADELINE ART DICTIONARY   N33 A223 1966
DICTIONARY OF LANGUAGE AND LINGUISTICS   P29 H34 1972b
DICTIONARY OF EUROPEAN LITERATURE   PN41 M3 1974
LITERARY TERMS: A DICTIONARY   PN44.5 B334 1975
MCGRAW-HILL DICTIONARY OF SCIENTIFIC AND TECHNICAL TERMS   Sci Ref
    Q123 M15 (1976)
COMPUTER DICTIONARY   QA76.15 S5 (1966)
BLACK'S MEDICAL DICTIONARY   R121 B598 (1976)
DICTIONARY OF AGRICULTURAL AND ALLIED TERMINOLOGY   S411 D47
    (1962)
ENCYCLOPEDIC DICTIONARY OF THE ENVIRONMENT   TD173 S27 1971
DICTIONARY OF TOOLS   TT186 S24 1975
GLOSSARY OF ARMS   U800 S8 1961
BOOKMAN'S GLOSSARY   Z1006 B6 1961

Data Grab: 69

GENERAL AND SUBJECT ENCYCLOPEDIAS

General encyclopedias contain informational articles of varying length on subjects in all fields of knowledge. Subject encyclopedias contain articles of greater depth and detail on topics within the particular subject area. Many subject encyclopedias are called "dictionaries," but a true dictionary includes short, concise, factual entries for terms on the subject.

Encyclopedias are useful for: factual information (including people and places); illustrations; an overview of a topic (including background information, scope, definitions, etc.); vocabulary control; and lists of additional sources.

When using encyclopedias, always: examine the organization; consult the index; follow through on cross-references; note bibliographies; note if a yearbook is published; consult several encyclopedias (note discrepancies, disagreements, consensus patterns, etc.).

General encyclopedias are located in the Library of Congress "A" classification of the Reference shelves. Subject encyclopedias are shelved in Reference in the LC class covering the particular subject area. Ask reference librarian for assistance in locating subject encyclopedias.

The Three Basic General Encyclopedias

ENCYCLOPEDIA AMERICANA   AE5 E333 1979
  Especially good for U.S. topics and clear explanations of technical subjects. Many shorter articles; longer articles have tables of contents.
ENCYCLOPAEDIA BRITANNICA   AE5 E363 1979 (15th edition)
  Divided into three parts:
  Propaedia (1 volume): organizes knowledge into categories; is not an index.
  Micropaedia (10 volumes): alphabetical arrangement of short articles; gives references to articles in the *Macropaedia* and to related articles in the *Micropaedia;* serves as an index to the *Macropaedia.*
  Macropaedia (19 volumes): longer articles alphabetically arranged by subject; also contains bibliographies.
  Famous earlier editions of EB: 7th, 9th, 11th.
COLLIER'S ENCYCLOPEDIA   AE5 E683 1977
  All bibliographies and a study guide are in the index volume.
(Another general encyclopedia is the WORLD BOOK, which is designed for children as well as adults and has many illustrations. WORLD BOOK is good for simple, clear explanations, but weak for bibliographies. It is not available in Norlin Reference Room.)

Examples of One-volume General Encyclopedias (Good for Ready Reference or Quick Factual Answers)

NEW COLUMBIA ENCYCLOPEDIA   AG5 C725 1975
RANDOM HOUSE ENCYCLOPEDIA   AG5 R25 (1977)
LINCOLN LIBRARY OF ESSENTIAL INFORMATION   AG105 L55 30th ed. (1967)

Representative List of Subject Encyclopedias

DICTIONARY OF PHILOSOPHY AND PSYCHOLOGY   B41 B3 1925 (3 vol.)
ENCYCLOPEDIA OF PHILOSOPHY   B41 E5 (7 vol.) 1967
ENCYCLOPEDIA OF PSYCHOLOGY   BF31 E522 (3 vol.) 1972
ENCYCLOPEDIA OF OCCULTISM AND PARAPSYCHOLOGY BF1407 E52 (2 vol.) 1978
ENCYCLOPEDIA OF RELIGION AND ETHICS   BL31 E4 1913 (13 vol.)
NEW CATHOLIC ENCYCLOPEDIA   BX841 N44 1967 (16 vol.)
DICTIONARY OF THE HISTORY OF IDEAS   CB5 D52 (5 vol.) 1973
ILLUSTRATED ENCYCLOPEDIA OF WORLD HISTORY   D21 L276 (2 vol.) 1975
MODERN ENCYCLOPEDIA OF RUSSIAN AND SOVIET HISTORY   DK14 M6 (16 vol. to date-through Ki) 1976
ENCYCLOPEDIA JUDAICA DS102.8 E496 (16 vol.) 1972
DICTIONARY OF AMERICAN HISTORY   E174 D52 1976 (8 vol.)
AFRO-AMERICAN ENCYCLOPEDIA   E185 A24 (10 vol.) 1974
ENCYCLOPEDIA DE MÉXICO   F1204 E5 (12 vol.) 1966
LAROUSSE ENCYCLOPEDIA OF WORLD GEOGRAPHY   G115 G5535 (1 vol.) 1965
ENCYCLOPEDIA OF WORLD COSTUME   GT507 Y37 (1 vol.) 1978
ENCYCLOPEDIA OF SPORTS   GV567 M46 1975 (1 vol.)
INTERNATIONAL ENCYCLOPEDIA OF THE SOCIAL SCIENCES   H40 A215 (17 vol.) 1968
ENCYCLOPEDIA OF THE THIRD WORLD   HC59.7 K87 (2 vol.) 1978
ENCYCLOPEDIA OF CAREERS AND VOCATIONAL GUIDANCE   HF5381 E52 1975 (2 vol.)

CYCLOPEDIA OF AMERICAN GOVERNMENT   JK9 C9 (3 vol.) 1914
ENCYCLOPEDIA OF AMERICAN FOREIGN POLICY   JX1407 E53 (3 vol.) 1978
ENCYCLOPEDIA OF EDUCATION   LB15 E47 (10 vol.) 1971
INTERNATIONAL CYCLOPEDIA OF MUSIC AND MUSICIANS   ML100 T47 1949
   (1 vol.)
ENCYCLOPEDIA OF WORLD ART   N31 E533 (15 vol.) 1960
ENCYCLOPEDIA OF WORLD LITERATURE IN THE TWENTIETH CENTURY
   PN774 L433 (4 vol.) 1967
McGRAW-HILL ENCYCLOPEDIA OF WORLD DRAMA PN1625 M3 (3 vol.) 1972
INTERNATIONAL ENCYCLOPEDIA OF FILM PN1993.45 I5 1972 (1 vol.)
ENCYCLOPEDIA OF AMERICAN LITERATURE PS21 R4 (1 vol.) 1962
McGRAW-HILL ENCYCLOPEDIA OF SCIENCE & TECHNOLOGY Science Lib. Ref.
   Q121 M3 1977 (15 vol.)
VAN NOSTRAND'S SCIENTIFIC ENCYCLOPEDIA   Q121 V3 1958 (1 vol.) ('76 ed.
   in Science Ref.)
ENCYCLOPEDIA OF BIOETHICS   QH332 E52 (4 vol.) 1978
INTERNATIONAL ENCYCLOPEDIA OF PSYCHIATRY, PSYCHOLOGY,
   PSYCHOANALYSIS, AND NEUROLOGY   RC334 157 (12 vol.) 1977
ENCYCLOPEDIA OF AMERICAN AGRICULTURAL HISTORY   S441 S36 (1 vol.)
   1975
COMPLETE ENCYCLOPEDIA OF MOTORCARS 1885-1968   TL15 G39 (1 vol.)
ENCYCLOPEDIA OF ESPIONAGE   UB270 S4383 1974 (1 vol.)
ENCYCLOPEDIA OF LIBRARY AND INFORMATION SCIENCE   Z1006 E57
   (29 vols. to date-through System) 1968

Data Grab: 68

The Hidden Agenda in the Measurement and Evaluation of Reference Service, Or, How to Make a Case for Yourself

Samuel Rothstein

Reference librarians often complain of their clients' tendency to "hide" the real point of their inquiries, perhaps even from themselves. When it comes to the question of the measurement and evaluation of reference service, my experience has been that practicing reference librarians are themselves guilty of a similar kind of evasiveness or self-deception. Reference librarians may talk and write a good deal about their need for better means of measuring and evaluating the services they provide, but my belief is that what they really want is guidance in—better still, recipes for—*justifying* their work and their contribution. They don't like to say so in public or in print, but when reference librarians talk with me in private I get the definite impression that they now feel their department's position to be threatened. They are anxious to find ways of making a stronger case for themselves.

I am not sure why reference librarians seem so reluctant to avow this goal of self-justification. Perhaps such a purpose is seen as running contrary to the professional ideal of dedicating oneself to the service of others. Are the two actually in conflict? I do not propose to argue the point here. Those reference librarians who find self-justification unnecessary or unworthy may simply avoid or dismiss all that follows. Those reference workers who feel as I do that the self-interest motive is perfectly reasonable in itself, consistent with

Professor Rothstein is on the faculty of the School of Librarianship, The University of British Columbia, Vancouver, BC; and is a member of The Reference Librarian editorial board.

This paper is based in part on a talk given to a reference librarians' workshop convened by the Greater Vancouver Library Federation in 1983.

high ideals of service and of particular urgency at present, may wish to have my suggestions on how they may put their best foot forward. Admittedly, my advice comes from the ivory tower rather than from the trenches, but I hope that it may still be seen as useful.

THE PROBLEM

The major problem in justifying reference service comes at the outset: determining at whom the case is to be directed. There seems to be at least two audiences for the reference librarian's pitch. One group—a rather obvious target—is the general public of users, actual and potential. The thinking here is that if you create in or elicit from these people a feeling of appreciation and need for reference services, then you can ultimately secure from them, directly or indirectly, the financial support required.

The second target group is, to judge from my impressions of the professional literature, seldom acknowledged as such. This group is the library's chief administrators—the people who make the decisions about allocating funds as between the various library departments. For understandable reasons, reference librarians are reluctant to state they are competing with their fellow staff-members for larger shares of the money pie. But that is just what they are doing in these days of financial exigency, and it is the high-level library managers who decide on the size of the slices.

Which of these two groups is the more important, and does the case to be made to the one necessarily differ from that made to the other? My own answer is that it is the administrators who are the primary concern, and that the arguments directed toward the general public will be useful only in so far as the administrators perceive the public to be genuinely aroused.

Let me put this another way: the fate of the reference department(s) is in the hands of the library administrators, and it would take a real outcry by the general public to affect the policy decisions made by the administrators. Such an outcry is very difficult to muster up in the case of reference services. Let's face it: the sort of public rallying round the flag produced by the closing of a branch, the cancellation of subscriptions or an intellectual freedom case is not going to be occasioned by the answering of reference questions, whether done extraordinarily well or not at all.

Nevertheless, the attention and appreciation of the general public is worth some effort in securing if only because any representation made by the users to the library administrators carries much more weight than do the arguments put forward by the reference librarians themselves. Inevitably the reference librarians' case for their own work, ''tainted'' by self-interest as it must appear to be, will be subjected to a considerable discount by the administrators.

THE PROCEDURE

I do not intend to offer a detailed prescription for how to win friends and influence people on behalf of the reference services because the techniques of public relations (for this is what we are talking about, aren't we?) are for the most part no different in respect of the reference department(s) than they are for any other library services. You can get such a prescription or guide in any good textbook on library management.[1]

There are, however, two points of special reference to reference that are worth singling out. One is the disturbing fact that only a small minority of the general public is even aware of the existence of reference services. Chen and Hernon are only the latest in a long line of researchers who have proven that reference is indeed the secret service.[2]

Reference librarians simply cannot afford to persevere in their present practice of doing good works surreptitiously, but unfortunately neither is a large-scale advertising campaign within their means. A little imagination might, however, serve in lieu of money. I would suggest that reference librarians (I am thinking here primarily of public libraries) associate and identify themselves closely with the two forms of information demand which affect the largest number of people: contests and school children's questions. Traditionally these two demands have tended to be met very reluctantly if at all, but I maintain that if you want to demonstrate the reference department's existence and usefulness to a great many people very quickly, these are the fastest highways to general recognition. (I append an example of how the Vancouver Public Library cooperated with a local newspaper on a trivia contest and reaped a huge harvest of effective publicity.)

My second point about getting better public recognition of reference service is that we must portray the nature and extent of that service more fully and accurately than is usually done. How is an account of the library's reference service usually presented to the general public? Aside from a smattering of well-worn anecdotes about the amazing variety of questions asked, the presentation normally limits itself to an indication of the number of reference inquiries handled, perhaps subdivided into categories ("directional," "ready reference," etc.) and compared with the previous year's figures.

The trouble with such reference statistics is that they take no account whatsoever of the fact that nearly all North American libraries are designed to operate mainly on the self-service basis. By far the greater part of the information work that is carried on in libraries is done, not by the librarians, *but by the patrons themselves, and most of the librarians' effort is indeed expended on enabling the patrons to help themselves effectively.*

The proof of this assertion is easily made. The numerous surveys of how reference librarians spend their time concur in indicating that they are seldom at the reference desk for more than three hours a day. Thus the usual statistics which libraries issue regarding their reference services—that is, a count of reference questions dealt with—*represent only a rather small part of what reference librarians actually do and contribute.*

A better measure is readily available. As De Prospo has shown, the use of library materials and services is generally closely related to the number of people who come into the library.[3] A fairly simple sampling procedure would indicate the number of people who use the reference facilities for any purpose. On the basis of this count one would construct a single statistic or measure which would reasonably represent the whole gamut of "reference activity"—that is, use of materials, staff, quarters and equipment. I have experimented with the construction of such a reference activity measure and while I cannot claim any proven validity for my results, my experience suggests that the total "reference uses" of a library are probably many times as great as the number of reference questions answered.

Support for this view also derives from the studies of De Prospo and Weech. De Prospo found that only about one-third of the patrons coming into public libraries actually took out any books;[4] it seems reasonable to suppose that many of the remaining two-thirds came to use reference facilities. Weech is more explicit; he cites studies indicating that some forty to seventy percent of library visitors came there specifically for reasons other than to take out books.[5] Put all these observations together and it seems quite clear to me that *reference librarians reporting only on questions answered have been guilty of selling their contributions seriously short.*

Which brings me now to the main item on the hidden agenda: how are reference librarians to persuade library administrators of the importance of their work? Or, to be more blunt, to accord it a higher priority in budget allocations?

One approach has already been suggested above: to make administrators better aware of the true extent of "reference activity" and especially of the degree to which the reference facilities act as a drawing card. A periodic questionnaire of users' reasons for coming to the library would, I suggest, yield very persuasive evidence on the extent to which the reference department(s) should be "credited" with attracting library patronage. One such survey, conducted in Ontario in 1977, indicated that about thirty percent of the times that patrons visited or telephoned the public library it was for informational needs (though only about half those times did they actually ask for help!).[6] Zweizig and Rodger give very useful guidance on how such a survey might actually be conducted.[7]

It would be even more persuasive and convincing if the above evidence on patrons' interest in information service were correlated with the proportion of total library staff time or dollars which were allocated to reference work. I do not know of a comprehensive study on this point but my own occasional calculations suggest that that proportion is only about ten percent. Given the well-known difficulties about library cost accounting, one would need to be cautious about the precise inferences one drew from this correlation, but on the face of it it looks as though the reference service yields a very handsome return, in respect of library patronage, for the money invested in it.

The same point—that is, regarding the "value" of reference service—might also be approached from another two directions. Perhaps the most direct means of ascertaining the cost-benefits of the reference service is to ascertain what it would cost the users thereof if they had to pay for it. As it happens, there are now quite a number of private sector information services, and it is quite feasible to determine what the going rate for such is in a given locality. For example, on my own campus in 1982, a "Rent-A-Librarian" information service charged students some $20 per hour or portion thereof. It would be most interesting, and I think also eye-opening, for administrators to view reference services in the light of their "market value."

Another and even more powerful means of justifying a high priority for the reference service would be to demonstrate the amount of time it saved its users. Unfortunately, I know of only one study of this kind. Kramer, testing the capacity of engineers to find needed information on their own as compared with having librarians secure it for them, found that the ratio in favor of the librarians was 9.1—that is, the patrons would spend about nine times as much time as did the librarian in finding the answer to a given answer.[8] Here again one must be very cautious about the inferences one draws from insufficient evidence, and yet here again one cannot but feel that further tests along these lines might well yield strong support for a high valuation of the contribution of library reference services.

I have one last suggestion to offer on how to make a strong case for the importance of reference service, and this approach comes very close to being a sure thing. It is simply to ask the patrons what they think of the reference service, i.e. to determine the "satisfaction rate." The reason why this approach can be so highly touted is that it has been tried many times and almost always has worked extremely well. For a generation and more, studies of the evaluation of reference services have indicated that satisfaction rates are usually in the 90% range.[9] So conduct your own bibliothecal equivalent of the "consumer taste test" and you are pretty certain to obtain results that should be flattering and impressive.

An interesting and potentially very useful variation on the usual consumer survey can be obtained for public libraries if one follows the procedure detailed in a book published by The Urban Institute and The International City Management Association and entitled: *How Effective Are Your Community Services? Procedures for Monitoring the Effectiveness of Municipal Services.*[10] The essential point here is that consumers' assessments of the library including specifically the reference services (p.75), are to be ascertained in conjunction and comparison with evaluations of the whole range of other municipal services such as fire protection, crime control, recreation, etc. If, as may be confidently expected, the library reference service ranks high in relation to municipal services generally, then its credit rating should soar.

SOME CONCLUSIONS AND EXHORTATIONS

I am not so naive as to believe that, even if the reference department gains the highest possible standing on a consumer survey, the battle for justification will be won. Hardheaded administrators may well dismiss such responses are analogous to being in favor of motherhood or as simply stemming from the patrons' ignorance of what they may rightfully expect. (The results of the various "unobtrusive tests" of the effectiveness of reference services do indeed lend some support for the latter view.[11]) Similarly, legitimate objections may be made to each of the other approaches which I have suggested.

Nevertheless, I firmly believe that if *my* particular measures are found wanting, something else of the sort *must* be found. A reference service that can make no better case for itself than to offer little stories about how much the service has meant to some users plus some almost meaningless statistics on the number of questions dealt with runs the serious risk of not counting with the people who count. The effective justification of reference service will depend largely on the ability and willingness of reference librarians to muster hard evidence in its favor. I think that this hard evidence can be found in data that represent the *full* array of reference activities; in surveys which indicate the "drawing power" of the service; in tests which suggest the worth of the service in terms of the time and money saved by the consumer; and above all in user studies which demonstrate the degree of consumer satisfaction achieved by the service.

It will take prolonged and concerned effort by reference librarians to devise reliable and practicable techniques for obtaining such evidence. To do so, they will first have to take the justification of reference service off the hidden agenda and place it prominently on their list of avowed priorities.

REFERENCES

1. See, for example: Joseph Wheeler and Herbert Goldhor, *Practical Administration of Public Libraries*. Completely revised by Carleton Rochell. (New York: Harper & Row, 1981), Chapter 15.

2. Ching-chih Chen and Peter Hernon, *Information Seeking: Assessing and Anticipating User Needs* (New York: Neal-Schuman, 1982).

3. Ernest De Prospo *et al. Performance Measures for Public Libraries* (Chicago: American Library Association, 1973), pp. 38-39.

4. *Ibid.*, p. 54-57.

5. Terry Weech, "Evaluation of Adult Reference Service," *Library Trends* 22: 320-321 (January, 1974).

6. Administrators of Medium-Sized Public Libraries of Ontario. Standards Committee, *Report on Performance Measures Surveys in Four Ontario Public Libraries*, by Sara Maley *et al.* (n.p.: September, 1977, mimeographed), p. 15.

7. Douglas Zweizig and Eleanor Jo Rodger, *Output Measures for Public Libraries: A Manual of Standardized Procedures* (Chicago: American Library Association, 1982.

8. Kramer, "How to Survive in Industry: Cost Justifying Library Services," *Special Libraries* 62: 487-489 (November, 1971).

9. Cf. Samuel Rothstein, "The Measurement and Evaluation of Reference Service," *Library Trends* 12: 464-465 (January 1964); Weech, *op.cit.*, p. 321; Charles Bunge, "Approaches to the Evaluation of Library Reference Service" *in Evaluation and Scientific Management of Libraries and Information Centres,* edited by F. W. Lancaster and C. W. Cleverdon (Leyden: Nordhoff, 1977), pp. 52-54. Bunge's study is particularly useful as providing the most comprehensive and thorough examination of all aspects of the evaluation of reference service.

10. *How Effective Are Your Community Services? Procedures for Monitoring the Effectiveness of Municipal Services,* by Harry P. Hatry, et al. (n.p.: The Urban Institute and The International City Management Association, 1977), pp. 69-76.

11. See, for example, the recent work by Marcia Myers and J. M. Jirsees, *The Accuracy of Telephone Reference/Information Services in Academic Libraries: Two Studies.* (Metuchen, N.J.: Scarecrow Press, 1983).

Tailoring Measures to Fit Your Service:
A Guide for the Manager
of Reference Services

Douglas L. Zweizig

> Managers are not confronted with problems that are in-
> dependent of each other, but with dynamic situations that con-
> sist of complex systems of changing problems that interact
> with each other. I call such situations *messes.* Problems are
> abstractions extracted from messes by analysis. . .Managers
> do not solve problems: they manage messes.
>
> —Russell Ackoff quoted in Donald A. Schon, *The
> Reflective Practitioner: How Professionals Think in
> Action.* N.Y.: Basic Books, 1983.

Managers of reference services are continuously aware of the
need to balance the complexity (''messiness'') of the service they
administer with the simplicity and clarity required of measures of
that service. No measure seems wholly satisfactory. No set of
measures will assess all the aspects of the service. Managers are
likely to conclude that they don't understand the measurement process or that those designing measures do not understand the reference process. The result is that measurement is not attempted or that
the data that are collected are not used.

This article will focus on how to think about measurement—how
to identify or design the kind of measure a manager might need in
order to tell how well a service is functioning. The article will not
emphasize statistical techniques. Statistics come into play after the
design process described here has been completed, and numerous
texts exist that deal with statistical techniques.

Professor Zweizig is at the Library School, University of Wisconsin, 600 N. Park St.,
Madison, WI 53706.

53

This focus has been chosen because the problem with evaluation does not relate to producing data. Community analysis techniques tell how to produce data about the service population. *A Planning Process for Public Libraries*[1] gives examples of surveys and of performance measures. *Performance Measures for Public Libraries* and *Output Measures for Public Libraries* give detailed instructions for applying specific measures.[2] Sources such as King and Bryant's *The Evaluation of Information Services and Products*[3] and Lancaster's *The Measurement and Evaluation of Library Services*[4] provide scores of example measures. Automated circulation systems will bury the manager in data. The current problem is to reduce the amount of time spent in looking at meaningless data and to use data efficiently to improve performance.

If data are to be useful to the manager, they must relate to the planning of the reference unit. The definition of planning used here is "a series of successive approximations to a moving target." The implication of this definition is that the function of data is to provide guidance, to give some indication of where the service is now and the direction in which it's moving. Because planning is done in a repeating series, measurement needs to be done periodically to inform the planning process. Because the goals of the organization will change over time (the moving target), measures must be adapted or replaced in order to remain relevant to the decisions being made.[5]

In identifying a measure to assist in the planning process, the reference manager might first specify the aspect of reference service that is of interest. Example aspects might be:

—community penetration (the degree to which the service reaches the community)
—user services (how well users are served)
—cooperation (how well a given library is able to share resources or services with other libraries)
—resources management (the degree to which the collection meets service needs)
—administration (the effectiveness of the management process)
—finances (the degree to which resources are adequate to the need)

When an aspect has been selected for focus (for example, user services), the choice of a measure will be aided by the articulation of a mission for that aspect. The mission expresses the intent of the service, its reason for existence. The mission is best phrased in terms of ends rather than means, in terms of the user rather than the library. An example mission for user services might be: to provide the most helpful responses to requests in the minimum time. The mission begins to direct attention to areas for possible measurements: helpfulness of responses, timeliness of responses.

IDENTIFICATION

Identifying a measure will also be assisted by listing the key functions of this aspect of service. For example, some key functions of reference user services might be: obtaining information from the user, identifying relevant sources of information, formulating the response, communicating the response to the user. Formally listing these key functions specifies just what services are being examined and suggests possible areas for measurement.

A further aid to generating measures is identifying desired areas of improvement. These are areas of the service that now are performed below some explicit or implicit standard. Since the totality of a service cannot be measured, attention to those areas of the service that are not working as well as they should will help to prioritize areas for measurement. If users complain about the time required for response, then a measure of time might be considered. If staff have noticed a reduction in requests for service, then monitoring of a measure such as number of reference transactions per member of the service population may be in order.

The purpose of articulating a mission, of listing key functions, and of identifying desired areas of improvement is to focus attention on just what aspects should be measured, why they should be measured, and how the results should be used in managing the service. This process involves the most difficult intellectual effort of the measurement process and is necessarily murky. But in the absence of such effort, measures are applied which do not fit the service being assessed, and the results obtained do not provide the information needed to monitor performance.

The product of this process is a list of elements of the service that may usefully be measured. These may relate to a variety of aspects such as the numbers of people served, the quality of the service in terms of time or accuracy, the number of inter-library requests filled, the degree to which materials in the reference collection are used, the staff turnover rate, or the proportion of materials requests for which funds are not available. If this process is a new one for the service, then the list of measures should probably be kept short. As experience is gained with this process, additional measures can be addressed.

The elements to be measured need next to be subjected to a refinement process that clarifies just what will be measured and how it should be measured. The refinement process involves testing candidate measures against a set of criteria.[6] The first set of criteria foster clarity in what should be measured. The second set test how well the proposed measure will work in practice.

WHAT WILL BE MEASURED?

Appropriateness and Validity

In general usage, the term "validity" refers to many aspects of measurement and therefore has lost precision of meaning. As used here, the term tests whether the proposed measure is the right measure for the aspect of interest. For example, if the aspect of interest is the helpfulness of service, a proposed measure may be the proportion of people served who answer "yes" to the question, "Did you find the service helpful?" But experience with such measures of "user satisfaction" shows that what is being measured by such questions is not the quality of service but the desire of users to be polite. Therefore, this measure lacks validity; it measures something other than it intends. A more valid measure would ask "In what way did the service help you?" or would focus more on behavior than on attitude: "How were the results of our service used?"

Establishing the validity of a measure is complex (recall the controversy over the validity of I.Q. testing), but for management purposes, it is enough to be able to speak to the question: Are you confident that the measure you are using measures what you think it does?

Interpretability

At some point, the results of measurement will need to be communicated to others. A test of a proposed measure is whether the results can be communicated in a sentence to staff or funders. Ohio State University Libraries were able to gain support for an automated circulation system in the mid-1960s by explaining, "We can save a quarter million user hours a year with the proposed system." Reference Fill Rate[7] translates into "We are presently able to complete 65% of our reference transactions by the end of the business day."

Controllability

There is an inevitable tension between the aspects of service of most interest and the aspects over which the library has control. Libraries provide materials so that users can gain new understanding, make better decisions, overcome problems, cope with worries, learn to live with difficult circumstances. But the library staff have virtually no control over the uses made of their materials. The library, on the other hand, has virtually complete control over which materials are owned. In between these extremes, the library shares control with the user: the library can control to some extent which materials circulate, to a small extent whether material that is circulated is read. The most satisfactory user services measures are those that point toward impacts of service but that also can be affected by management decision-making—measures in the middle range, such as circulation or demand for service.

Comparability

Some measures are of local interest only; some are more useful when the results can be compared with those from other libraries. Some measures are related to special projects; some are intended to be collected periodically over time. If comparisons with other libraries or over time are intended, then the measure needs to include definitions that are shared among libraries and needs to assess aspects of the service that are relatively unchanging.

Informativeness

This criterion tests whether the proposed measure will give the manager information on which to base decisions. One way to test a measure for informativeness is to ask: what decisions would be made if the results of measurement produced a high score? a low score? a moderate score? One public library administrator asked in a community survey whether respondents wanted the library to purchase more duplicate copies of popular items or to reduce duplication and purchase more unique titles. He intended to base the library's collection policy on the community's preference. The results of the survey were that 49% of the community wanted more duplicate copies and 51% wanted more unique titles.

The above five criteria (appropriateness and validity, interpretability, controllability, comparability, and informativeness) test proposed measures in terms of what will be measured. They provide tests which help clarify the thinking behind a proposed measure and help insure that a measure will produce useful data. The next criteria focus on how well the proposed measure will work in practice. They move beyond the considerations of the concept the measure is tapping to considerations of the design of the measure.

HOW WILL THE MEASURE WORK?

Practicality

This criterion asks whether the proposed measure is affordable in terms of time, money, and effort required to produce the results. In assessing reference service, many argue that unobtrusive testing of accuracy of responses to proxy-administered questions is the most valid measure. But libraries may question this methodology in terms of the expense involved. So validity is traded off against costs. Explicitly addressing this issue may bring to mind ways of making desired measures affordable.

Test questions that may be asked under this criterion are: Does the proposed method of measurement make maximum use of already collected data? Does it avoid duplication with already collected data? How can this measure be made less expensive? How would the measure be designed if money were no object?

Timeliness of Feedback

This criterion relates to the timing of the measurement. Results that arrive too late to affect decisions can be avoided by explicitly addressing this criterion. If data are needed in time for the annual budget request, the design needs to take that schedule into account. A second consideration of timeliness is how long it will take for a change in practice to affect results. For example, if document availability is the aspect being measured, how long will it take for a change in materials ordering practice to show up in increased document availability?

Accuracy and Reliability

This criterion deals with the trustworthiness of the data produced. A reliable measure is one that produces consistent results. Problems in reliability arise from staff using varying procedures to record data, from errors in transferring data from survey forms to tabulation forms, and from a host of other vagaries in measurement. A measure can be tested for reliability by inquiring where mistakes are likely to occur and then by pre-testing the measurement process. Sampling produces more accurate data than counting everything because there is less fatigue and boredom with the measure. Reference statistics suffer in reliability when staff neglect to accurately note transactions during busy periods or when staff definitions of kinds of transactions vary over time. Collections of sample reference statistics in confined periods of time allow improved staff attention to the measurement process, refreshed staff agreement on definitions, and closer supervision of the measurement process.

Representativeness

In selecting periods for measurement, the issue of representativeness needs to be taken into account. Some time periods are fairly typical, others are not. In public libraries, for example, the months of April and October seem representative of the school year months. In academic or secondary school libraries, the reference service will be strongly affected by the school calendar. If the aspect being measured is affected by the calendar, then the sample design needs to include periods to represent the entire year.

Precision Required

A final practical consideration is the precision that is required in the results. Metaphorically, the issue of precision refers to the fineness of mesh used in the screen. Since increases in precision involve increased cost, the issue here is a managerial one. It is wasteful to buy more precision than necessary, so the manager needs to decide how much precision is needed. For example, the precision of estimates obtained by sampling is directly linked to the size of the sample. Generally, a sample size of 100 will produce an estimate that has a 95% chance of being within ±10% of the value for the entire population. A result of 40% produced from a sample of 100 gives a 95% chance of the "true" value being between 30% and 50%. In order to increase the precision to ±5%, the sample size would have to be increased to 400. To increase the precision to +2%, the sample size would have to be increased to around 1500.[8]

Since increased precision involves an escalation in the sample sizes, and therefore expense, required, the manager needs to determine how much precision is required. For many library decisions, small differences are not of interest. If the library has introduced a service innovation, a five per cent increase in usage is not sufficiently different from no change. A five per cent decline in materials availability will probably not cause a manager to redesign ordering practices. For most areas of service, managers are only concerned with differences of ten per cent or more. Therefore, in most cases, managers are better off with smaller, less precise measures that are affordable and can be applied regularly.

The process described here is lengthy: focussing on an aspect of the service, articulating a mission, enumerating key functions, identifying areas for improvement, and then testing proposed measures against a set of criteria. But if the reference manager is to design a measure that fits the service (or to use a measure designed by someone else), some such process is necessary. After going through this process, the manager will be able to enlist the help of experts (statisticians, forms designers, survey researchers), as needed, to design the mechanics of measurement. In the absence of such a process, the manager is likely to receive data that are not helpful in managing the service.

The process described here can be carried out by an individual, but is probably better done in a small working group. Involvement of members of the staff brings the benefits of their perspective on the service, the potential of brainstorming alternative measures for the same aspect of service, and greater understanding by the staff of the purposes of measures to be implemented.

The quotation at the beginning of this article has several morals in terms of the measurement of reference services. The imposition of any measure on a reference service is an unnatural act. It requires that many complexities be ignored while selected aspects are isolated for examination. Even the most custom-designed measure will be unsatisfactory when compared to the reality of the service; ready-made measures are likely to be less satisfactory. The design of a measure requires a series of compromises: trading off validity for practicality, representativeness for timeliness of feedback. The manager must nevertheless apply measurement to the service in order to inform decisions. The process described here has the purpose of identifying for the manager just where the compromises are made.

REFERENCES

1. V. E. Palmour *et al. A Planning Process for Public Libraries.* Chicago, American Library Association, 1980.

2. Ernest DeProspo *et al. Performance Measures for Public Libraries.* Chicago, ALA, 1973; Douglas Zweizig and Eleanor Jo Rodger. *Output Measures for Public Libraries.* Chicago, ALA, 1982.

3. Donald W. King & Edward Bryant. *The Evaluation of Information Services and Products.* Washington, D.C., Information Resources Press, 1971.

4. F. W. Lancaster. *The Measurement and Evaluation of Library Services.* Washington, D.C., Information Resources Press, 1977.

5. This view of the use of data is in contrast to the prevailing practice of collecting the same library statistics year after year regardless of the goals of the library.

6. The application of criteria to measures that is formalized here has been aided by Richard H. Orr, ''Measuring the Goodness of Library Services: a General Framework for Considering Quantitative Measures,'' Journal of Documentation, Vol. 29, no.3 (September 1973) 315-332 and Harry P. Hatry *et al.,* How Effective are Your Community Services? Procedures for Monitoring the Effectiveness of Municipal Services, Washington, D.C.: The Urban Institute and the International City Management Association, 1977.

7. Zweizig and Rodger, 45-50.

8. Other factors are also involved in selecting a sample size; the figures used here are for purposes of illustration.

Definitions for Planning
and Evaluating Reference Services

Katherine Emerson

In order to express how good or bad any service is, one must first define what is under evaluation. Evaluation of reference service can be a review of the broad array of services that libraries may provide to the public and a consideration of whether the particular offerings of the library in question are a good match for the information needs of its public. Or evaluation may be an assessment of the correctness of responses to reference questions posed at the reference desk, or to reference questions called in by telephone or distinguished by some other characteristic. Or a group of library users may be asked to express the level of their satisfaction with the services offered by the reference department, or with the particular service of answering reference questions. Sometimes the focus of the evaluation, whether on the selection of services offered or on the quality of those services, is not altogether clear to those doing the evaluation, particularly if it is the public, which typically does not understand the implications of library terminology as specifically as librarians do.

Some of the difficulty of evaluation of reference service comes from the very different combinations of services that different reference departments offer. Cynthia Duncan identified no fewer than 118 different tasks performed in reference departments in just one type of library in one state.[1] Each department in any type of library has its own combination of tasks; the differences are attributable to

The author is an experienced librarian and a consultant. She may be reached at 130 Lake Ellen Drive, Chapel Hill, NC 27514.

different types of users, different levels of support, different philo-sophies and policies of service, and of course different histories. The variety of administrative structures that has grown up in libraries results from such factors and in turn causes further varia-tion. Reference service is divided in some libraries into departments or other separate locations based on subject specialization. In other libraries reference service is integrated to cover all or most subjects in one place, but there may still be separate service points carrying out some or all reference functions for different age groups or for different types of material, including but not limited to periodicals, microforms, audiovisual materials, manuscripts, maps, and govern-ment publications. The "not limited to" is important because by the very nature of its role as the library's interface with the public, reference service typically has very few limitations but is constantly facing rising expectations from its public. Joanne Euster, in an earlier issue in this series, pointed out the problem of overload and frustration brought by the diffuse array of services that any library might offer to the public, with new trends and technologies develop-ing in times when staff size cannot be expected to expand to match.[2] She points out that "it is essential to recognize the extremely broad scope and complexity of activities which are now subsumed into readers services or reference services departments, and to conscien-tiously separate the tasks into discrete units and activities so that the principles of time management can be applied." And, I would add, so that other evaluation and planning for improved quality or effi-ciency or preferably both, can be done.

DIFFICULTY

Fortunately, one other long-standing difficulty in evaluation of reference service—the lack of agreement in the profession on defini-tions of even the most basic service, that of answering reference questions—has recently been resolved. In response to a strong call in the profession for a standard system of measuring reference ser-vice,[3] definitions were developed during 1974-83 through extensive discussion in a series of program sessions, hearings, workshops, and committee meetings of the Reference Statistics Committee of the American Library Association's Library Administration and Man-agement Association, with frequent participation of the ALA Ref-erence and Adult Services Division and its relevant committees.

Definitions were developed and reviewed for acceptability by hundreds of librarians during these years. This was part of the major, multi-association effort that resulted in the publication of the *American National Standard for Library and Information Sciences and Related Publishing Practices—Library Statistics, ANSI Z39.7-1983* (New York, American National Standards Institute, 1983). The basic reference definitions incorporated in this *Standard* had reached something close to consensus as early as 1976, though some specific definitions, such as those for bibliographic instruction and other developing areas, reached final form only in the 1980s as the work of the ANSI subcommittee neared its end.

The achievement of consensus in an area as disputed as reference measurement provided some of the momentum needed to develop the rest of this long and complex *Standard.* In 1977 Jerrold Orne, chairman of the American National Standards Committee on Libraries and Information Science and Related Publishing Practices (better known as ANSI Committee Z39), called on me (I had chaired the ALA Reference Statistics and Statistics Coordinating Committees) to form a Z39 subcommittee to revise the original 1968 *Standard* for library statistics, whose recommendations were not very detailed and, for reference reporting, were internally inconsistent by type of library. Moreover, its definitions of a reference question, a concept not defined in the 1943 *ALA Glossary of Library Terms*—as ''Any request for information or aid which requires the use of one or more sources to determine the answer, or which utilizes the professional judgment of the librarian''—was unworkable because of its use of professional status and judgment as criteria, since staff members other than professionals were providing reference service in many libraries.

STANDARD

The subcommittee included Ellen Altman, Evelyn Daniel, Helen Eckard, Janice Feye-Stukas, C. James Schmidt, Ronald Dubberly 1977-79, and Glenn Miller 1979-83 in addition to myself. During the highly consultative process that developed the *Standard* as a whole, definitions evolved for information contacts other than typical reference questions handled at the desk: database transactions, bibliographic instruction, and cultural presentations; and agreement eventually was reached on a reporting system that will give libraries a clearer view of the scope of their reference and related public services than most of them have had before. Some performance measures important to reference service are also included. On the second, final, ballot the proposed standard was approved without a negative vote from any of the forty-five member organizations of Committee Z39, and the standard was subsequently adopted by the Board of Standards Review of the American National Standards Institute, Inc. Library association members of Z39 include the American Association of Law Libraries, American Library Association, American Society for Information Science, American Theological Library Association, Association of Jewish Libraries, Association of Research Libraries, Catholic Library Association, Council of National Library and Information Associations, Medical Library Association, Music Library Association, and Special Library Association. Other members include our three national libraries; networks, cooperatives, representatives of information services and publishing; and the U.S. Department of Education, which had funded the creation of several detailed handbooks that served as working papers for writing the standard.

The new edition of *The ALA Glossary of Library and Information Science,* edited by Heartsill Young (Chicago, ALA, 1983) uses the *Standard's* definitions for reference service, although it omits some details of counting that appear in the *Standard* but are outside the scope of the more general *Glossary.* (It also omits a definition of a database reference transaction, probably because of a failure on my part to supply it to Mr. Young.) ALA's Reference and Adult Services Division Board voted during the Midwinter 1984 meeting to adopt the definitions in *ANSI Z39.7-1983* that are relevant to reference and adult services. The action was taken at the request of Charles Bunge, chair of ALA RASD's Committee on Evaluation of Reference and Adult Services. RASD's Machine-Assisted Reference Section (MARS) had been a principal contributor to the definition of a database reference transaction, and to many other computer-related parts of the *Standard* as well; and the definitions and reporting system for bibliographic instruction were negotiated with several ALA groups in this area. These adoptions indicate that we have, in 1983-84, reached the long-sought national agreement on reference definitions.

The definitions and reporting structure in the 1983 *Standard* provide a needed conceptualization of reference service. While some libraries offer ''reference service'' and other libraries and more particularly information centers offer "information service," both services share the purpose of providing information to the public. Once this is recognized as the essential defining characteristic of references and information service, it becomes apparent that other functions offered by libraries, often under the rubrics of "outreach services" or "instruction," share the same purpose. So the *Standard* links these several related services as different ways of providing information. The basic definitions in the *Standard* are:

Information service. The personal assistance provided to users in pursuit of information. Consultation of circulation records requested by users is not included. For types of information service, see *information contact; information service to groups.*

Information contact. An encounter in person, by telephone, mail, or other means, between a member of the reference staff and a user, in which information is sought or provided. An information contact may be a directional transaction or a reference transaction, a bibliographic instruction or library use presentation, or a cultural, recreational, or educational presentation.

Reference transaction. An information contact that involves the use, recommendation, interpretation, or instruction in the use of one or more information sources, or knowledge of such sources, by a member of the reference or information staff. Information sources include: (1) print and nonprint materials; (2) machine-readable databases; (3) the library's own bibliographic records, excluding circulation records; (4) other libraries and institutions; and (5) persons both inside and outside the library.

A question answered through utilization of information gained from previous consultation of such sources is considered a reference transaction, even if the source is not consulted again. A contact that includes both reference and directional service is one reference transaction. Duration should not be an element in determining whether a transaction is reference or directional. See also *directional transaction.* [A footnote to this definition refers to further interpretation in my "National Reporting on Reference Transactions, 1976-78," *RQ* 16: 202-205 (1977), with the caution that some interim definitions in that article are superseded by definitions in the 1983 *Standard.* The 1977 article also contains history, rationale, and directions for application of the reference definitions, which will not be repeated in the present paper.]

Directional transaction. An information contact that facilitates the use of the library in which the contact occurs, or its environs, and that may involve the use of sources describing the library, such as schedules, floor plans, handbooks, and policy statements. Examples of directional transactions include: directions for locating facilities such as special rooms, carrels, and telephones; directions for locating library staff and users; directions for locating materials for which a user has a call number or which are designated on signs or floor plans; supplying library handbooks, policy statements, floor plans, and materials such as paper and pencils; and assisting users with the operation of machines. Directional assistance provided as a part of a reference transaction should not be counted here. See also *reference transaction.*

The reporting structure of the *Standard* calls for libraries to record all reference and directional transactions during a "typical week," and provides counting instructions in order to standardize reporting: count mail, telephone, and in-person contacts of the public with all staff members "whose assigned duties include the provision of reference or information service." And, a point necessary for reasons of practicality: "Staff members should report each contact separately, whether or not the user has already consulted either that staff member or another on the same information need." (It would be prohibitive for busy staff to ascertain that each contact was pristine before recording it, and the overlap, small in any case, does represent both workload and staff-public contacts.) The definitions for this weekly count deal with transactions resulting, typically at the reference desk, from individual users' questions. Reporting is called for in both the reference and the directional categories because some libraries have in the past made a single count including only reference questions proper, while other libraries have made a single count including all requests made of the reference staff, including directional. These different practices would persist in some libraries in any single count called for at present. The integrity of the count of reference questions proper can be protected, and continuity with different libraries' past reporting provided, only by making clear in the act of reporting itself, that directional transactions are different from reference transactions proper. A count of directional transactions is also worthwhile *per se,* if the effort of making it is held down, and the *Standard's* recommended count for only a typical week does minimize the counting effort.

Supplementing these definitions of transactions with individual users in traditional modes are definitions of other forms of information service not always recognized and in the past seldom reported as such. These are recommended for annual reporting since no single week can be considered typical for them:

Information service to groups. An information contact in which a staff member provides information intended for a number of persons and planned in advance. Information service to groups may be either bibliographic instruction or library use presentations; or it may be cultural, recreational, or educational presentations. Presentations both on and off the library premises are included, as long as they are sponsored by the library.

Bibliographic instruction. An information service to a group, which is designed to teach library users how to locate information efficiently. The essential goals of this process are an understanding of the library's system of organization and the ability to use selected reference materials. In addition, instruction may cover the structure of the literature and the general and specific research methodology appropriate for a discipline. This is distinct from library use presentation.

Library use presentation. An information service to a group designed to introduce potential library users to the facilities, organization, and services of a particular library—also called library orientation. It is distinct from bibliographic instruction.

Cultural, recreational, or educational presentation. An information service to a group that enriches the intellectual life of participants, provides wholesome entertainment, or provides formal instruction in some subject other than the use of the library. Examples are book reviews and discussions, media presentations, musical events, lectures, and story hours.

Database reference transaction. A reference transaction that results in a search of one or more machine-readable databases.

For information service to groups, the annual count includes the number of presentations made, a measure of staff effort and public opportunity. As a measure of the public's response that is compatible with the reporting of individual contacts and thus forms a consistent reporting system, attendance at each presentation is recorded separately, even if a presentation is one in a series that constitutes a course. Retention of the information contact as the basic unit in all of the library's forms of information service provides a comprehensive view that keeps any of the parts from being overlooked because they use a different reporting mode that does not have a place in the library's mainstream of numerical data on its activities. An additional count was added for bibliographic instruction, whose attendance is characteristically expressed in academic terms: "When bibliographic instruction is offered on an enrollment basis, report the number of individuals enrolled."

Information service to groups, and particularly cultural and recreational presentations, is a very different activity from answering reference questions that are asked by users. So are database searches that are intended to be exhaustive on a subject. But each is a form of selection of sources and presentation of information to meet the needs of users. If a library sponsors a recreational presentation, its purpose can be assumed to be consistent with the overall purpose of the library, either directly in the presentation of information (including the fresh ways of looking at previously existing information that contribute equally to research insights and to great comedy) or of library resources, or indirectly as a means of acquainting the public with the library so that library resources will be used and information transferred later.

REPORTING

This comprehensive reporting is not intended to substitute media presentations, lectures, etc. for basic reference service, the provision of information requested at reference desks. Rather, it is to recognize that information is provided by library reference/information staff in more than one form and more than one context. It brings the reporting system out of the past, with its limitation to desk work, and into the present greater diversity that reference service has reached.

The nationally adopted standard definitions should bring direct savings in time to individual libraries or systems wishing to evaluate reference services, since libraries will no longer need to invest time to create definitions on their own. A second advantage is that these and other definitions in the *Standard,* developed cooperatively by a great many librarians and endorsed by a number of library and information associations through their participation in the national organization for voluntary standardization, will be used widely by libraries and researchers, so that soon there will be a body of data, some published and some on record in libraries, systems, or state agencies, with which individual libraries can compare their performance on the same functions, defined in the same way. Translation of one library's categories and inclusions and exclusions should not have to be made in order for its results to provide information useful to another library. While the conceptualization of reference service provided in the *Standard* is an important means of understanding the service called for and provided, and alternatives to it, the use of comparable data on the operations of other libraries sharpens perception of a single library substantially.

To illustrate the value of the definitions and of following them fully rather than making local exceptions, let us consider only the one most obvious case, the role of definitions and quantitative measures in assessing the accuracy of answers provided to reference questions. This accuracy is expressed most easily and clearly as the percentage of correctly answered questions out of the total questions received. Without quantitative units of measure, qualitative evaluations of this service can be expressed only very inexactly. Compare the information conveyed in the statement "Our reference service is above average" with the information conveyed in "Our reference staff is providing correct and complete answers to 70% of the reference questions received." If a survey of a library's reference users rated the service as "above average" and the library thereupon instituted a program of staff development in reference skills, everyone involved should want to know if any change resulted. But without quantitative measures, progress could be reported only in some such terms as "improved from 'above average' to midway between 'above average' and 'very good.' " The ability to make and express discriminations of quality is on a different order if one uses quantitative measures. Even the assigning of numerical values to a ranking scale, so that it becomes a ranking "on a scale of 10," gives rankings whose relationships are so widely understood that "Ten" or "Nine" can be used as the title of a film without any of the ambiguity inherent in "Far Above Average" or "Outstanding." Use of a number scale like 0 to 100 provides means of expressing even finer gradations meaningfully because the notation is both clear and succinct as well as widely understood.

ASSUMPTION

The use of a scale of 100 to express ratings, however, carries with it an implication of exactness that calls for all libraries that may be comparing data with each other to adhere to the same definitions. The assumption that reference departments correctly answer very nearly all the reference questions they handle is no longer tenable since the development of testing of reference performance, particularly unobtrusive testing. But it is still a reasonable assumption that the success rate is substantially higher on directional transactions than it is on reference transactions proper, since directional requests are not the brain teasers that reference questions can be, and normally do not need skillful interviews to ferret out the real question. In order to illustrate the desirability of separating these two—of applying the *Standard* definitions consistently—let us use an estimate that 96% of directional transactions are handled correctly, which is as close to 100% as we ought to calculate, since no service is fail-safe; and an estimate that 60% of reference transactions proper have correct results, a figure slightly higher than that indicated by the growing body of literature of unobtrusive testing. (It should be noted that this literature in order to obtain data that provides comparisons of success and failure rates among different libraries, must use questions that are hard enough for reference staffs in some but not all of the tested libraries to fail to answer. The typical set of unobtrusive test questions is not selected to typify the *average* level of difficulty of reference service in the libraries tested, even though the questions fall within the broad range of difficulty represented by the libraries' typical service; the aim is at a level where there will be some successes and some failures.)

The ratio of reference to directional transactions varies from library to library, but for our purposes we can use the ratio of 45 reference to 55 directional transactions reported in both the 1977 and 1979 surveys of over 2,000 academic libraries by the National Center for Education Statistics,[4] which used the reference definitions in nearly final form.

If a library fails to exclude directional questions when calculating its success rate, even if it performs otherwise valid testing of its reference staff's success in answering questions at the desk its calculation will be misleading. Let us assume that two libraries both average 55 directional questions for every 45 reference questions proper, that each is successful with 96% of directional transactions and with 60% of reference transactions, and that those success rates miraculously turn up in the sample of 100 desk transactions that each library evaluates.

If Library A fails to exclude directional queries, it will find a success rate of 80% (representing successes on 96% of 55 directional transactions, or 53; and on 60% of 45 reference transactions proper, or 27; 53 plus 27 = 80 successes out of 100 contacts). But this is not a useful figure, since Library A does not know how many of the transactions are the reference transactions it set out to evaluate. In truth 55% of the contacts surveyed are directional transactions, which should be routine, usually are not worth the time and effort that must be expended to obtain a valid estimate of reference service quality, and if they are worth it, should be evaluated separately because of their different nature.

Library B, on the other hand, understands that such an effort is worthwhile only for the more varied and more difficult requests that have been defined as reference questions proper, and that evaluation of the two together is like performing the same type of testing on the flavor of oranges and apples and reporting results that do not identify the fruits separately but treat them as one group of fruit. Therefore in the transactions Library B monitors it omits directional questions, and finds a success rate of 60% on what it does monitor, reference transactions proper.

SATISFACTION

If it wants to know how well it is satisfying its public in directional transactions, Library B will monitor them separately or record and evaluate them separately if they are monitored in the same survey as reference transactions.

Library B may appear to be behind Library A by a score of 60% to 80%, but in fact it is far ahead because it has measured what it set out to measure, has not confused the issue by intermingling two different types of service, and can repeat the measurement later in confidence that any real improvement (or deterioration) in the interim will show up. Library A, on the other hand, has not used a tight enough definition to learn what it needs to know and is subject to an embarrassing drop from 80% to 60% when it realizes it has confusingly measured directional service along with reference service proper in this evaluation. This is one reason the ALA Reference Statistics Committee recommended that reference and directional transactions never be presented as a single composite figure.

The two cases also illustrate why evaluation should be understood as a step in the process of planning services and keeping them on target, not as an independent process whose outcome has not been designed to provide information that can be acted on. It is apparent also that any local decisions a library makes to except certain types of transactions from the standard definitions—for example, to treat explanation of library policies as reference rather than directional service—will result in a hybrid success rate that is partly directional and partly reference, partly orange and partly apple; comparisons with other libraries will not be valid and usefulness even within one library is limited.

The reporting system in the *Standard* gives further guidance for evaluation, and the full *Standard* should be consulted for different periods of time during which information can be collected that has been found to be both obtainable without a diversion of staff effort that would threaten ongoing services, and valid; for sampling methods within the capability of any library staff; and for a few performance measures that assess the context within which reference help is provided. Among the performance measures, for example, are indicators of the on-shelf availability of books and periodicals owned by the library, the proportion of users' interlibrary loan requests actually obtained, the average time for obtaining them, and how many items are having to be borrowed from other libraries per hundred circulations of the library's own materials. These are measures of the adequacy of the library's collection for the needs of its users that provide strategically important information on the context of reference service.

As information of this sort becomes available about a number of libraries, we will obtain an idea of the ranges in which libraries of different types are operating. The ratios and time-elapsed figures are telling and, like percentages, are usable at face value rather than having to be multiplied, divided, or otherwise manipulated to convey their message to libraries of all sizes and shapes. While there are varying conditions which affect the operations of all libraries, a large body of information about other libraries will normalize the variations and give library managers a solid comparative basis for assessment of any library's needs and achievements. Since there are expected to be significant differences in characteristics by type of library, the *Standard* recommends that information be cumulated only among libraries of the same type.

REDUCTION

Because a number of articles in recent years on professional versus nonprofessional staffing of reference desks have used reference measurement to argue for the reduction or virtual elimination of professionally trained librarians as the regular staff of reference desks, some comment on the relationship of these definitions to that question is in order here. In libraries with reference staffs large enough to allow the scheduling of different numbers of staff at the desk at different hours, it is unlikely to be economical, or to promote high quality service, if the department fails to take advantage of that fact.

The simplest goal of evaluation for scheduling purposes is quantitative: to determine the number of desk contacts hour by hour and to schedule available staff so that the number of contacts per staff member scheduled on the desk is as nearly the same as possible during each service hour of the day and the week. Unfortunately the desk hours of many reference departments resemble the office hours of a business even when their user population may start the day later, come in most heavily at midday when offices are least fully staffed, and continue coming in after the office worker has been able to close for the day. At the risk of stating the obvious, let me say that the scheduling of reference desks should be responsive to the patterns of users rather than of traditional office hours where there is any difference between the two.

In a forthcoming unobtrusive study of reference service at thirteen major universities I report on some flaws in staffing patterns such as having a single library assistant staffing the main reference desk alone every day during an always-rushed noon hour though the desk staff included over ten librarians, and having two librarians on the desk from 8 to 9 a.m. every day with very few users ever present, while at the other end of the day the service ended during the evening while the library was packed. Few people would argue that caseloads varying from one per staff hour on the desk to thirty or forty per staff hour make the most effective of staff resources. Some present-day staffing patterns are probably carried over from a past in which they may have been effective, but these cases, which are not isolated, illustrate that quantitative evaluation should be done frequently enough to maximize the ability of available staff to meet the needs of today, not those of yesterday. Such evaluation also needs to be done carefully enough to produce results that can be used, and used with confidence. For example, records of periods longer than one hour tend to lose their value as their duration is increased. A busy lunch hour may be followed by an early-afternoon slump, and a report on a two-hour period containing one hour from each of these periods does not help either to get extra help on the desk during peaks or to release unneeded staff from the desk to make productive use of their time during slack periods.

GOAL

A more functional goal of evaluation for scheduling purposes is both quantitative and qualitative, and is relevant to the professional versus nonprofessional composition of reference departments as well as to scheduling. The use of staff with different levels of qualifications will be successful in maintaining service, or minimizing reductions in it despite tight budgets, only to the extent that staff at different levels are on the desk at times when their services are appropriate. If there are periods of the day or week when the most challenging reference questions are asked, no amount of additional help from students or others with only minimal training will improve the service unless those same periods also have a large number of directional questions. If there are periods abounding in calls for addresses or phone numbers in obvious sources or directions about the library, those are the times to schedule less skilled staff if there are any on the staff. Only if the definitions of reference and directional transactions are used to record the service load hourly by type of transaction will the necessary information be gained for staffing at more than one level of qualification and for decisions on future hiring at different levels.

It sometimes seems that questions answerable from a limited number of "ready reference"-type tools kept at the reference desk can be answered by a staff member without training or with minimal training. This is true in some cases in almost any situation; with some staff members it is almost always true; and in some reference situations it is true often enough to be taken into account in planning service. But one of the great truths of reference service is that one person's easy question is another's hard one. This was mentioned with feeling, over and over at the meetings leading to the adoption of the standard reference definitions, and it was and is irrefutable. It was for this reason that duration of a transaction was explicitly prohibited in the definitions from playing any part in the distinction between directional and reference transactions. This was also part of the reason for a significant omission from the definitions: there is no definition of a ready reference transaction. The *ALA Glossary* of 1983 does define a ready reference *collection,* but that is not the same as a separate category of transaction.

In my unobtrusive study of university reference service, the number of errors in using one tool alone, the *Statistical Abstract of the United States,* a common ready reference tool, revealed difficulties with finding the latest information from several tables in the same volume giving different figures for the item sought, as well as problems with selecting items in the right column from headings whose terminology did not exactly match the wording sought, failure to read into the table three or more zeros from foot or headnotes stating "in thousands," "in millions," and numerous similar errors. A library degree is not necessary to find and read tables with consistent correctness (and it is no guarantee of that), but some ability and, for most people, some training are. It may well be that an undergraduate majoring in marketing is the best reader of economic tables, but that is a different case from any nonprofessional or any paraprofessional. Further, is the marketing major good with the other kinds of requests he will receive, or only "his" kind? Similar conditions exist for extracting correct and complete information from many other tools, even those in a ready reference collection.

PROBLEMS

Often when it is suggested that desks be staffed wholly by nonprofessionals, it is expected that they will call in a librarian on the infrequent occasion of a demanding reference question. This optimism about the ease of recognizing a reference question hidden behind an inquirer's opening request flies in the face of the commonly recognized need for skillful reference interviews to determine users' true information needs from their opening questions; indeed, question negotiation is one of the most professional of library tasks if not *the* most professional. If the reference desk is considered only a switching center, from which a small number of questions will be referred to professionally trained personnel, we can be sure that a large number of reference questions, introduced by directional or unclear inquiries, will never be recognized and the inquirers' information needs will not be met. Even the published library literature does not lack examples of "routine directional questions," cited as such, that contain unmistakable evidence that they are reference queries opened on a directional note. Can we expect students or others with little training or experience to be more perceptive than the professional authors of such articles? What percentage of them, and in what percentage of the cases? Only a study using carefully defined categories can provide this information, so necessary for correct decisions.

In addition, the mere fact of being transferred from one person to another and having to repeat the whole inquiry is time-consuming and frustrating for the inquirer, and in turn often causes the inquiry to be less well stated the second time, by either the first staff member, who couldn't handle it, or the now somewhat harassed inquirer, thus reducing its chances of a successful outcome. (To get the whole view of the disturbance created in referring the transaction we need to recall that a measurable number of inquirers have already placed their request elsewhere in the library and thus are placing it for at least the second time when they come to the reference desk from the circulation, information, catalog information, or reserve or other desk.) Both the user's frustration and the reduced chances of success with a repeated question tend to be ignored or given slight consideration by advocates of regular staffing of the desk by nonprofessionals who are supposed to call on professionals when needed. But even if we omit the putative reduction in success rate for referrals (which I have never seen documented), the desirability of avoiding user frustration has been given a high priority in reference service by a great number of evaluative studies in library science and other fields that indicate that the public values courteous treatment at least as high, and in many cases higher than concrete results in its contacts with service personnel.

So I would say in conclusion that evaluation of reference services, quantitative and qualitative, will not result in the same decisions in all libraries about such issues as the most efficient means of maintaining a desired level of effectiveness, or the amount of efficiency that can be introduced without lowering effectiveness. Each situation has to be evaluated carefully in terms of demand and available resources; priorities need to be assigned, decisions made on the basis of reliable quantitative information that bears on the points under consideration, and the results of change need to be measured the same way for confirmation or modification of decisions.

The role of the definitions, procedures, and supporting structure of *ANSI Standard Z39.7-1983* is to enable us to acquire, for individual libraries and nationally, quantified information essential for evaluation, including:

• the present quality of reference service, or any component of it;

- distribution of user demand by type or level of service, and throughout the schedule of desk service;
- distribution of staff time by type or level of service, and throughout the schedule; and
- the results of changes made after the initial evaluation, and their effectiveness and costs.

The *Standard* also enables us to express both quantitative and qualitative evaluations of reference service in quantitative terms that make comparisons easy and indicate first whether changes indicated in an evaluation will be worth their costs, and second, if changes are adopted provides us with a means of staying on target.

REFERENCES

1. Cynthia Duncan, *An Analysis of Tasks Performed by Reference Personnel in College and in University Libraries in Indiana.* Ann Arbor, Mich., University Microfilms, 1974.

2. Joanne Euster, "Helping the Manager: Defining Reference Services," *The Reference Librarian* 3: 35-37 (1982).

3. See particularly the *Proceedings of the Symposium on Measurement of Reference, 1974,* ed. Katherine Emerson (Chicago, American Library Association, Library Administration Division, 1974), excerpted in *RQ* 14: 7-19 (1974); and ALA Reference and Adult Services Division. Standards Committee, "A Commitment to Information Services," *RQ* 14: 24-26 (1974), which called for continuing measurement for evaluation and other purposes.

4. Figures for both surveys are reported in U.S. Department of Education. National Center for Education Statistics, *Library Statistics of Colleges and Universities, 1979 Institutional Data,* by Richard M. Beazley (Washington, the Center, 1981), p. 2.

QUESTION, ANSWER
AND LIBRARIAN

Referred Reference Questions: How Well Are They Answered?

Terence Crowley

Patrons of public libraries ask all sorts of reference questions, including some which cannot be answered, at least with local library resources. In some libraries which belong to cooperative systems, a proportion of these unanswered questions are referred to other, usually larger libraries which have been designated as referral centers. Often the Headquarters Library of the system, the referral—or second level—center has larger collections of reference material, a staff trained in reference work, and, increasingly, access to online databases and long distance telecommunications. At most second level centers the questions are either answered or returned, but in California, there is a third level to which referral centers can themselves refer. In Los Angeles, the Southern California Answer Network fulfills this function for Southern California, while in the North, the Bay Area Reference Center serves Central and Northern California system.

This is a study of how well reference referral centers answer the reference questions referred to them by local public libraries. Specifically, it compares the quality of answers provided by a second level center, the San Joaquin Valley Information Service (SJVIS) located in Fresno, with those provided by a third level center, the Bay Area Reference Center (BARC) and with a commercial service, Information on Demand (IOD), which has some experience in answering reference questions from public libraries.

The method used in comparing SJVIS with the other two systems is to compare the answers provided by each system to thirteen reference questions, judging the answers with various criteria to deter-

Professor Crowley is at the Division of Library and Information Services, San Jose State University, CA 95192.

mine the "best answer" for each. No other element of reference service is taken into account. More importantly, the individuals asking the questions have not been consulted about their reactions to various answers. Because of the constraints imposed by the preliminary nature of the study, there is no extensive literature search, although a brief bibliography is appended.

The outline of the overall reference study poses several questions to be answered. Briefly summarized, they ask 1) if a second-level reference center could answer questions now referred to third level centers if more money for resources and staff were provided; 2) how much would that cost and would it be cost effective; 3) does the cost of answering questions and the quality of the answers from SJVIS compare favorably with BARC and IOD; and, 4) what questions can only be answered by third level centers.

Conversation with the SJVIS director and an examination of the documentation reveals that there are larger, more involved questions than those relating just to the SJVIS comparisons. The question of funding second and third level centers is obviously important and just as obviously in need of additional research. Although this study provides some additional light on the question of comparative quality of second and third level centers it is clear to the author that the sample of questions is too small, the selection too biased, and the funding inadequate for this study to reach any firm conclusions. The results of the study suggest some possibilities for further research.

OVERALL COMMENTS

The thirteen reference questions represent a range of subject interests; six appear to be related to a business, hobby, or self-improvement project while another six could be characterized as curiosity or enlightenment inquiries. One question is medical (or pharmaceutical). These labels are tentative because we have almost no information about the uses to which the answers will be put or the situation of the inquirer. Without that background, we cannot be certain if the categories really fit. But assuming that the labels are valid, a higher percentage of the six "curiosity" questions is answered than of the "business" type. Four out of five of the former are answered, while only two of the six business questions are completely and unequivocally answered.

Another way to characterize these questions is according to

whether they are requesting extensive material or brief information. The business questions, with one exception, seek material on how to do something. The curiosity questions require shorter, more defined information.

Methods used in answering questions: These include 1) checking indexes to periodicals and reference books; 2) searching computer data bases; 3) writing local or out of town sources of information; 4) telephoning local or out of town sources of information; 5) scanning files compiled by a library; and 6) testing "collective memory" by soliciting answers in a newsletter to librarians. Collective memory was probably tested by discussing the question(s) with one or more colleagues, but that was not documented.

Quality criteria. There are several components to any judgement of the quality of the answers. The first one is objective; it rests on numerical assessment and a stated, "reasonable number" judgement. For instance, in a request for a list of companies, a list with five companies is better than a list with one company although no assumptions are made about how much better the larger list is. Also, there is probably a point of diminishing returns, when the size of a list diminishes its utility. The judgement can be made only when there is an unequivocal answer to a question. It cannot be made when the request is for "material on subject X" and one is comparing different quantities of material; in such a case, "more" is not always "better."

The second criterion is more qualitative. An answer which is "enhanced" with additional information which is clearly relevant to the question is better than one which is not enhanced. For a question about fish exporters a letter from FIJI detailing the kinds of fish handled by each exporter is better than the answer which provides no information about the kind of fish exported, even though the original question did not specify wanting to know.

A third criterion is speed. An answer provided in 24 hours is better than one provided in 60 days, other things being equal. It is also true that for some inquirers, speed is not a criterion. For the purposes of this study, we assume that speed is a criterion.

A fourth criterion is appropriateness, which consists of matching the level of technical expertise of the inquirer with the material. Again, this is impossible to judge without interviewing the inquirer, although in a few cases judgements can be made tentatively.

It seems clear that these criteria are not always distinct and separable, and that without interviewing the inquirer we have no way of judging whether a fast, brief, unenhanced answer is to be preferred to a longer, slower, enhanced one. We employ our own best judgement in determining the quality of answers, trying to make our own biases and assumptions explicit so that the reader may take them into account.

In addition to these criteria, there are other issues on which reasonable reference librarians will disagree depending upon the individual situations. One is the question of how far to go in obtaining information on behalf of a patron, and at what stage of the inquiry to refer the patron to the sources of information, print or personal. Some libraries have policies in this matter; others do not. Closely related is the issue of policy regarding questions which call for legal or medical judgements. We know of no professional consensus on the issue of when a question calls for judgement. A third issue is when to refer to an expert outside of the library. In our opinion, referrals should be made only after the librarian has determined that the expert is 1) appropriate to the inquirer's need, and 2) willing to share his or her expertise. Blind referrals, wherein the reference librarian is guessing about the ability of the place or person called to respond appropriately, should be avoided.

The answers compared. The catchword for each question is in capital letters.

1. Setting up a COURIER business in a rural county. SJVIS did not know the county of origin, and hence could not make any calls to appropriate local officials. IOD called local county offices and obtained some specific details of county requirements. BARC's written material included some that was judged less relevant. In a meeting with SJVIS staff there was some indication that SJVIS staff would dispute the propriety of making those calls instead of referring the patron, but in our opinion the IOD calls were appropriate and helpful. SJVIS noted that "part of our function is training local staffs. This is an opportunity to teach them how to use their own local resources. We would recommend they call." SJVIS included some references to the *United States Code* and the *Federal Register* which we found inappropriate. The SJVIS DIALOG search apparently did not yield the same results as the BARC database search, but there was no documentation.

2. Fish exporters from FIJI. BARC answered this question with a single company name after some dialog with the inquirer which SJVIS had no opportunity to match. IOD made a call which BARC had suggested the patron make and generally documented the pro-

cess better. SJVIS followed up a call to the Fiji UN mission with a letter to the Fiji Economic Development Board. Approximately eleven weeks later a letter listing five companies and their fish specialities was received. Was this enhanced but delayed answer useful? Without recourse to the inquirer we cannot judge. This is one of two clear examples of enhanced answers being received later than simple answers.

3. Biographical information on an artist named RUDISUHLI. This is one of the questions in which a difference seems to emerge. The art references available at San Francisco Public Library are clearly superior to those found at either Fresno Public or the California State University in Fresno. Because the BARC and IOD staff had access to more scholarly sources they could compare sources and resolve what was apparently an error in one of the standard reference sets.

4. Identification of DYN, an Argentinian news agency. SJVIS called New York; the Associated Press provided the literal answer to the question within one day. An enhanced answer with additional information was received by BARC two weeks after they sent a letter to Argentina. As with question 2, FIJI, we do not know how the inquirer would have responded to each of the two answers.

5. Words and music to SONG: ''It is somebody's birthday . . . '' SJVIS did not find the answer to this question, an example of a genre question which is reported by BARC to be extremely difficult to answer. BARC did not find it in the SFPL Art Department's Song Title Index because of a misleading reference to a verse which did not match the chorus being searched. IOD found the words and music through a reference from the same Song Title Index. This is another example of a source which SJVIS could not duplicate because it is unique.

6. Title, author and full text of a POEM which begins ''If you put your nose to the grindstone rough . . . '' No library answered this, another of the quotations—poem—song genre. SJVIS did not do an original search on this question according to the documentation but tried their own Collective Memory vehicle, the newsletter IMPULSE.

7. Ideas and plans for building a WATERFALL indoors. Both BARC and IOD found complementary material, with one IOD book particularly helpful. SJVIS found ''dribs and drabs'' but was handicapped by having to use ILL for ''magazine articles which might be helpful but which [we] have not yet received.'' The smaller period-

ical collection available in Fresno played a part in the response to this question.

8. Is STEVIA Rebaudiana, a South American plant substance contained in a pill patron is taking, harmful? This question contained incorrect information from the patron in the form of the pill name. Both SJVIS and BARC called the manufacturer who was very guarded with information. IOD did not catch the erroneous pill name and thus provided a printout which the referring library thought might give "false reassurances." The medical pharmaceutical nature of this question made it difficult to judge.

9. Patron wanted material with which to teach his four-year-old son ENGLISH. Of the thirteen questions, this one proved to be least satisfactory in terms of receiving a responsive, satisfactory answer. BARC's initial response was modified by its inquiry into the qualifications of the father-as-teacher. BARC learned that the father was "essentially non-English-speaking" and had no teaching experience and then responded with a variety of material, citations, and a promise of a catalog from the Bay Area Bilingual Education League. IOD's material came from four groups "involved with bilingual education." SJVIS sent "several books that may help." In the author's opinion, this question was not answered well by any of the Reference Centers, in part because it is an example of a question asking for assistance of a kind that may not exist in the County of origin. The father wanted help in teaching his son English, but 1) his son was only four and 2) the father did not speak English. Although there may be services in larger cities for foreign language speaking children to help them learn English, it seems unlikely that those services would be available in an essentially rural county. If they were, then perhaps the best approach would have been to put the father in touch with them. Not every problem has a solution, nor every question an answer.

10. Patron wanted to know the stall speed of a torque converter necessary for an automobile transmission being used in a MARINE installation as well as general information. Both BARC and IOD queried boat equipment shops. In successive calls about converting auto to marine transmissions, BARC was told by three experts: 1) it can't be done; 2) it is possible but not worth it; and 3) we do it all the time. The last expert also asked not to be identified to the patron as a source of free information. SJVIS answer was much less adequate: a note that they were borrowing a 1978 edition of a title mentioned by the referring center and three nonspecific references to professional

associations, *Thomas Register,* and transmission manufacturers. The lack of marine equipment companies locally probably diminished the potential for SJVIS to answer this question. It was also a technical question for which some reference librarians would feel that the patron would be better off calling sources of information directly.

11. Patron wanted breeding information about a type of chicken called FRIZZLES. SJVIS had more material which appeared to be relevant to this question than either of the other two centers, perhaps because of the agricultural nature of the question. A very useful complement to the print material was BARC's contact with a professor at the school of Agriculture at the University of California, Davis, who was an expert on chickens. The professor offered to help the patron both with information and also with direct services at UCD.

12. Source of a quote identified by Referring Library as originating with GOETHE: "No one has ever loved as much as we have loved . . . " BARC obtained the answer to this question eventually by writing to the curator of the Goethe collection at Yale (a source identified in Ash's *Subject Collections,* according to BARC staff) who found the source and full text. SJVIS checked eleven titles (eight in German) and followed up on a (false) lead from another reference librarian who thought that the quote "sounds like it came from" two titles, neither of which was the right one.

13. Detailed information on making a HAWAIIAN quilt. Both SJVIS and BARC found an additional, appropriate title, when IOD did not.

CONCLUSIONS

It seems clear that there is no "winner" in this three-way contest of "referencemanship." Each of the three centers answered some questions better than either of the other two centers, and each failed to answer questions which other centers answered.

Comparing SJVIS with BARC on these questions shows BARC to be somewhat more successful. BARC had access to superior art reference books for RUDISUHLI, and more appropriate experts in MARINE; their strategy was better in Goethe and their expert accessible in FRIZZLES. SJVIS had a better "enhanced" answer for FIJI and a faster, unenhanced answer for DYN.

Responding specifically to the question of whether second level centers can answer some questions now referred to third level centers, we suggest a qualified yes. More funds would have to be spent by second level centers on reference books, long-distance telephone budgets, and ad hoc purchases from local bookstore. On the other hand, second level centers will never match the quantity of highly trained staff nor can they duplicate SFPL collections, files and contacts which BARC uses to advantage. It should be noted that the second level centers vary a great deal in resources, and that SJVIS may be among the strongest centers, both in collection and in the quality of staff. No judgments about other second level centers should be made on the basis of SJVIS as an example.

What levels of staff and resources would it take to make SJVIS the functional equivalent of BARC? This question can't be answered because of the unpredictability of questions and the resources needed. A far more extensive study would have to be undertaken to determine if it would be cost effective to raise the resource and staff levels of SJVIS.

The cost questions of the outline are particularly hard to address because of the small number of questions and the different strategies adopted by SJVIS—sometimes re-doing another library's search and sometimes building on a search. Because of these variables, the only conclusion reached concerning cost figures is that on the surface, BARC and SJVIS seem closely comparable in hourly costs. (BARC estimated $15/hour for staff time, SJVIS estimated $13.62.)

A more controlled, rigorous study might reveal cost figures in which all parties could be confident. If such a study is designed, it should control the way in which the center receives the question, the description of prior work accomplished, the standards for documenting the search, and the criteria for evaluating answers. These should be worked out in consultation with the staffs of the centers and if at all possible should involve the end-user's evaluation. Panel judgement on the appropriateness of answers such as the King Study employed might avoid the problems inherent in a single judgement. The sensitivities of the staff to what may appear to them to be a "waste of time" on stale reference questions should be taken into account, as well as the natural disinclination to accept another's professional judgement. The advantages of contrived questions, carefully designed to test certain elements of potential service, should also be considered.

Finally, any study should consider the advantages of independent, multiple approaches to the measurement of reference capacity. Collection evaluation, staff review, and testing of delivery can effectively complement each other when attempting to "measure reference quality"; the strengths of one approach will tend to offset the weaknesses of another approach, and used in concert, several methods strengthens one's confidence in the overall conclusion.

QUESTIONS

1. Patron wants to establish a local COURIER (messenger) service to transport documents, medical papers, etc., locally. He needs to know the legal requirements and any general information on such a service.
2. Patron wants a list of companies based in the South Pacific that export seafood from the FIJI islands to the U.S. Patron needs names, addresses, telephone numbers, etc.
3. Patron needs information on Herman RUDISUHLI. Anything available.
4. Patron wants to know what "DYN" stands for. They were used in an AP news story on the Falkland's war 6/10/82: "The privately owned news agency DYN said . . . "
5. Words and music to the SONG "It is somebody's birthday."
6. Title and text of POEM which begins "If you put your nose to the grindstone rough and hold it down there long enough you will forget there are such things as brooks that babble and birds that sing . . . "
7. Patron wishes material with ideas and construction plans for building a WATERFALL indoors. He has seen one made of a redwood stump with water falling from bucket to bucket. The measurements he plans to stay within are approximately 6′ tall and 2′ wide. He particularly needs to know pipe sizes to use with various pumps.
8. Patron is taking a pill called Magnolol, manufactured by Marathon Nutrition. It contains a substance from the South American plant STEVIA Rebaudiana, which he believes is a "natural steriod" but which CRC Handbook of Food Additives (1972) identifies as a sweetening agent. Patron wants to know if the substance is harmful.
9. Patron wants to teach a very young child ENGLISH. The child, around age four, is of Spanish-speaking parents.

10. Patron wants to convert an automobile transmission to MARINE use.
11. Patron wants breeding information about a type of chickens called FRIZZLES, which are genetically incomplete.
12. Patron heard on the soap opera Days of Our Lives (May 21, 1982 program) a GOETHE poem that went something like "No one has ever loved as much as we have loved . . . " Patron wants a full source and quote.
13. Patron wants detailed information on making a HAWAIIAN quilt.

BIBLIOGRAPHY

1. "Your Best Buy: the System Reference Coordinator" by Susan Holmer. *RQ* 23 (Fall 83): 75-80.

2. "Cooperative Reference in an Illinois Library Service" by Jane Levine. *Illinois Libraries* 65 (April 83): 252-261.

3. "The 200 Questions" by Barbara Newlin. *Library Journal.* (January 15, 82): 151-53.

4. *California Statewide Reference Referral Service: Analysis and Recommendations* by Nancy Van House DeWath. (King Research, Inc.) Sacramento: California State Library, 1981 (ED206 311) 214p.

5. "Cooperative Reference: Hazards, Rewards, Prospects" RQ 18 (Summer 1979): 355-68.

APPENDIX:
BARC/IOD/SJVIS REFERENCE STUDY
OUTLINE

Purpose

Given certain resources/staff can a second level reference center adequately answer questions now referred to 3rd level centers?

If so, what are those resources/staff levels that make it possible? Is it cost-effective?

How does the cost and quality compare to BARC? To Information on Demand?

Are there questions that can't be answered at the 2nd level? Why not?

What changes to 2nd level would make it possible to answer those questions?

Are there questions that must be answered by a 3rd level center? What kind?

Method

1. Questions received from BARC as they originally came in.
2. Questions divided among the SJVIS staff.
3. Staff works on questions using normal procedures with the exception of NOT sending questions to 3rd level reference.
4. SJVIS staff keeps careful track of time spent and sources used, contacts made.
5. BARC sends SJVLS answers to questions done by BARC and IOD.
6. Answers are reformated so the source of the answer (BARC, SJVIS, IOD) is not identified.
7. Answers given to independent reference librarian for evaluation of content. Rank them as to best answer for each question, 1,2,3. Report why one answer was better than another, e.g., more library materials found, more in-depth search, better strategy, more creative, "non-traditional" methods used, etc.
8. SJVIS staff discusses answers to determine why or why not questions were answered by SJVIS.
9. Calculate SJVLS costs per question using different methods: 1. total interlibrary reference budget (take out liaison activity?) ÷ number of questions answered in a year; 2. time spent on question × salary; 3. reference question answering portion of budget ÷ number of questions in a year; 4. time spent × part of salary apportioned to direct question answering.
10. SJVIS writes report.

Factors Influencing the Effectiveness of Question-Answering Services in Libraries

F. W. Lancaster

The literature relating to the evaluation of library services can be traced back many years. Nevertheless, diagnostic microevaluations (i.e., detailed analytical studies intended to identify causes of failures and suggest possible remedies for these), based on objective methods, have been applied to information services for only a short time. In fact, the prototypical diagnostic studies appear to be those applied to bibliographic searching services (e.g., Lancaster, 1968) some fifteen to twenty years ago. Since that time, somewhat equivalent procedures have been applied to the document delivery capabilities of libraries (e.g., Kantor [1976], Saracevic et al. [1977], Schofield et al. [1975], Urquhart and Schofield [1971, 1972]).

As a result of these studies, a considerable body of knowledge has been accumulated on the factors affecting the performance of bibliographic searching services (e.g., Lancaster, 1979) and the document delivery services of libraries (e.g., Buckland, 1975).

While obtrusive and unobtrusive methods have both been applied to the evaluation of question-answering in libraries (e.g., Crowley and Childers [1971], Bunge [1967], Powell [1976], Childers [1972], Weech and Goldhor [1982], King and Berry [1973], Myers and Jirjees [1983]) these have failed to reveal all of the factors influencing the probability that a factual-type question, when posed to a library, will be answered completely and correctly. One reason is simply the fact that diagnosis is more difficult in this situation than

The author is one of the world's leading authorities on evaluation of reference services and is on the faculty of the Graduate School of Library and Information Science, University of Illinois, Urbana, IL 61801.

in most others. For example, it is not easy to observe the reference librarian in action by any unobtrusive method or to collect many of the data needed for a complete microanalytical study.

The present paper is an attempt to identify those factors likely to influence the probability that a factual-type question will be answered completely and correctly by a particular library. Empirical evidence on the importance of a few of these factors can be derived from the evaluations mentioned earlier. Many other factors have been arrived at intuitively rather than empirically. This paper must therefore be regarded as speculative rather than definitive. The author arrived at these factors through interaction with several hundred students of library science over more than a decade and would like to acknowledge the considerable assistance received from these students in their formulation and refinement. The factors identified are summarized in ten exhibits.

WILL LIBRARY RECEIVE A QUESTION?

Exhibit 1 relates to the probability that questions will arise in the minds of members of a community and that these individuals will approach a library to have their questions answered. An underlying assumption is that a library is readily accessible to members of the community.

Exhibit 1
Probability That Question Will Arise
and be Submitted to Library

Sequence of events	*Factors affecting probability that event will occur*
1. Question arises in the mind of some individual.	Individual's education; background, interests, experience and level of intelligence and literacy.
2. Individual recognizes that he needs to have question answered.	Individual's education, background, interests, experience and level of intelligence and literacy.

Exhibit 1, continued

3. Individual is sufficiently motivated to seek answer.	As for Event 1, plus: (a) the value of the answer to the individual, and (b) the individual's perception of the probability that the question can be answered by some source.
4. Individual approaches library to have question answered.	Is individual aware of existence of library? Is individual aware that library provides this service? Is library perceived to be appropriate and convenient source to use? Has individual had good or bad experiences with libraries in general and this library in particular? Is the library open at the time answer is needed? Can individual visit or contact library at time answer is needed?

It seems reasonable to suppose that level of education and intelligence, as well as diversity of professional and personal interests, will strongly affect the probability that questions will arise in the minds of individuals, information be needed by them, and information needs actually be recognized. These same factors also seem likely to influence motivation, i.e., whether or not an individual actually seeks to find the answer to some question.

There are at least two other factors likely to influence motivation. The first is the perceived value of having a question answered. In many cases, an answer will have no financial value. Nevertheless, it will have some intangible value to the questioner, such as curiosity satisfied or mind set at rest. Even if the reward is intangible, when an individual seeks the answer to a question, he or she is making a type of value judgment: that the answer is worth the effort (a cost) of pursuing.

In some instances, of course, an answer will have financial value. In these situations, the amount of money involved will probably determine the motivation. For example, in buying a major appliance, such as a refrigerator, one could save $100 or more by finding that some consumer magazine judges one brand as effective as another. In buying an electric toaster, on the other hand, one may decide that the potential savings are so small that the consumer information is not worth the effort of seeking.

Finally, although no hard evidence exists on this, one suspects that the motivation to find an answer to some question will be influenced by the individual's perception of the probability that an answer exists, is recorded and can be found. The answers to many questions may never be sought because the individuals, in whose minds they are raised, believe (perhaps quite erroneously) that no recorded answers exist.

The next step illustrated in Exhibit 1 relates to the probability that an individual, once decided to seek the answer to some question, will go to a library rather than to some other source. Clearly, he must know that a library exists, that he is qualified to use it, and that the library does attempt to find answers to many types of question. If these conditions apply, the library will presumably be selected if (a) the questioner perceives the library to be the most convenient information source to use, (b) he retains favorable impressions if he has used the library in the past, and (c) the library is open at the time the information is needed.

WILL LIBRARY ACCEPT THE QUESTION?

Given that it is approached by some member of the community, will the library seek to find the answer to his question? Clearly, the question must first be understood by the librarian receiving it. Whether this occurs will depend on the communicating abilities of both librarian and questioner. If the question is understood by the librarian, will it be accepted? Perhaps the questioner will be refused because he is not a qualified user (e.g., in the case of some industrial library). If the questioner is acceptable, the question may not be. It could be of a type that the library, as a matter of policy, refuses to answer (e.g., homework questions, quiz questions or certain kinds of medical or legal questions). See Exhibit 2.

Exhibit 2
Will Library Attempt to Find Answer?

1. Communication factors:
   Questioner
   Librarian
2. Policy factors:
   Is questioner acceptable to library?
   Is question acceptable to library?

CAN ANSWER BE FOUND?

For some questions, while an answer may be considered to "exist," at least in a theoretical sense, it has not been recorded or even, perhaps, determined. This might apply, for example, to a question on the height of a relatively obscure building or one on the thermal conductivity of some uncommon alloy. Given that an answer has been recorded somewhere, the question arises as to whether or not the librarian can locate it. Six groups of factors influencing this probability are identified in Exhibit 3 and elaborated on in Exhibits 4-9.

Exhibit 3
Will Questioner Receive a Complete
and Correct Answer?

1. Is answer recorded somewhere?
2. Can librarian find answer?
   Policy factors
   Collection factors
   Librarian factors
   Question-related factors
   User factors
   Environmental factors

Exhibit 4
Policy Factors

1. How much time is librarian willing and able to spend?
2. What expenditures can librarian incur?
   Long-distance telephone
   Access to online sources

Exhibit 5
Collection Factors

1. Does the library own a source that contains the complete and correct answer?
2. How many sources does the library own that contain a complete and correct answer?
3. How accessible are these sources to the librarian?
4. How well organized and indexed are these sources?

Exhibit 6
Librarian Factors

1. Knowledge:
   Of collection
   General knowledge
     Current awareness
     Language abilities
2. Ability and willingness to communicate
3. Decision-making abilities
4. Perception of professional responsibilities and commitment to these responsibilities
5. Efficiency:
   Speed
   Accuracy
6. Education and training
7. Experience as a librarian and as a reference librarian

Exhibit 7
Question-Related Factors

1. Subject
2. Obscurity
3. Complexity
4. Stability of answer (in particular, how recently did answer change?)

Exhibit 8
User Factors

1. Status
2. Personality and attitude
3. Ability to comprehend answer

Exhibit 9
Environmental Factors

1. Stress
2. Physical/mental health of librarian
3. Pure environmental:
   Temperature
   Humidity
   Lighting

POLICY FACTORS

Most questions can be answered if one is willing to put enough time, energy and money into the endeavor. Whether a particular user gets a nonroutine question answered completely and correctly will partly depend on how much time the librarian is willing and able to devote to it. This will be determined in part by library policy. But other factors also come into play: how busy the librarian is at the time the question arrives, how important the librarian perceives the question to be (which may relate to how important the librarian perceives the questioner to be), how interested the librarian is in the question (and, under certain circumstances, the questioner!), and so on.

There are other library policies affecting the probability that a question will be answered completely and correctly. An important one relates to how money can be spent. In some cases, the most up-to-date or accurate information could be obtained through a long-distance telephone call. In other cases, such a call might save many minutes of the librarian's time. Exactly the same could be said of access to online data bases and data banks. Library policies are very shortsighted if they do not allow reference librarians to use the most cost-effective approach available. Regrettably, in most libraries, ownership represents a more legitimate expenditure of public funds than access does.

COLLECTION FACTORS

It seems fairly obvious that a question is more likely to be answered if the library owns a source that could provide the answer than if it does not. Some of the other collection factors identified in Exhibit 5 may be somewhat less obvious.

It is hypothesized (without any hard data to offer in support[*]) that the probability that a question will be answered completely and correctly increases with the number of sources owned by the library in which the answer is recorded. This is really a matter of probability: the more substitutable sources that exist, the greater the probability that the librarian will use one of them. This probability is related to the relative obscurity, or otherwise, of the question. "What is the capital of Argentina?" is a question that could be answered by any one of several hundred sources in some libraries. On the other hand, consider the following question: "What is the origin of the name Tigre, a resort close to Buenos Aires?" This question can be answered by few (if any) sources in even a large library. The probability that this question would be answered correctly is very low.

Another hypothesis, untested as far as this author is aware, is that the physical accessibility of the information source to the librarian influences the probability that an answer will be found. In many libraries, a "quick-reference" collection exists immediately adjacent to the reference desk. If the correct answer to a question is contained

---

[*]Powell (1976) studied the relationship between collection size and success in answering questions but in the aggregate. He did not determine number of possible sources for each question.

here, it seems highly probable that the librarian will find it. This probability is likely to decrease successively when the answer exists: elsewhere in the open-access reference collection, in reference materials in closed-access stacks, in circulating materials, in a circulating item that is now on loan, in an item in a remote storage facility.

Finally, the organization of the information source needs to be taken into account. For example, for a particular question the only answer may exist in one history of art. The probability that this answer will be found by a librarian, given that the book itself is looked at, will depend on how the book is organized and how well it is indexed.

In Exhibit 5, collection factors are considered from the aspects of a single factual question. Primary factors, rather than secondary, are identified. Such factors as "size of collection" are purely secondary since, viewed at the level of the individual question, these factors merely influence the primary factors (e.g., the probability that the library will own multiple information sources that are equally complete and correct).

LIBRARIAN FACTORS

A number of these are identified in Exhibit 6; some are more important than others. First and foremost, the librarian must have a detailed knowledge of the information sources available. However, general knowledge is not insignificant. In particular, the librarian should have a good grasp of current events. Without this, he may well give an answer that is no longer accurate (e.g., to the question "Who is the world record holder in the 1500 metres?", when the record was broken two days before the question was asked). Ability to read foreign languages may be important to some libraries but, for most questions, is not likely to be a major factor influencing the probability that an answer will be found.

The communicating abilities of the librarian affect his understanding of the question in the first place as well as his ability to convey a correct answer to the user. Decision-making abilities affect the efficiency of the librarian's search strategy. Other important decisions include: when to refer to an outside source and when to give up completely.

The librarian's perception of his professional responsibilities may influence whether or not he accepts a question (e.g., questions should not be rejected out-of-hand because they seem too difficult) as well as how much time he is willing to devote to it.

The efficiency of the librarian is another important factor. The more quickly he finds answers to the routine questions, the more time he can devote to the nonroutine. He must also be accurate, in checking indexes, in reading text or tables of data, and in relaying answers to users.

Certainly one would expect that, all other things being equal, the more experienced the librarian in reference work, the more likely the question to be answered completely and correctly. To a lesser extent, one might also expect this probability to be related to the education and training of the librarian, although a study by Bunge (1967) tended to indicate that reference librarians without formal education (i.e., without attending library school) were no less likely to answer questions than those with formal education in librarianship.

QUESTION-RELATED FACTORS

The complexity of a question (Exhibit 7) will affect the probability that the librarian will understand it, that a complete and correct answer can be found, and that the answer can be transmitted successfully to the user. The obscurity of the question will affect the number of sources in which an answer appears and, thus, probability that an answer will be found. The subject matter involved, since this relates to the strengths and weaknesses of particular collections, as well as of particular librarians, is another significant factor.

More important than all of these, however, may be the stability of the answer and, more particularly, how recently the answer changed. The question "When was Smetana's *The Bartered Bride* first performed in the United States?" is orders of magnitude more easy to answer correctly than "When was *The Bartered Bride* performed most recently by a major opera company in the United States?" The first answer, presumably, cannot change while the second may have changed as recently as yesterday.

USER FACTORS

While some librarians may deny it, it is hard to believe that "human" factors do not enter into this picture. In an industrial library, a vice president receives more care and time than a design engineer recently appointed. In an academic health science library, the same situation applies to the dean of the medical school.

But status is not the only "human" influence. Whether consciously or unconsciously, it seems reasonable to suppose that a librarian will try harder for the questioner judged "simpatico" (or, for that matter, "simpatica") than for one considered rude, arrogant or ignorant.

Finally, although an answer may exist, and the librarian can comprehend it, the user may not be able to. This might apply, for example, in the case of a questioner who is a child. Alternatively, the librarian may locate a source for the answer but neither the librarian nor user can understand it. For example, the user may be a practicing engineer and the answer, appearing in the literature of applied mechanics, is incomprehensible to him because it is too mathematical.

ENVIRONMENTAL FACTORS

Environmental factors (Exhibit 9) may be more important than they seem at first sight. If a questioner calls at 9:05, shortly after the library has opened, it may be more likely that his question is answered correctly than if he calls at 12:05 at which time two of the three reference librarians are at lunch, five people are waiting at the reference desk, and two telephones are ringing. Stress influences the accuracy of the librarian, his effectiveness, and his perseverance.

Quite apart from these stress factors, the efficiency of librarians varies from one day to the next depending on health factors, how much sleep they have had, whether or not they have quarrelled with their spouses that day, and a whole host of related factors that are frequently overlooked and are difficult to categorize. Also frequently overlooked is the fact that human efficiency diminishes as physical environmental conditions deteriorate. In a building without air conditioning, time of day may significantly influence the probability that a question will be answered correctly.

REFERRAL FACTORS

Exhibit 10 relates to the probability that a librarian, unable to answer a question himself, will refer the library user to another source. One factor has to do with the librarian's own self-assurance.

Some librarians seem reluctant to refer a questioner elsewhere, especially to another professional colleague or department, because they feel that such an action is a sign of their own incompetence. Others may refuse to refer because they adopt a tenacious and proprietary interest in a particular question. Tenacity is an admirable quality but not if it results in failure to answer an answerable question.*

Exhibit 10
Referral Factors

1. Is librarian willing to refer question
   (a) to a colleague in the library,
   (b) to an outside source?
2. How extensive is the librarian's knowledge of the resources, abilities and interests of individuals or institutions?
3. Do referral directories appropriate to this question exist, does the library own them (or can access them online), and does the librarian know of them?
4. Is the questioner willing to be referred?

If the librarian is willing to refer, the quality of his referral will depend on his knowledge of primary or secondary information sources, as well as the relevance and accessibility of these sources and the willingness of the questioner to be referred elsewhere. Once the question is referred, of course, all of the performance factors previously identified will tend to apply to the new situation.

CONCLUSION

Not all the factors listed, obviously, are of equal importance. Their range and diversity do indicate, however, that the effectiveness of question-answering activities is governed by a rather complex set of variables. Moreover, chance enters into the situation: if

---

*In a study of public libraries in Illinois, Wallace (1983) discovered some reluctance to refer a question to system resources when the reference librarian was unable to answer it locally.

one telephones a public library, for example, the probability that one's factual question will be answered completely and correctly may depend on the time selected and how the reference librarian happens to be feeling that day. It is little wonder that several studies have indicated that the probability of complete success in this situation may not be much more than .5 to .6. On the other hand, it should also be recognized that the factors identified imply some redundancy and counterbalancing. For example, that a particular question can be answered correctly from several sources might tend to compensate for the fact that a librarian may not be feeling at his very best on a certain day.

Finally, as electronic information sources are increasingly used to support question-answering activities, the importance of some of these factors will decline. Clearly, access will be more important than ownership and the size and redundancy of the collection will no longer be a significant variable affecting the quality of reference service. Moreover, online indexes to the contents of electronic resources will tend to ensure that a librarian will choose the best source for any particular question. At the same time, the ease with which an electronic source can be updated will tend to ensure that the information is the most current available.

REFERENCES

Buckland, M.K. *Book Availability and the Library User.* New York, Pergamon Press, 1975.

Bunge, C.A. *Professional Education and Reference Efficiency.* Springfield, Illinois State Library, 1967.

Childers, T. "Managing the Quality of Reference/Information Service," *Library Quarterly,* 42, 1972, 212-217.

Crowley, T. and T. Childers. *Information Service in Public Libraries: Two Studies.* Metuchen, N.J., Scarecrow Press, 1971.

Kantor, P.B. "Availability Analysis," *Journal of the American Society for Information Science,* 27, 1976, 311-9.

Kantor, P.B. "The Library as an Information Utility," *Journal of the American Society for Information Science,* 27, 1976, 100-112.

King, G.B. and R. Berry. *Evaluation of the University of Minnesota Libraries Reference Department Telephone Information Service. Pilot Study.* Minneapolis, University of Minnesota, Library School, 1973. ED 077 517.

Lancaster, F.W. *Evaluation of the MEDLARS Demand Search Service.* Bethesda, Maryland, National Library of Medicine, 1968.

Lancaster, F.W. *Information Retrieval Systems: Characteristics, Testing and Evaluation.* Second Edition. New York, Wiley, 1979.

Myers, M.J. and J.M. Jirjees. *The Accuracy of Telephone Reference Information Services in Academic Libraries.* Metuchen, N.J., Scarecrow Press, 1983.

Powell, R.R. *An Investigation of the Relationship Between Reference Collection Size and*

Other Reference Service Factors and Success in Answering Reference Questions. Ph.D. Thesis. University of Illinois, Graduate School of Library Science, 1976. (Also see *Library Quarterly,* 48, 1978, 1-19).

Saracevic, T. et al. "Causes and Dynamics of User Frustration in an Academic Library," *College and Research Libraries,* 38, 1977, 7-18.

Schofield, J.L. et al. "Evaluation of an Academic Library's Stock Effectiveness," *Journal of Librarianship,* 7, 1975, 207-227.

Urquhart, J.A. and J.L. Schofield. "Measuring Readers' Failure at the Shelf," *Journal of Documentation,* 27, 1971, 273-276.

Urquhart, J.A. and J.L. Schofield. "Measuring Readers' Failure at the Shelf in Three University Libraries," *Journal of Documentation,* 28, 1972, 233-241.

Wallace, D.P. *An Index of Quality of Illinois Public Library Service.* Springfield, Illinois State Library, 1983.

Weech, T.L. and H. Goldhor. "Obtrusive Versus Unobtrusive Evaluation of Reference Service," *Library Quarterly,* 52, 1982, 305-324.

Who's Giving All Those Wrong Answers? Direct Service and Reference Personnel Evaluation

Terry L. Weech

The literature of reference service evaluation is extensive. Rothstein, Weech, Lancaster, and Bunge are a few of the authors who have published reviews of reference evaluation literature.[1] Murfin and Wynar list 127 citations under "Measurement and Evaluation" in their reference service bibliography.[2] It is evident from these reviews and bibliographies that few reports or articles specifically on reference personnel evaluation have appeared in the literature. The lack of attention to reference personnel evaluation is perhaps understandable given the service rather than administrative orientation of most reference librarians. The focus has thus been on the evaluation of the service provided rather than on the personnel providing the service.

An exploration of the library management literature is not much more successful in uncovering items specifically on reference personnel evaluation. The basic texts on library administration approach performance evaluation in a general way, rather than differentiating among the various functional positions within the library. Although a reference position may be used on occasion as an example, there is little in library administration literature which focuses on the special problems of reference personnel evaluation.

The author is Associate Professor and Coordinator of Advanced Studies at the Graduate School of Library and Information Science, University of Illinois, Urbana-Champaign, 61801.

Admittedly much of the methodology of reference service evaluation can be applied to reference personnel evaluation. One might ask, "why the fuss?" Part of the concern is based on some research findings which indicate the user has not much more than a fifty-fifty chance of getting a correct and complete answer to a reference question. Although factors other than staff performance may be influencing the success rate, most reference evaluations have avoided evaluation of the performance of specific staff. This is consistent with the social science research tradition of protecting the identity of the research subject. This author is not suggesting a change in that tradition, but if we are to determine the extent to which the performance of individual reference staff may affect the overall performance of the library's reference service and if we are to improve the level of service provided, the next step in reference service evaluation would seem to demand the evaluation of individual staff performance. It is in this sense that the term "reference personnel evaluation" is used in this paper. It is distinguished from "reference service evaluation" by being concerned with the evaluation of the performance of specific staff rather than the performance of specified groups of staff (e.g., grouped by experience, education, or other variables).

Another concern is that reference personnel evaluation is sufficiently different from the evaluation of other library personnel to warrant special attention. What makes reference work different? Certainly the diversity of the tasks of reference staff and the independent, professionally isolated nature of many of these tasks tend to distinguish the reference function from other library staff functions. While reference librarians may be asked to undertake a wide variety of tasks, often termed "reference support duties," which may result in the staff having a limited number of hours at the reference desk, it is the provision of direct reference service which is the focus of this discussion. This is not to say that other direct and indirect services, such as library user instruction, material selection, database searching, bibliographical and other research and reference activities, are not important. Any comprehensive evaluation of reference personnel will need to take into consideration all activities which are included in the job descriptions of reference librarians.[3] But in the interest of building on related research and recognizing that evaluation of direct reference service and the evaluation of reference personnel share common concerns in the area of staff performance, this paper will focus on evaluation of reference personnel in the provision of direct reference services to users.

LITERATURE REVIEW

Although several sources were found that discussed personnel evaluation as part of a more general discussion relating to the administration of reference service, a review of the literature uncovered only two sources specifically on the evaluation of reference personnel. One source is the paper focusing on reference personnel evaluation presented by Ellen Hoffmann at a 1977 Canadian Library Association symposium on the reference interview. She reviews the issues relating to performance appraisals of reference librarians and identifies four principles of performance appraisal relevant to reference personnel evaluation: 1) clarify what you want to accomplish; 2) evaluate what matters; 3) make it a group process; 4) performance appraisal is not a universal solvent, it will not solve all your problems.[4] Hoffmann critiques some of the traditional methods of reference performance appraisal and calls into question user surveys and the "pseudo-scientism" of infatuation with forms and numbers.[5] Whether we agree or not with Hoffmann's opinions, she has done a great service by reviewing some of the traditional personnel evaluation procedures and assessing their relevance to reference staff evaluation.

The other source focusing on reference personnel evaluation, as opposed to reference service evaluation, is the article by Ellison and Lazeration which presents and discusses a model reference personnel accountability form. The form, which is designed for academic reference librarians, includes evaluations on almost every variable discussed by Hoffmann and covers indirect and support reference activity as well as direct reference service.

Beyond these two sources, one must turn to the more general literature of administration of reference service. The spring 1982 issue of *The Reference Librarian,* which is on "reference services administration and management," contains a number of articles which refer to reference personnel evaluation as part of the function of administering reference service. But the discussion of reference personnel evaluation is not extensive. In "Questions Sheehy Can't Answer . . . ," Mary W. George is left "wondering how to go about objective, positive evaluation and reinforcement . . . ."[6] Kathleen Voigt, in her article on guidelines for beginning academic reference managers, specifies the development of an evaluation form for staff as the last of eight guidelines and suggests a separate evaluation for reference staff instead of the general form used for all library personnel.[7] In discussing the revision of the reference and professional services policy at Enoch Pratt, Peggy Glover notes that "Evaluation raised questions about methods of evaluation and the collection of usage data," but no further comment appears to have been made on evaluation of reference personnel in the Enoch Pratt policy manual.[8] Judith W. Devine, in "Considerations in the Management of a Reference Department," does go into some specifics on evaluation of reference personnel. She recommends direct observation of the employee's performance at the reference desk and the use of reference practice questions.[9] Geraldine B. King details a "management information system for reference service" utilizing a 4 × 6 reference transaction slip which she suggests can be used for evaluation of the work of individual staff members.[10] King also suggests a "staff log" to detail activities when not at the reference desk.[11]

Although these articles contain some valuable comments and observations on reference personnel evaluation, the lack of a cumulative knowledge base for reference personnel evaluation is evident from the bibliographic citations in the issue. Neither Hoffmann nor Ellison and Lazeration were cited in the articles or in the bibliography included in the issue.

REFERENCE SERVICE EVALUATIONS VARIABLES RELATED TO CHARACTERISTICS OF STAFF

From the variables described in the literature of reference service evaluation, a list of staff characteristics may be derived and used in constructing a model for reference personnel evaluation. The variables identified in the reference services evaluation literature include certain demographic and personal characteristics of librarians such as education, experience, and personality. Attempts have also been made to determine or explore the search strategy or searching style of reference staff. In reference service evaluations, these variables are often measured against the accuracy and completeness of the answer provided, the speed and/or cost-effectiveness of the librarian, and the satisfaction of the user. As they apply to reference personnel evaluation, each of the variables relating to staff characteristics will be discussed separately.

Education

Education, when used as a variable, is usually used to distinguish between those staff members with graduate professional degrees in library and information science and those without such degrees. Bunge's study, which found that trained librarians tend to answer factual questions more quickly, is one of the earlier studies using education as a variable.[12] Halldorsson and Murfin focused on the ability of professionals and nonprofessionals to discover when the user is providing faulty information in the reference interview and found that the professionally trained librarian is more likely to obtain corrected information than the nonprofessional.[13] In a study conducted in Australian academic libraries, Schmidt observed that staff with more education appear to perform better in answering factual questions.[14] In a study of academic librarians in the southeastern U.S., Myers found that having a graduate degree is positively correlated with the accuracy of answers provided to questions asked by surrogate users, but the association is not as strong as that between the accuracy of answers and the number of reference volumes held and the hours of reference service provided.[15] Weech and Goldhor found very little correlation in a public library setting between library education and time spent searching for answers to reference questions and they found no significant correlation between the education of the staff and user satisfaction.[16]

Experience

Experience is usually interpreted as an indication of the number of years of work. Bunge matched the trained/nontrained reference librarians in pairs to hold years of reference experience constant, so reference experience is not a variable in his study. He did, however, find a positive relationship between the number of hours assigned at the reference desk and reference efficiency of the staff.[17] This might be interpreted as one form of experience and may be a more valid measure of ability to perform than total years working as a reference librarian. Jirjees found a high correlation ($r = .70$) between reference experience and the percentage of correct answers provided by the academic librarians, but the correlation has a p = .094, which calls the statistical significance of the results into question.[18] Weech and Goldhor also failed to find a statistically significant relationship between experience of public library reference staff and performance as measured by user satisfaction.[19]

Personality/Interpersonal Communication

The personality of the reference librarian has been the subject of numerous articles in the literature, but only a few have attempted to apply research methodology to measure personality and its relationship to reference desk performance. Lopez and Rubacher used psychological tests to measure such characteristics as empathy, respect, genuineness, concreteness and specificity of expression. They found a significant relationship between these factors and user satisfaction in a university library setting.[20] Markham, Sterling, and Smith reported on the effect of academic librarians disclosing something about themselves to patrons in an attempt to establish interpersonal communication. They found that the patron responded more positively to questions about the librarian's communication skills when the librarian participates in self-disclosure.[21] Self-disclosure, however, seems not to affect the patron's evaluation of the librarian's ability to answer questions accurately and factually.

Searching Styles

Search strategies or searching style, also referred to as cognitive style, is a variable focusing on how the reference librarian pursues the information needed to answer the user's question. It might be viewed as the interaction of the librarian with the sources for information while "personality" as a variable is concerned with the interaction of the librarian with the poser of the question. In one of the earlier comments on the topic, Mittal suggested that a "split-mind," which can recall previous answers provided to other users, can be important in enhancing problem-solving abilities. He suggested that a psychological test might be developed to identify staff with such "split" or associative minds.[22] Johnson and White use the psychological construct of "cognitive style" to contrast those reference librarians who tend to take the "global" or wholistic view of problem-solving with those who take the narrower, analytical approach. Using terms from perception research, "field dependence" (the tendency to view an object as integrated with its surroundings) and ''field independence'' (the tendency to view an object apart from its surrounding field), they found that reference librarians with social science undergraduate majors are more field dependent and those with arts and science undergraduate majors are more field independent.[23] Their research thus suggests that the undergraduate major may be a factor in predicting the searching style or information retrieval patterns of a reference librarian.

SUMMARY OF STAFF CHARACTERISTICS VARIABLES

Although it was noted earlier that most of the reference service evaluation literature avoids the evaluation of specific staff members, this review of variables related to staff characteristics suggests some conclusions which may be helpful in developing staff evaluation procedures. There is little evidence that staff performance, as measured by accuracy of the answers to factual questions, is associated with education, experience, or personality. User satisfaction does not seem to be related to these variables. The few studies that do suggest some association between these variables are limited in terms of sample size, strength of association, and other factors. There is some indication that professional education may be a factor in the ability to conduct the reference interview more effectively and to identify faulty information within the interview situation, but even here further research would be warranted before drawing definite conclusions. But one conclusion which might be drawn is that research results seem to confirm the need to go beyond the paper credentials of education and experience and the subjective assessment of personality to properly predict and evaluate the performance of individual reference staff. Clearly much more research remains to be done.

THE ONLINE/SEARCH ANALYST LITERATURE

In the course of carrying out their duties, reference librarians and online search analysts may perform many similar functions and thus share similar concerns of performance evaluation. In many library and information center settings, the staff perform both functions. But the evaluation literature is fairly distinct, probably because of the traditions of search analysts to publish in the online and information science rather than the library science literature. A review of the online literature resulted in the following impressions: 1) the online literature and the reference literature are concerned with many of the same variables; 2) there seems to be much more emphasis on staff accountability and evaluation of individual performance in the online literature than in the reference service evaluation literature. Fidel and Soergel present an excellent summary of the factors which might be considered in evaluating online bibliographic retrieval and include in a discussion of "the searcher" most of the variables found in the reference service evaluation literature relating to reference staff.[24] Dolan and Kremin report on an attempt to measure "innate skills of searchers" by administering a test to beginning search analysts.[25] The following skills were measured: concept analysis, flexibility of thinking, ability to think in synonyms, anticipation of variant word forms and spellings, and self-confidence. The authors claim to have used the test successfully to screen individuals for training as search analysts. Fenichel analyzed the relationship between experience, searching process (number of commands used), and search results.[26] She found that experience was associated with speed of search. New searchers worked more slowly than experienced searchers, but only slight evidence was found that experience was related to greater searching success (recall). Helen Howard conducted a similar study of database searchers and found no relationship between training of the searchers and their performance.[27] When experience of searchers was compared to overall search results, Howard obtained mixed results. Those with the greatest experience had the highest precision ratios and more cost-effective searches, but tended to expend more search effort in their search procedure than less experienced searchers.[28] Glunz and Wakiji describe a search analyst peer review system in a medical library which uses the following criteria for evaluating the search analyst: 1) correct interpretation and use of stated information requirements, 2) topical vocabulary; 3) indexing policies; 4) online system mechanics.[29]

It seems obvious from these sources in the online literature that both search analysts and reference librarians have much to learn from each other, yet the extent to which the online literature and the reference service evaluation literature are isolated from each other is indicated by the lack of overlapping citations. The online literature does seem to place greater emphasis on evaluation and accountability of staff. This may result from the availability of documented records of the search analyst's search strategy, time used in search, and cost of search. Undoubtedly, in our economically oriented society, cost and time are important motivations for search strategy evaluation. In balance, however, the online literature is also concerned with the quality of results.

TOWARD A MODEL FOR REFERENCE PERSONNEL EVALUATION

What personnel managers have known for some time is confirmed by the literature reviewed. Generalizations about education, experience, and personality are no substitute for documented performance evaluation of individual staff members. Given the need for such evaluation, the next question is, How to proceed? Various methodologies are available for evaluating staff performance. Some of the more common methods are subjective insight, interviews, questionnaires, tests, and observations.

Although subjective insight may be one of the more attractive methodologies for the evaluator, it leaves much to be desired from the point of view of the evaluatee. Since subjective considerations almost always are factors in evaluations, one should try to become aware of one's subjective impressions and, where possible, compare them to ''objective'' or externally verifiable sources of information relating to the evaluation. One of the primary methods of checking subjective impressions is to interview the subject of the evaluation, and the coworkers and clients of the evaluatee. Interviews usually attempt to measure perceptions of performance, but may also measure the ability of the evaluatee to communicate and assess patron needs.

The questionnaire can also be used to verify or reject subjective impressions. Examples of questionnaires and evaluation forms used in academic libraries can be found in the American Library Association's Association of College and Research Libraries *CLIP Notes,* published in 1980.[30] Often data on the number and type of reference questions answered and not answered are the focus of questionnaires and evaluation forms. Other background data on direct reference service may also be gathered by this method. Although often categorized as ''reference statistics,'' data from questionnaires may include more than mere counts of number of questions asked. *The Planning Process for Public Libraries* also includes sample questionnaires and survey forms.[31]

Tests usually involve "practice-type" questions of a factual nature administered either obtrusively or unobtrusively (with or without the knowledge of the person being tested). The performance criterion usually involves the correctness and completeness of the answers provided. Although "practice-type" tests have been used extensively in reference service evaluation, there is little evidence in the literature of such tests being used for individual personnel evaluation. Nor is there any indication that the various psychological tests discussed in the literature have been used in reference personnel evaluation. These latter tests, of course, use validated psychological constructs as measurement criteria.

Like testing, observation can be done obtrusively or unobtrusively. Unlike testing, some forms of observation are very informal and may be unintentionally unobtrusive. One is likelier to have a valid evaluation if the observation method is more formal in structure. Observation may use many of the measurement criteria used by the other methodologies discussed above, but there is always the danger of having the subjective impression influence what is observed and recorded when formal procedures are not followed.

In terms of who does the evaluation, four categories or sources of evaluation might be considered: 1) supervisor evaluation; 2) peer evaluation; 3) self-evaluation; and 4) patron evaluation. Each of the four categories of evaluation will be examined separately with their strengths and weaknesses noted.

Supervisor Evaluation

This is probably the most common and potentially the most subjective of all the evaluation categories. Evaluation by the supervisor need not have these negative characteristics. Time constraints on the supervisor and the nature of direct reference service often lead to less-than-complete evaluation by the supervisor. This is not to say that the supervisor should not or cannot be part of an evaluative process of reference personnel. In a 1972 survey of academic libraries, Johnson found that 74 percent of the libraries responding to her questionnaire indicated that the director or administrator prepared or participated in the preparation of performance appraisals.[32] But the limitations still exist, especially in the area of providing reference service on a one-to-one basis at the reference desk. The use of tests, observations, and interviews can take some of the subjective elements out of supervisor evaluation, but it is probably best to balance such evaluation with one or more of the other evaluation categories.

Peer Review

Peer review of reference personnel is especially appealing since it is consistent with the concept of a "professional" and allows input from multiple sources. Johnson reported in her 1972 survey that 29 percent of the responding libraries had one or more committees, councils, or peer groups involved in the appraisal process.[33] Most of those attending a reference personnel evaluation discussion group at the 1983 ALA Conference reported that peer evaluation was used in their reference personnel evaluation process.[34]

Self-Evaluation

Perhaps the most difficult evaluation to validate is self-evaluation. Although essential to professional development, self-evaluation can obviously be abused and become trivial. The Public Library Association's *Output Measures* call for the reference librarian's perception of the number of reference questions answered correctly and completely at the reference desk.[35] Self-evaluation has thus become "institutionalized" as a recognized performance measure, but even the most avid advocate of self-evaluation would probably agree on the necessity to balance its results with those of some outside evaluation source.

Patron Evaluation

The Public Library Association's *Output Measures* call for patron evaluation as the second level of evaluation of reference service.[36] As the construct "user satisfaction," patron evaluation has been a part of reference service evaluation and online search analyst performance measures for some time. "User satisfaction" has been defined and redefined. In most instances, users seem to be more generous than staff in terms of evaluating the reference process. In fact, the generosity of the user in evaluating reference service has raised the question "Do users really care if they receive accurate and complete answers?"[37] Most patron evaluations are solicited by the library as part of a formal evaluation program. Unsolicited patron evaluations also occur. Unsolicited evaluation may include written or verbal communications of praise or complaint. The obvious problem is that unsolicited praise tends to be shared and unsolicited complaints misplaced or handled as special patron problems. Although it is inevitable that unsolicited evaluation will continue to be part of the total evaluation process, it is probably the least reliable in terms of providing consistent evaluation data for reference personnel.

CONCLUSION

Clearly, we have many options to choose from when it comes to evaluating reference personnel. But we need to draw from all potentially beneficial sources for reference staff evaluation techniques. There must be more exchange of ideas between reference librarians and online search analysts. The adaptations of some of the screening tests developed for search analysts might be explored for reference librarians. The peer review techniques used in some online searching situations might also be appropriate for traditional reference staff. But the first step has been taken in establishing an evaluation program for reference staff if the special problems of evaluation are recognized. Certainly, some element of the evaluation of reference personnel should include peer evaluation. The peer evaluation process recognizes the unique function and the professional nature of the reference librarian's work. Peer evaluation is also used in other fields, such as medicine, and thus may enhance the standing of our field by signaling the concern we have for maintaining quality. But most important, attention to staff evaluation may result in improved performance and thus improved reference service for users of libraries and information centers.

REFERENCES

1. Rothstein, Samuel. "The Measurement and Evaluation of Reference Service," *Library Trends* 12 (January, 1964), 456-472; Weech, Terry L. "Evaluation of Adult Reference Service," *Library Trends* 22 (January, 1974), 315-335; Lancaster, F.W. "Evaluation of Reference Service," *The Measurement and Evaluation of Library Services* (Washington, DC: Information Resources Press, 1977), pp. 73-139; Bunge, Charles A. "Approaches to the Evaluation of Library Reference Services," in *Evaluation and Scientific Management of Libraries and Information Centers,* edited by F.W. Lancaster and C.W. Cleverdon. (Leyden: Noordhoff International Publishing, 1977), pp. 41-71.

2. Murfin, Marjorie E. and Wynar, Lumbomyr R. *Reference Service, an Annotated Bibliographic Guide* (Littleton, CO: Libraries Unlimited, 1977).

3. Ellison, John W. and Lazeration, Deborah B. "Personnel Accountability Form for Academic Reference Librarians: A Model," *College & Research Libraries* 16 (Winter, 1976), pp. 142-48.

4. Hoffmann, Ellen. "Reference Librarians and Performance Appraisal" in *The Reference Interview, Proceedings of the CACUL Symposium on the Reference Interview,* held . . . June 9 to 15, 1977. (Canadian Library Association, 1979), pp. 108-116.

5. Ibid., p. 111.

6. George, Mary W. "Questions Sheehy Can't Answer: Reflections on Becoming Head of Reference," *The Reference Librarian* (Spring, 1982), p. 13.

7. Voigt, Kathleen, "Selective Guidelines for a Beginning Manager of an Academic Library Reference Department," *The Reference Librarian* (Spring, 1982), p. 44.

8. Glover, Peggy. "Updating a Reference Services Policy," *The Reference Librarian* (Spring, 1982), p. 53.

9. Devine, Judith W. "Considerations in the Management of a Reference Department," *The Reference Librarian* (Spring, 1982), p. 65.

10. King, Geraldine B. "Try It—You'll Like It: A Comprehensive Management Information System for Reference Service," *The Reference Librarian* (Spring, 1982), p. 71.

11. Ibid., p. 77.

12. Bunge, Charles A. *Professional Education and Reference Efficiency* (Springfield, IL: Illinois State Library, 1967), p. 61.

13. Halldorsson, Egill A. and Murfin, Marjorie E. "The Performance of Professionals and Nonprofessionals in the Reference Interview," *College and Research Libraries* 38 (September, 1977), pp. 385-395.

14. Schmidt, Janine. "Reference Performance in College Libraries," *AARL (Australian Academic & Research Libraries)* 11 (June, 1980), pp. 87-95.

15. Myers, Marcia J. and Jirjees, Jassim M. *The Accuracy of Telephone Reference/Information Services in Academic Libraries: Two Studies* (Metuchen, NJ: Scarecrow, 1983), pp. 94-95; 108.

16. Weech, Terry L. and Goldhor, Herbert. "Reference Clientele and the Reference Transaction in Five Illinois Public Libraries" accepted for publication in *Library and Information Science Research.*

17. Bunge, Charles A. *Professional Education and Reference Efficiency* (Springfield, IL: Illinois State Library, 1967), p. 62.

18. Myers, Marcia J. and Jirjees, Jassim M. *The Accuracy of Telephone Reference/Information Services in Academic Libraries: Two Studies* (Metuchen, NJ: Scarecrow, 1983), p. 201.

19. Weech, Terry L. and Goldhor, Herbert. "Reference Clientele and the Reference Transaction in Five Illinois Public Libraries" accepted for publication in *Library and Information Science Research.*

20. Lopez, Manuel and Rubacher, Richard. "Interpersonal Psychology: Librarians and Patrons" *Catholic Library World* 40 (April, 1969), pp. 483-87.

21. Markham, Marilyn J.; Stirling, Keith H.; and Smith, Nathan M. "Librarian Self Disclosure and Patron Satisfaction in the Reference Interview" *RQ* 22 (Summer, 1983), pp. 369-374.

22. Mittal, R.L. "Split-Mind & Reference Service," *Indian Librarian* 14 (September, 1959), pp. 70-72.

23. Johnson, Kerry A. and White, Marilyn Domas. "The Cognitive Style of Reference Librarians" *RQ* 21 (Spring, 1982), pp. 239-246.

24. Fidel, Rayo and Soergel, Dagobert. "Factors Affecting Online Bibliographic Retrieval: A Conceptual Framework for Research," *Journal of American Society for Information Science* 34 (May, 1983), pp. 163-180.

25. Dolan, Donna R. and Kremin, Michael C. "The Quality Control of Search Analysts," *Online* 3 (April, 1979), pp. 8-16.

26. Fenichel, Carol Hansen. "An Examination of the Relationship Between Searching Behavior and Search Background," *Online Review* 4 (no. 4, 1980), pp. 341-347.

27. Howard, Helen. "Measures that Discriminate among Online Searchers with Different Training and Experience," *Online Review* 6 (August, 1982), pp. 315-327.

28. Ibid., p. 325.

29. Glunz, Diane and Wakiji, Eileen. "Maximizing Search Quality Through a Program of Peer Review," *Online* 7 (September, 1983), pp. 100-110.

30. *Performance Appraisal—CLIP Notes: College Library Information Packets, #1-80* (Chicago: American Library Association, Association of College and Research Libraries, College Libraries Section, 1980).

31. Palmour, Vernon E.; Bellassai, Marcia C.; and DeWath, Nancy V. *A Planning Process for Public Libraries* (Chicago: American Library Association, 1980).

32. Johnson, Marjorie. "Performance Appraisal of Librarians—A Survey," *College & Research Libraries* 32 (September, 1972), pp. 359-367.

33. Ibid., p. 364.

34. *RASD Update* 4 (July/September, 1983), p. 11.

35. Zweizig, Douglas and Rodger, Eleanor Jo. *Output Measures for Public Libraries: Annual of Standardized Procedures* (Chicago: American Library Association, 1982), pp. 45-50.

36. Ibid., p. 50.

37. Myers, Marcia J. and Jirjees, Jassim M. *The Accuracy of Telephone Reference/Information Services in Academic Libraries: Two Studies* (Metuchen, NJ: Scarecrow, 1983), p. 109.

Evaluating the Reference Librarian

William F. Young

See the Reference Librarian and the joys that appertain to her;
Who shall estimate the contents and the area of the brain to
her?
See the people seeking wisdom from the four winds ever
blown to her,
For they know there is no knowledge known to mortals but is
known to her . . .
How they throng *to* her, all empty, grovelling in their insuffi-
cience,
How they come *from* her o'erflooded by the sea of her omni-
science . . .

This poetic effort appeared in a 1906 issue of *Library Journal.*[1]
Literary merit aside, the sentiments are sincere and, however the
grandiloquent tone, represent a perception and ideal not entirely of a
bygone and more innocent age. Library users remain appreciative of
the Reference Librarian's skills or, at the very least, seem satisfied
with reference service as it's currently provided in American libraries. Typical are the results of a 1975 Reference Services Department User Survey taken at the University Libraries, State University of New York at Albany. In a five point scale, the average
user expressed a degree of satisfaction of 4.5 with the answer given
to a reference question. With little variation, faculty, staff and
students all indicated similar appreciation nor was there any significant divergence by time of day.[2] These highly positive findings
coincide with other studies of user opinion of reference services in
both public and academic library.[3] The work of reference librarians
is favorably perceived by the public. However, as is well known
within the profession, there does exist a rather extraordinary contradiction. The often cited unobstrusive studies by Crowley and

The author is Head of Reference at the State University of New York, Albany, Library.

123

Childers,[4] supported by more recent research,[5] indicate that reference librarians as a group answer questions correctly just slightly more than 50% of the time. While there are some variations in these results according to such factors as collection size and type of library,[6] the total picture is nonetheless disturbing.

The fact that library users seldom possess the expertise to evaluate the quality of reference service might partly explain the contradiction between user satisfaction and the results of unobstrusive testing. Perhaps some library patrons don't care about the "right answer"? Recently it has been pointed out that the value of information supplied may not be judged by the same objective criteria established by the library profession.[7] The very fact of receiving help or the pleasant demeanor of the reference librarian, rather than accuracy of information, will inevitably influence patron perception of service. This phenomenon of almost invariable user satisfaction further complicates the question of evaluation. The difficulty of judging reference librarians' performance is a common complaint for those in the position of evaluating. As one recently appointed head of reference observed;

> Reference presents a paradox in that the work involves infinite, unpredictable variety and permits unlimited creativity, yet by its one-to-one idiosyncratic nature it lacks both standard evaluation criteria and the range and hierarchy of internal responsibilities found in technical services . . . [8]

COMMON OPINION

The view that reference librarianship is an "art" not a "science" is a commonly held opinion. This being the case, so the reasoning goes, the human variables and creative values implicit in the reference process cannot be quantified or analysed. Within the burgeoning body of literature on evaluating reference this viewpoint is often set up as a strawman to be demolished. Yet much of the same literature focuses on quantitative studies useless in making any evaluative judgment.[9] Discussion on the subject of evaluation, to cite one specific example, point to "measuring" reference for providing "a means of evaluating the quality of the [reference] service we offer" but end up in suggesting the collection of only "the most basic and routine statistics on a day-to-day basis: for example, the number of questions handled, classified by rough breakdowns of the amount of time spent on each question".[10] Certainly, low cost methods for reporting reference statistics in a way which may be transformed into a measure of librarians' performance do exist. Such methods are however dependent on the librarians' view of "user satisfaction" and hence raise serious questions of accuracy in reporting.[11]

The concern of the novice head of reference mentioned previously was noted in her discomfit in having to evaluate her reference librarians. As she observes:

> More has been written with less good result about evaluation of reference service than about any other facet of librarianship . . . not only are there no widely accepted evaluation methods to draw on, but being continually aware of my own fumbles and inadequacies at the desk, I feel presumptuous judging and rating colleagues . . . I am left wondering how to go about objective, positive evaluation and reinforcement, especially in regards to the conduct of the reference interview and the follow through of complex questions.[12]

Almost any reference department head will be sympathetic to this complaint. The literature of reference evaluation is almost useless since it fails to provide practical guidance in what is necessarily the area of primary concern: evaluating the reference librarian as differentiated from the overall quality of reference service. We have learned that there are feasible techniques for assessing the latter. The aforementioned unobstrusive studies by Crowley, Childers, Myers and Jirjees indicate that the results of such research is reliable and valid.[13] The studies measure what is unquestionably the major facet of reference service, namely what Charles Bunge calls the "question answering aspect".[14] Can, however, these measures be applied to individuals? Cost factors aside, questions of professional propriety and the ethics of disguised observation are magnified.

LITERATURE VIEW

The inadequacy of the literature directly relevant to evaluating reference librarians is surprising in that the discussion related to reference evaluation implicitly or explicitly agrees that "the solution to most problems concerned with reference service is to be sought in the individual librarian".[15] The problem of evaluating reference service is, therefore in the final analysis, principally a question of personnel evaluation. The literature of personnel administration in libraries is however equally unhelpful. When reference librarians are mentioned it is invariably within the context of a problem or a special case.[16] Joyce Veenstra pointed to the difficulty at Columbia University Libraries in establishing "measurable and meaningful performance objectives, especially in an area like reference". She notes that it was easier in the Health Sciences Library where there was terminal access to data bases and hence amenable to one concrete standard: "All data base monthly updates are initiated no later than one work day after the current data base becomes available." She next points to another measure which she characterizes as "questionable in the reference area":

No reader complaints of a substantial nature are received OVER HOW LONG A PERIOD OF TIME? AND WHAT IS SUBSTANTIAL? AND WHAT ABOUT READER'S COMPLIMENTS?[17]

MEASURES

Ms. Veenstra concludes by noting that "initially you measure the things for which it is easiest to articulate measurement but often they are not the most important things".[18] Indeed, they are often not the most important considerations as any Head of Reference, who has seriously attempted to deal with evaluation, well knows. Obviously there are measurable aspects. A goal, for example, may be established by which reference librarians are called upon to learn and provide data base searching. Measurements of training success and quality of data base searches may be ascertained,[19] but such an indicator remains a secondary aspect. This should be a serious concern for reference librarians since individual performance evaluation has become a measurement intrinsically related to organizational goals.

A document put forward by an ALA Committee expressed this relationship in its opinion that personnel appraisal "shall be used as a means towards the realization of organizational goals". Among the ways this is to be achieved: "human resources . . . are inventioned for utilization and development", "individual employees are motivated to improve their performance and to work toward organizational goals''.[20] Unfortunately, in evaluating by measurable objectives the result, particularly for academic reference librarians, is an inevitable emphasis on such factors as continuing education, faculty consultations, publications and committee work.[21] Quality of service provided by the reference librarian is necessarily de-emphasized simply because it is intrinsically far less measurable. It is evident, moreover, from what we have see that the literature on reference evaluation contributes to this distortion in priorities.

Attention must turn away from evaluating reference service to evaluating the performance of the reference librarian in relation to his or her primary function. Some discussion has already begun.[22] It will be difficult. Reference Librarianship *is* an art. There are many paths toward providing the ''right answer''. Is it enough some of the time or most of the time to direct users to information sources where they may find the information sought? An obvious starting point is for libraries to establish their own staff performance standards.

POLICY STATEMENT

A reference service policy statement should realistically state what the expectations are based on known capabilities. Perhaps an ability to provide guidance or consultation on information requests should in some cases be the standard performance goal rather than providing the actual correct data or answer? Once standards are established who should evaluate? Direct observation of the reference librarian's work is essential but in large libraries Heads of Reference may not frequently work at the desk with all their colleagues. In such a situation peer input might be individually elicited from those who are directly familiar with someone's work. Points to consider in such an evaluation should be consistent and specific, for example: an awareness of new reference titles, a knowledge of those bibliographies providing control over the documents collections, reference technique capability i.e., the ability to find sources which will successfully meet information needs, courtesy and patience in dealing with patrons, a demeanor or attitude which encourages patrons to approach the reference desk etc. Such a method, properly implemented, could at least provide a consensus regarding performance. This is merely one suggestion. Concern must turn to ways and means of assessing how that ''flower of perfect knowledge'', characterized in the poem,[23] individually performs at the task of reference. The far more difficult question of remedial action lies before us.

REFERENCES

1. Samual Foss, "Song of the Library Staff," *Library Journal,* 31 (August 1906) p. 35. The author was a journalist who late in life became a librarian. The poem was read as part of the ALA Conference program in 1906.

2. State University of New York at Albany, University Libraries, User Survey Committee, "Final Report and Recommendations of the User Survey Committee" (October 22, 1975, Mimeographed), appendix 2, p. 1#3, appendix 2, p. 1, 3d, appendix 2, p. 2, section e.

3. Samuel Rothstein, "The Measurement and Evaluation of Reference Service," *Library Trends,* 12 (1964), p. 464-465.

4. Terence Crowley and Thomas Childers, *Information Service in Public Libraries: Two Studies* (Metuchen, N.J.: The Scarecrow Press, 1983).

5. Marcia J. Myers and Jassim M. Jirjees, *The Accuracy of Telephone Reference/Information Services in Academic Libraries* (Metuchen, N.J.: The Scarecrow Press, 1983).

6. *Ibid,* p. 105-109.

7. Alma Christine Vathis, "Reference Transaction and End Product as Viewed by the Patron," *RQ,* 23 (Fall 1973), p. 60 61.

8. Mary W. George, "Questions Sheehy Can't Answer: Reflections on Becoming Head of Reference," *The Reference Librarian,* (Spring 1982), p. 8.

9. Rothstein's, "The Measurement and Evaluation of Reference Service" and Terry L. Weech's, "Evaluation of Adult Reference Service," *Library Trends,* 22 (1974), p. 315-335 are the standard surveys.

10. Candace Morgan, "The Reference Librarian's Need for Measures of Reference," *RQ,* 14 (Fall 1974), p. 11-12.

11. See, for example, Paul B. Kantor's data collection method outlined in "Quantitative Evaluation of the Reference Process," *RQ,* 21 (Fall 1981), p. 43-52.

12. George, "Questions Sheehy Can't Answer," p. 13.

13. Marcia J. Myers and Jassim M. Jirjees, *The Accuracy of Telephone/Information Services in Academic Libraries,* p. 104, 235.

14. Charles A. Bunge, "Approaches to the Evaluation of Library Reference Services," in *Evaluation and Scientific Management of Libraries and Information Centers,* ed. by F. W. Lancaster and C. W. Cleverdon (Leydon: Noordhoff, 1977), p. 52.

15. Earl Tannenbaum as cited by Manual D. Lopex, "Measurement, Costs and Value: Academic Reference Service," *RQ,* 12 (Spring 1973), p. 240.

16. See, for example, Maxine Reneker, "Performance Appraised in Libraries: Purpose and Techniques," in Sheila Creth and Frederick Duda, eds., *Personnel Administration in Libraries* (New York: Neal Schumen, 1981), p. 252, 255.

17. Joyce Veenstra, "Performance Standards for Librarians, Are They Coming or Not? Library Personnel and Performance Standards," (paper presented at the American Library Association, Annual Conference, New York, N.Y., July 7, 1974). ED 096956, p. 7.

18. *Ibid,* p. 8.

19. Richard W. Blood, "Evaluation of Online Searches," *RQ,* 22 (Spring 1983), p. 266-277.

20. Staff Development Committee. Personnel Administration Section. Library Administration and Management Association. American Library Association, *Personnel Performance Appraised—A Guide for Libraries* in Reneker "Performance Appraised in Libraries: Purpose and Techniques," p. 231.

21. See, for example, John W. Ellison and Deborah B. Lazeration, ''Personnel Account-ability Form for Academic Reference Librarians: A Model,'' *RQ,* 16 (Winter 1976), p. 142-148.

22. A discussion group on performance standards for reference personnel within ALA's Reference and Adult Services Division was established in 1983.

23. Foss, ''Song of the Library Staff,'' p. 35.

Evaluating Reference Librarians: Using Goal Analysis as a First Step

Mignon S. Adams
Blanche Judd

How does one go about evaluating reference librarians? This is a question which concerns many librarians. Over a year ago, an RASD discussion group on "Performance Standards and Evaluation of Reference Personnel" was formed; at the 1984 ALA Midwinter Meeting in Washington, evaluating reference librarians was a major area of interest at an ACRL discussion group for heads of public/readers' services. Academic librarians who have acquired faculty status, or have otherwise been asked to participate in formal evaluative procedures, are especially concerned. They find themselves in the position of having to evaluate reference performance, a major activity of many librarians, with no guidelines or criteria save those designed for teaching faculty.

Turning to the professional literature is not of great help. While there is much written on the evaluation of reference, almost all of it concerns the evaluation of reference *services,* not the evaluation of individual librarians.[1]

Discussion with librarians from other institutions indicates that academic librarians are meeting requirements for evaluation in several different ways. Some avoid entirely evaluating reference service, relying instead on consideration of external measures such as publications or committee work. Under these circumstances, there is little incentive for a librarian to improve skills or even to perform more than adequately at the reference desk.

Many institutions depend upon informal and anecdotal evalua-

The authors are at the Penfield Library, State University of New York at Oswego, NY. Ms. Adams is Coordinator of Information Services. Ms. Judd is Head of Reference.

131

tions. Many others rely on a form of management by objectives: individual librarians set their own goals and objectives, discuss them with a supervisor or coordinator, and then after a period of time demonstrate how (and how well) they meet these objectives.

A major problem with the latter two approaches is the difficulty of determining just what is meant by being a "good" reference librarian. What is meant when I describe librarian X as being "good" at reference, and librarian Y as being "poor?" Is X more knowledgeable or more personable, or is X's style closer to my own? When two people make judgments on the same person, is each referring to the same characteristics, or only to those traits most important to each?

Examining standard reference texts gives a little more insight into identifying the characteristics of a good reference librarian. For example, the latest edition of Katz's *Introduction to Reference Work* refers to Taylor in listing skills every librarian should try to develop:

1. The ability to organize data and information for people to use;
2. awareness of the totality of information resources and the probabilities of success of strategies for searching for information in any specific situation;
3. awareness of and ability to use the range of information technologies, from print to sound and image to computing;
4. sensitivity to use, uses, and users of information, and a strong tradition of services, which demands attention to client satisfaction.[2]

Katz goes on to suggest other important traits: imagination, perseverance, judgment, accuracy, thoroughness, and orderliness.[3] Most would agree that these are important, but there is still the difficulty of trying to evaluate them. My perseverance may end after five minutes, while you may consider this as barely starting.

Further descriptions of competencies required for all kinds of librarians in various work settings are being developed by King Research, Inc., under a contract from the U. S. Department of Education. Competencies are assembled under the headings of "Knowledges," "Skills," and "Attitudes." For example, a senior level reference librarian should be able (among many other skills) to "establish rapport with users; communicate well by written, verbal, and non-verbal means; negotiate a reference interview."[4]

Such lists of competencies are valuable in ascertaining the breadth of knowledge and skills required, and pinpointing important attitudes. Reading the competencies could perhaps prompt many librarians to examine and think about what they do. However, when it is time to evaluate work at the reference desk, these competencies supply only a framework. Perhaps others have been faced, as we have, with librarians who think of themselves as being approachable when in fact they are hunched above a book at the reference desk, glaring over their glasses at people who interrupt them. In order to determine what "approachability," or good communication, or other competencies, mean, those behaviors which make up the competencies need to be determined. Only then is there a basis for evaluation or for guidance towards the improvement of a reference librarian.

THE PROCESS OF GOAL ANALYSIS

How can appropriate behaviors be determined? One way to solve this problem is to turn to a model of "goal analysis," popularized by Robert Mager (an author whose provocative yet readable books, particularly on objectives, have been widely used by educators).[5]

Mager's point is that it is not possible to tell if someone has reached a goal unless it is decided what behaviors are exhibited when the goal is reached. It is, for example, easy to tell when someone is a good runner: he or she wins the race (or at least finishes). People can readily agree when the goal of *running well* is reached. When, however, the goal is an attitude or possession of knowledge, progress towards the goal is not visible. I cannot see into your mind to be able to tell when you have "awareness of the totality of information resources," or sufficient knowledge to answer reference questions. I can, however, see you using a variety of sources and selecting appropriate ones to answer reference questions. If I can define those behaviors which demonstrate that someone has reached a goal, then I can look at those behaviors to evaluate how well the goal is reached. To paraphrase Mager, I should not label someone as being a poor reference librarian when I don't even know what I would accept as evidence of achievement.[6]

For example, one of the competencies from the King report (previously mentioned) is the ability to "establish rapport with users." Mager would call this a goal, rather than a competency; he would say that its meaning is too "fuzzy" for someone to be able to tell when a librarian possesses it. (If I tell you to teach someone how to establish rapport, do you know how to go about it?) Establishing rapport is an important goal, but in order to determine behaviors which indicate the achievement of a goal, Mager suggests going through a process of several steps.

STEPS IN GOAL ANALYSIS

The first step is to determine an important goal (such as the ability to establish rapport) and write it down. The next step is to brainstorm, alone or with others, those things that someone should do or say to cause you to agree that he or she has reached this goal. What does someone do or say when he or she can establish rapport with a user? It might help to think of someone who can, and to write down the behaviors that person exhibits. Some behaviors which might come to mind include smiling, good eye contact, acting as though the question is important.

Thinking of negative behaviors may help; for example, good rapport is not established when the librarian is abrupt, points to a source, or acts as though the user's question is an interruption. Then these negative behaviors can be transposed to positive ones: the librarian takes time to listen, gets up and goes with the user to a source, immediately puts aside materials he or she may be working on and reassures the user that the question is not an interruption.

Mager suggests asking other questions in order to determine appropriate behaviors. Given a group of librarians, what criteria could be used to sort them into two groups, those who meet the goal and those who don't? What could others be told so that they would know one when they say one?

Step three involves tidying up the preliminary list. The list should include everything that has been thought of, but then it needs to be examined for consistency and for the refinement of its language. Part of the process should be testing the list for adequacy: if a person exhibits these behaviors, is it agreed that the goal is indeed met? This part of the process ensures that all the behaviors which are important are included, and those which are not important are excluded.

As an example of the importance of selecting important behaviors, a recent text on reference work lists three attributes for personal interaction. While there's no evidence that these attributes were derived from a goal, the authors obviously feel them important. They say that

> A reference librarian must maintain a pleasant expression (rather than a scowl that is easily read as disapproval of present company), speak clearly in a voice that can be readily heard but is not loud or abrasive, and dress to avoid appearing to demand comment . . . [7]

While we certainly agree on the importance of a pleasant expression, we are not so impressed with the necessity of the other two attributes. We have known one librarian in our institution who spoke so softly as to be barely audible, and another librarian whose resonant tones bounced off the reference walls; and several librarians whose dress bordered on the bizarre. In none of these cases did these particular behaviors interfere with the people's ability to be effective reference librarians. In fact, the soft-spoken librarian often received gifts from students (concrete evidence of establishing rapport) and this perhaps was due to her quiet voice's invoking a feeling of intimacy.

Of course, while undergraduate students will probably not be put off by slightly strange attire, the users of a bank's special library may well be. Behaviors which are important for reaching a goal in one situation may not be important at all in another. While librarians in different institutions may easily agree on general goals, the lists of behavior they consider important may (and probably should) vary widely. A goal analysis should reflect the needs of one particular work situation.

BUT IS IT TRIVIAL?

One criticism that often arises when a goal is broken down into its component behaviors is that often the individual behaviors seem trivial, even though the goal is considered important. Are we really suggesting that a reference librarian should receive a poor evaluation for not smiling enough? To rely again on Mager, "the test of triviality is in the consequence of not achieving the performance."[8] If there is no consequence when the librarian doesn't smile (or wears funny clothes), then there is no reason to evaluate him or her on it. If, however, students always go to another librarian for help, or complain of unfriendly librarians, then failing to smile is no longer trivial.

IMPLEMENTING A GOAL ANALYSIS

If a library decides to go through a process of goal analysis, who should do it? If the head of reference is asked for either formal or informal evaluation, then he or she should feel justified in establishing a list of appropriate behaviors. In that case, the reference head has been given the authority to define what good reference service is in that particular library. If, however, reference librarians are to be asked to evaluate each other, then they as a group should work together to formulate those behaviors which they agree are important. In this case, the group has been given the authority to establish norms for reference service.

In either case, the developed list should be available to all who are being evaluated by it. It is patently unfair to expect people to exhibit behaviors when they have only a fuzzy idea of what those behaviors are. Of course, general acceptance of the criteria will be greater if many librarians have had input into developing them.

The next part of this article presents an example of how goal analysis can be applied to a particular library. The goals and the behaviors which are thought to meet these goals were developed over a period of several years by the head of reference at Penfield Library, State University of New York at Oswego.

INSTITUTIONAL BACKGROUND

SUNY at Oswego is a primarily undergraduate, public college of about 7000 students. Penfield Library, with a collection of about 350,000 volumes, has a strong program of library instruction and a well-established reputation of providing good public services. Its director has placed a top priority on providing good reference services; there is at least one librarian available at all times the library is open. All librarians serve on the reference desk, and all reference librarians participate in some other library activities, such as instruction, data base searching, and collection development.

Librarians at Oswego have full faculty status, and are evaluated for retention, continuing appointment, promotion, and merit in the same way that other faculty members are. An elected personnel committee considers each candidate. The director sends both her own and the committee's recommendations on to the next administrative level.

The head of reference is responsible to both the director and the personnel committee for evaluating each librarian's performance at the reference desk, although not for the other activities in which the library may be involved. She is also responsible for training new reference librarians, and has worked out procedures on goals and expected performances.

This particular analysis, then, reflects the circumstances of one institution. The behaviors we list may or may not be important at another institution, but they are considered important at ours. The list may be useful to others either as an example of goal analysis, or as a source of ideas for others who might want to initiate a similar process.

Goal

Reference librarians should be knowledgeable, i.e., they should be able to find factual and background information, and to explain the use of reference sources to users; they need to know library policies and procedures and where to find this information; and, finally, they need to have an in-depth knowledge of reference sources in at least one needed subject area.

Performances

A. First level; the librarian:

1. uses ready reference materials, reference files (such as Penfield's key word file), and the library's policies and procedural manual kept at the reference desk.
2. uses subject guides produced by librarians for library instruction classes.
3. attends colleagues' subject-related library instruction classes.
4. participates in professional development workshops.
5. reviews new reference books during the one-month period they are shelved in a separate area.
6. asks questions of colleagues.
7. refers problem questions to a subject specialist librarian or to the head of reference.

B. Second level; the librarian:

1. uses a variety of sources to answer questions.
2. uses a varied search strategy.
3. uses the most specific subject source available.
4. refers questions to a subject specialist librarian or the head of reference only after first consulting obvious sources.

C. Third level; the librarian:

1. is able to find and use the research materials in a subject field.
2. writes reviews for reference books in subject area for the library newsletter.
3. presents staff workshops to share subject expertise with colleagues.

Discussion

Being considered "knowledgeable" can seem an overwhelming goal to many reference librarians. Determining whether or not a librarian is "knowledgeable" can seem equally difficult to an evaluator. Using goal analysis to determine those performances which will result in a librarian's being considered "knowledgeable" is of benefit to both. Dividing the performances into different levels allows for equitable evaluation of librarians with different reference experience; librarians will no longer fear being unfairly compared to their more experienced colleagues. This division also provides librarians with a much needed framework for establishing priorities in reaching the goal of being considered "knowledgeable."

At the first level librarians are asked to become familiar with the sources and subject areas most in demand in this library; they are encouraged to view the reference process as a team experience in which all librarians are willing to share their expertise. As a librarian gains experience, his or her knowledge should develop to include the performances at the second level. When each reference librarian is hired, or shortly thereafter, he or she agrees to become one of the library's "experts" for a particular subject. The final level includes the performances necessary to demonstrate in-depth knowledge of a librarian's chosen subject specialty.

Being able to speak to specific performances should provide a more meaningful review of a librarian's work at the reference desk.

A librarian who is advised to improve his or her knowledge of reference sources might not know where or how to begin. A librarian who is told, "You've overlooked ready reference sources in helping students," "You need to use the key word index to find more specific subject sources," has some concrete suggestions for reaching this goal.

Each library needs to decide what is meant by a "knowledgeable" reference librarian. Levels of performance appropriate to a librarian's experience and responsibility need to be established. Each librarian needs to then know the level at which he or she is being evaluated.

Goal

Reference librarians should be able to relate positively to patrons.

Performances

The librarian:

1. appears approachable to patron by smiling, maintaining eye contact, being attentive, and listening carefully.
2. shows concern, is tactful, and non-judgmental.
3. reassures the unskilled, unsure patron.
4. assists patron in complex search or in using complex materials; leaves desk to go with patron.
5. is able to solicit from the patron the background information need to accurately determine the patron's needs.
6. does not respond to an angry patron with anger; the librarian tries to reduce the patron's anger.

Discussion

A recent study documents what many librarians have suspected, namely that patrons' satisfaction with reference service is based first upon their perception of the librarians' concern for their needs, and second on their perception of the degree to which the librarians satisfied their needs.[8] Most patrons do not have the ability to know whether or not the best source was found, or was found efficiently, but they do know when the librarian appeared preoccupied, indifferent, or rude.

The patron's first impression of a librarian is usually made by an interpretation of that librarian's "body language" or non-verbal communication. First impressions are important; it would benefit a librarian concerned with this goal to follow the suggestions in performance one. Boucher lists characteristics which demonstrate a "preoccupation mode" and an "availability mode."[9] This list is one which might be used to provide examples of positive and negative body language.

To further clarify verbal performance, here is an example of a situation in which a librarian shows concern and is non-judgmental: the student who tells the reference librarian he can't find any books for his paper which is due this Friday feels more positively towards the librarian who responds, "Yes, you do have a problem; let me see if I can help you find some journal articles," than he will towards the librarian who responds, "You shouldn't have waited until the last week; all the books are probably checked out." Although the latter statement may be true, saying so serves no constructive purpose.

There are many times at the reference desk when there is an opportunity to reassure an unskilled patron. When a patron says she can't find any books written by Mary McCarthy in the card catalog, the librarian might respond that libraries alphabetize "Mc" as if it were "Mac." A better response is to also add that library filing rules confuse many patrons. Being told other users have similar problems, and having the librarian assume some of the responsibility for that problem, leaves the patron feeling better about herself and the reference encounter.

Willingness to assist a patron in using complex tools is best demonstrated by the librarian who goes with the student to provide assistance. A student should not be left alone to struggle through a first-time use of the *Social Sciences Citation Index.*

In a successful reference interview, the librarian is able to determine what the patron's actual information needs are. Many librarians start to find information for a patron only to discover the information being sought is not what the patron wants. Recently a student asked in this library for a list of social service agencies in each state. Upon questioning the student, the librarian found out what the student really wanted was a job with an adult care facility. A list of such facilities in the *Health Services Directory* is more relevant to that student's needs.

Librarians will on occasion find themselves confronted with an angry or upset patron. For example, the patron who complains that all the copying machines aren't working and he needs to copy an article for the next day should not be briskly told, "The copying machines aren't my responsibility; complain to librarian X." To that patron the librarian on the reference desk represents the library, which is responsible for his dilemma. Some positive approaches are to find the person responsible for fixing the machine; copy the article on a staff machine; or, at least, to recognize the library's responsibility and the patron's position by stating, "I'd be upset too if I were in your situation. I'll see that the librarian responsible hears of your complaint."

Again, librarians who are told during an evaluation that they have problems in relating to patrons might not know what steps to take to improve their performances. However, being told, "You need to appear more approachable; smile; look at the patron and appear interested," provides specific behavioral guidelines. Also, being told, "You need to take time to go with patrons and assist them with complex sources," or "You should not express criticism of patrons who wait until the last minute to do their research," are assessments of specific performances which librarians could try to improve.

Goal

The librarian shows good judgment when providing reference service; he or she is able to balance the needs of the patrons, the needs of the library, and the relative merit of sources and then make wise decisions.

Performances

The librarian:

1. asks for assistance from colleagues when desk becomes too busy for one librarian to serve, when the librarian needs to assist a patron in an extensive search in another area of the library, or when he or she is lacking the in-depth subject knowledge needed.
2. chooses materials consistent with patron's level of expertise and particular needs.
3. makes exceptions to library's policies by weighing the patron's need against the reasons for the library's policy.

Discussion

What is "good judgment?" The *American Heritage Dictionary* defines judgment as:

>   The mental ability to perceive and distinguish relationships or alternatives; the critical faculty; discernment. The ability to make reasonable decisions, especially in regard to the practical affairs of life; good sense; wisdom . . . [10]

Good judgment is thus the ability to discern relationships, to balance one need against another, and, when required, to decide wisely. This ability often separates the adequate reference librarian from the good or exceptional one. This goal is more difficult to evaluate compared to others because greater subjectivity is possible. Assessment of this goal like the other goals, however, must depend on the extent to which a librarian's behavior corresponds to the performance standards. Some exhibiting poor judgment with great frequency will doubtless be viewed as not meeting the standards for possessing good judgment.

The first performance deals with the librarian's ability to balance the conflicting needs of patrons. If another librarian or the subject specialist librarian is not available, the library needs a procedure to handle these situations. At Penfield we have a tutorial-by-appointment service (PLUS) for patrons with extensive searches or who need a subject specialist librarian. The librarian on duty then has the option of having such a patron fill out a form requesting a PLUS appointment. He or she is then free to give assistance to other patrons.

In choosing materials consistent with a patron's needs and expertise, the librarian weighs a number of possible choices and chooses the ones most appropriate. For example, an undergraduate student needing information for a speech on heart attacks is probably best served by pamphlets in the vertical file and some general magazine articles found using the *Readers' Guide*. Referring the student to *Index Medicus* would not serve this student's needs.

A librarian is often requested to make exceptions to a library's policy when he or she is the only professional in the building. For the librarian's decision to be considered "good judgment," he or she needs to know the library's philosophy regarding exceptions to policies in general and the rationale for the policy in question. In this library a major consideration in allowing exceptional overnight circulation of a reference book is the possible inconvenience to other students if the book is not returned the next morning. Thus we rarely circulate ready reference books as they are used daily by many students.

Though it may be more difficult to evaluate, "good judgment" should not be overlooked in determining goals for reference librarians. It is often the area where an otherwise good librarian needs improvement. Referring to specific instances, statements such as, "You leave the reference desk uncovered too long when answering research questions in documents," or "You should not have circulated ten phone books; they were not available to patrons who needed them the next day," aids the librarian in understanding what is meant by "good judgment" in your library.

Goal

The librarian is dependable.

Performances

The librarian:

1. is on time for assignment at the reference desk.
2. provides service throughout the scheduled time, leaving only when required time at desk has been completed.

Discussion

This goal may seem unimportant until a library finds itself with a librarian who is consistently late for scheduled time at the reference desk, or who leaves early, or who forgets scheduled reference time entirely. As librarians are human, and it is human to err, all librarians will probably exhibit this behavior on occasion. Each library needs to decide at what point it is concerned about each episode . . . the first time a librarian is late? the second? during what period of time?

It is more productive to tell a librarian, "You've been late for morning reference work twice this semester. If you're late again during this evaluation period, you'll be rated poorly on dependability," than "You need to be more dependable."

CONCLUSION

Once a library or reference head has decided upon the qualities which define an effective reference librarian at that institution, as we have at Penfield, what then should be done with the list? Even if nothing more than identifying the behaviors is done, such a list of behaviors is useful. The head of reference can share the list with reference librarians, so that they have a clear idea of behaviors which are expected of them. Many reference librarians may not have thought through the effects of all their behaviors; the list may therefore serve as a kind of self-assessment.

If the reference head, or other librarians, are asked to describe a librarian's reference performance, they have a list of criteria to consult in order to derive specific examples of the librarian's ability. A letter of recommendation, for example, is more convincing if it makes clear what is meant by "good" performance.

In a formal evaluation, either to a personnel committee or to a director, the reporting librarian again has a basis for the comments he or she makes. When behaviors are defined, then it also becomes possible to comment on an individual's strengths and weaknesses and to compare them with others.

The list may also be used informally to assign librarians to reference duty. If, for example, librarian X is extremely knowledgeable, but tends to be somewhat brisk with users, it might make good sense to assign X with librarian Y, whose knowledge might not be so extensive, but whose people skills are good. The strengths and weaknesses of each can bolster the other's performance—and each can learn from the other.

Once a library has identified important characteristics, then it also has a clear indication of activities which can promote these characteristics. For example, at our institution, we have a monthly in-service training session (called RAPS). Most of these sessions are devoted to information sharing (good science sources, strategies for locating texts of speeches, etc.) thus contributing to an increase in librarians' knowledge. However, other sessions have been devoted to interpersonal behaviors such as "how to say no without making a patron angry" (a session given by a member of the college's counseling department) or developing good listening skills (led by a county extension agent). Once it's known what skills reference librarians should possess, selecting appropriate learning experiences becomes much easier.

Finally, the list may be used as part of a more formal evaluation procedure. The University of Arizona has developed a list similar to ours (under the direction of Rebecca Kellogg, then Head of Reference at Arizona) but with a number of differences, reflecting the needs and perceptions of a different institution. Each reference librarian at Arizona evaluates each other reference librarian, using the list of behaviors. The head of reference then compiles these and shares with each librarian the evaluation of his or her own peers. Since what is expected from each librarian is clearly understood, such feedback can provide valuable guidance and direction for the person being evaluated.

Whatever the final utilization of the list of behaviors which make for an effective reference librarian, it is the process of formulating the list which is most important. One is forced to focus on these qualities which are most important, leaving out those like dress or individual style which may have little bearing on performance. When faced with a librarian with weak skills, the supervisor has available a basis for concrete suggestions for improvement.

Even those who are opposed to performance behaviors must have some basis for evaluation. We feel that evaluation is not only easier, but fairer to those being evaluated, if it is based upon specific criteria which clearly define the behaviors expected from a ''good'' reference librarian.

REFERENCES

1. See, for example, the extensive literature review in F. W. Lancaster, *The Measurement and Evaluation of Library Services* (Washington, D. C.: Information Resources Press, 1977), Chapter 3.

2. Robert S. Taylor, ''Reminiscing about the Future,'' *Library Journal* 104 (1979): 1873. As cited in William Katz, *Introduction to Reference Work,* 2 vols., 4th ed. (New York: McGraw-Hill, 1982), 1: 28-29.

3. Katz, ibid.

4. A sample preliminary competency list for a senior level reference librarian in a special library is reprinted in the article by Jose-Marie Griffiths, ''Our Competencies Defined: A Progress Report and Sampling,'' *American Libraries* 15 (1984): 43-45.

5. Robert Mager, *Goal Analysis* (Belmont, CA: Fearon Press, 1972).

6. Ibid., 110.

7. Diana M. Thomas, et al., *The Effective Reference Librarian* (New York: Academic Press, 1982), 96.

8. Alma Christine Vathis, ''Reference Transaction and End Product as Viewed by the Patron,'' *RQ* 23 (1983): 60-64.

9. Virginia Boucher, ''Nonverbal Communication and the Library Reference Interview,'' *RQ* 16 (1976): 27-32.

10. ''Judgment,'' *American Heritage Dictionary of the English Language* (Boston: Houghton Mifflin Co., 1978), 709.

The Accreditation of Reference Services

Bernard Vavrek

One of the fascinating things about writing for a journal (word-processing these days), is being able to say what you want even if there is always the assumption that there may be far fewer readers than would satisfy the author. So it is with this present essay, which is concerned with strengthening the perceptions and realities of reference services—an ambitious undertaking at the very least. This article is specifically concerned with the need to accredit the reference services of libraries in the same fashion in which, e.g., hospitals, schools, etc., are certified to be "professionally pure." While the ideas inherent in this commentary pertain to all types of libraries, the public library will be the model that will be specifically considered. Before getting to this issue, however, the author would like to provide some subjective comments on reference/information service as a matter of background. Parenthetically, to simplify things the author will use the term "reference" throughout this paper instead of the more cumbersome label "reference/information service" which is utilized in RASD's document, *A Commitment to Information Services: Developmental Guidelines.* [1]

It's an interesting endeavor to consider what are the motivating forces or Furies that generally drive librarianship at the present time. These also propel reference librarians, of course. The reader will find no difficulty in constructing a list of concerns. The following ones are the author's favorites. Without question, the top category in importance is the headlong concern most librarians have with technology, particularly microcomputers, at the present time. While this author has suggested, in other places, that he frequently is tempted to sell his micro and that other librarians might consider similar action, this has been branded by some as a rather regressive

---

The author is Coordinator of The Center for the Study of Rural Librarianship and a member of the faculty of the College of Library Science at Clarion University of Pennsylvania, Clarion, PA 16214.

147

attitude to maintain. Even at the risk of being labeled as the old man on the mountain (Clarion is 7,000 feet above sea level, so I would qualify), my concern emanates from the fear that library basics are being forgotten at the expense of individuals wanting to be au courant. It is also my view that librarians, whether they know it or appreciate it or not, have confused means and ends. There must also be a concern that those who see themselves as information scientists (what a heady category) and now wish to interpret the entirety of library practices in nanoseconds, are nicely playing into the hands (nay, motherboards) of companies manufacturing electronic components, information utilities, and electrical engineers. The future library needs no librarians nor information scientists. Hopefully, reference librarians will not need to be constantly reminded that human beings still require the prerequisite attention in all libraries.

ANOTHER CONCERN

"Professional anonymity" is a second concern. The National Commission on Excellence in Education handed librarianship another jolt by pretending that we don't exist, i.e., ignoring us in the grand scheme of pursuing educational excellence. Almost humorously, but with the best intentions in mind, the U. S. Department of Education, is holding seminars around the country asking what librarians can now do to respond to achieving excellence in education. To now begin asking questions of ourselves such as, "What is the role of the library in the educational process?", infers that this is a new direction for librarianship. Sadly, it also indicates that we have been asleep professionally. In my view, a major part of the problem is explainable through the fact that librarians have not been concerned enough with providing the basic research necessary to explain library services to themselves and particularly for others. Neither, have we the statistics to adequately describe what libraries provide for society. For example, the reader is challenged to discover the number of adult readers who use public libraries in the United States on an annual basis. How many reference questions, as another example, are asked annually in academic libraries? There are many such unanswered questions.

Historically, of course, librarians have not been insensitive to the fact that society does not easily project its sympathies on libraries and librarians. It rarely occurs to us that the lack of identity in the community may be our fault rather than someone else's. This situation is relevant to all librarians, of course. Unfortunately, reference librarians, particularly those in academic settings, tend to use the application of technology as a boot strap operation (pun intended) to overcome role uncertainty.

THIRD ISSUE

The third issue facing librarianship has to do with the reciprocal matters of library training and professional placement. Concerns over the accreditation of schools of library and information science are juxtaposed with efforts to alter standards for federal librarians and the hiring of staff on what might be described as a type of temporary service contract. Added to this is the fact that there will only be a modest amount of growth in the number of library positions available in the future with most of these being of the replacement type. Although, some growth is projected for rural areas. While it is unfair and incorrect to place the total blame on the corporate shoulders of the American Library Association, the fact that anyone can function as a librarian with impunity helps to erode both the philosophical and practical reality of being a librarian.

Currently, e.g., there is concern being shown by the American Medical Association that unqualified individuals (in the legal sense) are practicing medicine in the United States. My thought here is not to ridicule librarianship or the ALA, but can any person of reason, recall a circumstance where librarians were challenged on the job because they have not met the minimal levels of education necessary to perform as a librarian. What are these qualifications in practice? Who enforces them? Clearly, circumstances do exist, e.g., where institutional requirements must be met as in school or academic libraries. But this is not necessarily true in most special or public libraries. Also, it is not necessarily true where library contractors are at work. This author will have more to say shortly about accreditation, particularly as it relates to reference librarians, since it is a major thrust of this paper.

Other problems facing American librarianship also leap from the disk of my word processor with some celerity as, e.g., the less than overwhelming financial support for libraries, the information explosion, marketing library services, etc. The patient reader will be delighted, undoubtedly, that the author will not be tempted to extrapolate these any further than as a listing. But one is challenged, for completeness sake, to continue and to identify a subset of problems that particularly confront reference librarians. And if the reader has now forgotten what is going on with this list, the author is still providing background.

In addition to those general problems cited above, reference librarians must also contend with the ever-growing number of resources, data bases, etc., that comprise their reference collections; attempt to deal dynamically with the varied personalities of individuals (including problem patrons) who frequent our libraries; contend with administrators who have little perception of the complexities of what we call reference service; and, strive to remember, in addition to everything else, that the reference librarian is really the person who represents the library to the public, i.e, through his/her visibility on the job. While there are other problems which might have been added to this listing, the author has exercised some frugality in the choosing.

ELEMENTS

At this point, even the patient reader may wonder about the necessity of referring to the previously cited problems. The question now becomes one of what have technology, image perception, etc., to do with this paper? All of these elements are directly, or indirectly related to the education of the reference librarian. In fact, there can be no greater priority for American librarianship than the matter of how well reference librarians are educated. The necessity of having academically trained reference librarians is an easily accepted concept, since it is obviously the normal thrust of things. It should be noted, however, that in some facets of librarianship, notably among public libraries in rural areas, that only 25% of those full-time staff members performing as librarians are academically trained, while the national average for all public libraries is approximately 50%. And regardless of the best of intentions, reference service in these libraries lacking trained persons suffers. Unfortunately, the individuals involved may not really perceive their inadequacies due to the enthusiastic level at which most of them perform. Emotion, however, is not really a substitute for formal training.

Concerns over the training of librarians is not a new issue. Furthermore, it is a credit to American librarianship, that the matter continues to be debated, otherwise it might suggest a complacent profession. Recently, questions have been newly raised about accreditation procedures including such matters as who should comprise the majority members of the Committee on Accreditation. What is missed, however, in this continuing enthusiasm about considering educational techniques, is that attention has been given to only one-half of the training phenomenon. If the overall goal is to insure a quality trained librarian in order to provide quality service, then in addition to the certification of schools of library and information science, libraries must also be accredited. Owing to the dynamic nature of libraries, this then suggests that the key element must be at the focal center, i.e., reference services.

This idea was first proposed by the author in the publication, *Reference and Online Services Handbook,*[2] over a year ago. To report that it created only a mild amount of interest, would be a gentle characterization of the truth. Undaunted by its immediate lack of overwhelming success, however, this individual would again like to plead the case.

It seems to me that the heated attention given to the accreditation of schools of library and information science by the American Library Association falls short of a holistic approach of insuring quality library services. Insisting that students come from centers of learning which have been given the imprimatur of excellence by ALA is not unimportant, quite the contrary, but it doesn't go far enough. For example, any library administrator clearly understands the need for a newly hired librarian to "learn the ropes" on the job. That is, not only should there be a period of time in which the new recruit must master the idiosyncrasies of his/her new library position, formal, i.e., classroom learning must now be complemented by on the job experience. And considering the fact that a majority of jobs require previous experience, it is relatively clear in practice, that experience is valued more highly than classroom exercises by the hiring librarian.

EFFORT NEEDED

Perhaps, then, there should be some accreditation effort aimed at the library administrator. Considering, however, that the librarian is only one aspect of the library information system, an inspection of personnel is not enough. A more sensible approach would be to certify the quality of the library's information function (since our concern in this paper is with reference services)—by no means an easy task. Because of the author's often repeated refrain that it, the information function, is the essence of any library and comprises all of its parts, a review of the information function would not only include the administrators—even if there is only one—but everything else as well. Therefore, a dual approach, including both the accreditation of library schools and libraries, would give a decided measure of completeness presently unavailable. Even at the risk of offending the reader who has long since tired of comparisons of librarians with physicians, etc., since hospitals, schools, churches, etc., are subject to accreditation procedures by their respective agencies, there are valid parallels that librarianship might emulate.

But why accredit libraries; what would be gained? Hopefully, the long range goal would be the general improvement of library services throughout the nation. Some short range accomplishments would include the strengthening of services within individual libraries and the improvement of the reference librarian's skills. It should be stressed, again, that the evaluation process being proposed is meant to be a positive, constructive force. The intent, however, is that accreditation would result in a winnowing process in that only qualified librarians and library collections would remain. For some time, it has concerned this author that librarians offer no form of guarantee for their work. Think of it, being able to certify that one's information is 100% pure and enable the library consumer to return it in 90 days if not satisfied, i.e., if the reference librarian gives you the wrong information. Since few other professions give guarantees, however, it is unlikely that librarians would be leaders in this endeavor. We should be able to at least guarantee that libraries meet minimal levels of acceptability. This is accomplished only indirectly at the present time, i.e., to the extent that mandates for libraries receiving state aid are implemented. Even in the light of state requirements, there are no national standards to insure uniform library services throughout the United States. Further, there is no standard to measure.

It would be an important development for librarianship, e.g., if every American citizen could expect a uniform quality of library service whether he or she were in Big Springs, Texas; Stone Mountain, Georgia; or White Pine, Pennsylvania. This is not to suggest that there wouldn't be variations created by community differences. It is probably somewhat overly ambitious to contemplate thousands of librarians around the country all shouting in unison, "Here's the beef," since American librarians seemingly don't even have the political clout to implement a national logo in the form of highway signs. Other challenges seem Herculean by comparison.

Implementing the scheme of accreditation being advanced in this paper, would first suggest that national *quantifiable* standards would have to be instituted. While the author is aware of the fact that this suggestion seems to be contrary to the trends that have been observed over the last decade, it should be noted that the promulgation of *Output Measures for Public Libraries*[3] is really a return to the quantifiable days. The difference is, however, that numerical models are expected to emerge inductively from data collecting using the *Output Measures* rather than being stipulated beforehand.

MODUS OPERANDI

The author would like to advance the following modus operandi in pursuing the concepts of accreditation suggested in this paper.

One, as a beginning thrust, it would be essential to have PLA/ RASD and representatives of state library agencies meet together to develop national standards that would be used for library accreditation practices. Owing to the fact that the *Output Measures* document does not deal with reference services at the intensity level needed for the type of evaluation being discussed here, this author would like to suggest that the publication, *A Commitment to Information Services: Developmental Guidelines* be also employed. Those familiar with this document (many are yet to discover it) will remember that it is also a product of the "Mission Statement"[4] mentality, i.e., a descriptive rather than prescriptive source. Numbers would have to be related to its generally useful framework. For example, while it (RASD's publication) gives the reader the advice that a reference specialist should be available all hours that the library is open, this admonition isn't really specified numerically. Converting this would not appear to be a major challenge, though. Although this individual has come to "appreciate" the deliberate speed with which American librarianship sometimes works. Quantifiable standards used by state library agencies would be another source of input here and throughout the remainder of the steps to be highlighted subsequently.

In my view, the following elements would necessarily be vital in the evaluation of library services: overall collection size; size of the reference collection; number and type of staff; hours open, etc. In short, those things that we usually associate with numerical evaluation. As an aside, although the author has no immediate proof to support his view, it is my belief that the lack of tangible guidelines (quantifiable standards) defining such things as optimal collection size and more specifically actual reference titles has had an injurious effect on library services, particularly in the small library. The information explosion makes it difficult for everyone to make sense of things. This is understood. But it is more trying for the individual in the small library (in a population of 25,000 or fewer people) to determine what is basic, i.e., judging such things as where does one begin and with what.

PROCESS

Since the accreditation process quite clearly involves a consideration of the human elements of service, i.e., the library staff, criteria would be needed that measure the relative efficiency and accuracy of the reference person in answering questions, the quality of interpersonal skills, online talents, degree of bibliographical instruction, extent to which the library serves as a community information center, etc. Yes, the author quite agrees that developing a rating scale for these last items would not only prove more difficult to organize, there would be a commensurate difficulty in implementation. It may, however, be less of a problem than perceived. For example, on the matter of ''bibliographical instruction,'' one might be logically concerned with the question, ''Is bibliographical instruction being provided by the reference staff (or person) and what techniques of instruction are used?'' The assumption, of course, would be that bibliographical instruction or whatever else that is used for the ratings, are desirable items and the absence of the same is an indication of a library which needs some help. Again, remembering that this accreditation activity is supposed to have a salubrious effect on the library being accredited rather than being viewed as an IRS audit—with all due respects to our colleagues in government.

Parenthetically, it should be noted that owing to the variety of libraries that comprise public librarianship in the United States, i.e., particularly small institutions, accreditation practices and procedures may more frequently be concerned with the one-person library rather than complexities of reference departments. Regardless of the size of the institution, however, the procedures should essentially be the same.

The second step in the accreditation process being suggested is for field testing to be conducted on a regional basis. After the evaluative criteria are drawn, which should not take any longer than six months, well, maybe one year, it would be useful to put the scenario through some rigorous testing for feedback and improvement.

Third, a series of hearings should be scheduled throughout the United States, sponsored both by ALA and the state library agencies. Perhaps, this could be coordinated with the summer ALA meeting which would allow differing and geographically representative views to be heard. If it is not immediately apparent, the reason for the hearings, in addition to permitting as much input as possible, is to enable the framers of this ''declaration'' of accreditation to implement any needed change.

Fourth, the dissemination of the accreditation document would be next in order. Coupled with its distribution, would be another obligatory round of hearings, but this time conducted by state library agencies within individual states.

Fifth, assuming that the third year has now passed since step one was instituted, we would now be at the implementation stage. Importantly, it should be noted that, it would be left to the state agencies to decide the actual, i.e., final techniques to be utilized. That is, the states would decide matters such as, e.g., how many individuals would be included in the sight visit, format of the final report, etc. Also, if it has been unclear, it would be now the prerogative of the state agencies to accredit libraries. Remember, this is now being based on national standards.

PENALTY

What would be the penalty for failing the accreditation process? While one is not advocating that some nefarious McCarthy type of list be generated and circulated about, clearly, there must be some relative pain felt by the library judged lacking in services. It would be my suggestion that this library's state aid should be held in jeopardy until observed deficiencies are corrected. Perhaps, each library should be given two years to conform to the accreditation requirements, and the whole process might by cycled on a five or six year basis.

Finally, owing to the fact that American librarianship now has available national standards of service, a responsibility of the states should be to provide statistical data to the National Center for Education Statistics to be published on a annual basis. The availability of these statistical data is a viable reason, in itself, to proceed with what has been described in this document.

American librarianship—a euphemism for all types of libraries—is is in danger of becoming extinct. Unknowingly, but inexorably, we have contributed to this destiny and hastened its arrival with the inappropriate application of technology for library practices. While the author is not foolish enough to assume that a new Rosetta type stone has been discovered (and explained in this document), it is my distinct view that positive change is needed in the collective manner with which we deal with library services—in all libraries. We have not only been too casual in setting standards of achievement, we have frequently acted as if library/information service is something for which society has more responsibility than individual librarians.

The author understands the difficulties inherent in trying to implement the ideas suggested in this paper. Further, once again, one would reiterate that the context of this document has been oriented toward all libraries. Academic institutions, e.g., are no less an ingredient in the need for library change and improvement. Academic librarians simply escape society's scrutiny that is characteristic of life in a public library. It remains to be observed how well, if at all, librarians respond to the challenges of 1984 and beyond. There are, of course, alternatives to action. And we have already demonstrated our talents in that regard.

REFERENCES

1. *A Commitment to Information Services: Developmental Guidelines.* (Chicago: Standards Committee, Reference and Adult Services Division, American Library Association, 1979.)

2. "After the Guidelines and Reference Policy" in Bill Katz and Anne Clifford (eds.) *Reference and Online Services Handbook.* (New York: Neal Schuman Publishers, 1982), pp. 3-7.

3. Zweizig, Douglas and Eleanor Jo Rodger. *Output Measures for Public Libraries: A Manual of Standardized Procedures.* (Chicago: Public Library Association, American Library Association, 1982.)

4. *The Public Library Mission Statement and Its Imperatives for Service.* (Chicago: American Library Association, 1979.)

THOSE WHO ARE SERVED

A Community Based Approach to Evaluation of Public Library Reference Service

Mary Lee Bundy
Amy Bridgman

We are today seeing an upsurge in professional interest in evaluation of public library reference service. This interest may be a measure of the field's sophistication in using management tools and it may be a most welcome development.

But there is reason for caution. Unless appropriately applied, this evaluation could have negative consequences. The primary reason for concern is the narrowness of current evaluation focus. Because the *status quo* of reference—that body of interrelated traditions, assumptions, values, and practices which characterize current practice—is not being substantially questioned, evaluation may have the effect of "locking in" reference service at a time when it may be propitious for it to be both re-oriented and expanded.

Unless serious questions are raised about *who* is being served in terms of community elements and with regard to *what kinds of information* are being provided to communities, evaluation will support improvement in existing practice, but not change. Indeed, failure to raise these and other questions regarding the goals of reference leaves libraries unable to fully respond to their social mandate and unable to intelligently exploit the newer technologies.

In this article we take a community-oriented look at the evaluation potential. We overview what we consider central issues regarding today's reference practice, outline the ingredients of a community-based approach to reference planning, and then spell out its implications for evaluation.

Mary Lee Bundy is a professor in the College of Library and Information Services, University of Maryland. Amy Bridgman is a free lance reference librarian and researcher, specializing in health information in San Diego County, CA.

159

To get some indication of current reference evaluation and related practices, information was solicited from a sample of public libraries across the country, serving populations of 100,000 or more, and the findings reported here.

There can, of course, be no question that evaluation is closely linked to quality of service and that reference service under any terms must commit itself to the highest of performance standards.

THE QUALITY QUESTION

There is now a body of studies which examine how well public libraries respond to reference inquiries. Those using unobtrusive measures, that is, studies carried out by having questioners pose as real clients of the library, have the advantage that they are not dependent on either the subjective judgment of the librarian or the user as to whether the correct information was supplied. These studies were usually conducted by telephone and in general, but not exclusively, have focused on questions calling for a factual answer.

They vary widely in size and methodology. But when the findings regarding how many questions were answered correctly are compared, they show remarkable consistency. While there may have been variation in success rates among the libraries in a given study, the overall rate was nearly always around 50 percent (Bundy, Bridgman and Keltie, 55%;[1] Childers, 55%;[7] Childers 58%;[6] Crowley, 54%;[8] House, 40%;[10] Peat, Marwick, Mitchell and Co., 40%[19] Ramsden, 49%;[20] Weech and Goldhor, 70%.[24]

This same rate was also found in college studies (Jirgees, 56%;[11,17] King and Berry, 60%;[12] Myers, 50%;[16,17] Schmidt, 50%.[22] And in a recent study by Charles McClure and Peter Hernon of academic government depository libraries, only 37 percent of the questions were answered correctly.[15*]

Most significant of all, the success rate of 50 percent involved questions readily answerable from standard reference sources. With the more difficult questions asked in the study of government depository libraries, the rate dropped to 18 percent.

In any profession the low success rates found in these studies would be taken most seriously and librarians must be equally concerned, even alarmed.

---

*Jirgees, King and Berry, and Peat, Marwick, Mitchell and Co. were not seen. Percentages are from McClure and Hernon (15).

WHO BENEFITS

Quality is one key question. But any public service, though purportedly available to all, must also ask and answer who its main beneficiaries are. It must also ask what is being supplied to them in terms of social good. It is extremely important to know the answers to these questions when it comes to public library reference service because user studies of public libraries through the years and today have identified that the public library is an institution used primarily by the middle class, largely unused by and alien to the poor of American communities.

While there is a lack of research into reference use, studies of information seekers and libraries provide some insight. Most striking is the apparent small percentage of adults who use public libraries as an information source. In 1977 Douglas Zweizig generalized from past research that while perhaps 20 percent of the adult population may use a public library frequently (at least once a month), five percent or less, call on public libraries for needed information.[26]

Later, a study by Ching-chih Chen and Peter Hernon of information needs and behavior of adults in the six New England states, found that only 17 percent of respondents in seeking information used libraries.[4,5] In percentage of respondents consulting them, libraries ranked ninth among all information providers and fourth among the institutional source providers, coming after professional people, businesses, and government agencies. The investigators also dismally concluded from what respondents told them that people seeking information in the library sense a latent inability to deliver pertinent, accurate, and up-to-date information.

This interesting study found that professional and technical workers, managers and administrators, and students accounted for 56 percent of the situations in which libraries were used. But clerical workers, craftsmen and service workers each accounted for nearly ten percent of use. Libraries received at least some use for a range of reasons, but were most often consulted for job-related: technical, education and schooling, and consumer related purposes.

Two research studies give some direct, although contradictory, evidence as to how activist groups make use of libraries.* Pauline Wilson, who studied individuals in a midwestern metropolitan area

---

*Both these studies offer insights into how to determine/predict group information needs as a function of their activities and with regard to types of information sources used by groups.

who had recently been most active in an organizational effort to effect social change, found that *none* of them used a public library in connection with that effort.[25] Joan Durrance, some eight years later in Toledo, Ohio, in an analysis of the role of citizen groups in information transfer, studied neighborhood, special interest/advocate and public affairs organizational information seekers.[9] She found that over one-half (56%) had tried to use the library as one of many sources of information in connection with an activity, and that most found it to be a minor contributor to the project. These and other studies have found, however, that organizational leaders and people with community involvements tend to use public libraries heavily for their personal use in far greater proportion than the general population.

SAD EVIDENCE

This is mostly, but not entirely, discouraging evidence. If we consider that probably only one-third of information seekers using public libraries get help from a librarian, we conclude that public library reference use is negligible in terms of percent of the population served, particularly out-of-school adults. We expect public libraries to be of minor information assistance, if at all, to groups working on social change.

There is a related concern. The writers' unobtrusive measure study focused on how public libraries respond to inquiries challenging the *status quo.*[1] In this case study of how public libraries answered questions regarding draft registration, few of the libraries surveyed could refer questioners to major organizations opposing the draft and few had material in their collection from the peace movement, thus seriously limiting their ability to provide anti-draft information. If libraries are habitually excluding information from the various social movements, rather than being non-partisan, they are functioning unduly as rationalizers and supporters of the *status quo* with social change interests only incidentally served.

A LOOK AT TODAY'S REFERENCE PRACTICE

Low use and indifferent quality may well be the result of failure to adequately fund and otherwise support a service. It seems clear that unless libraries make an overt effort to seek out reference use, they will continue to be used by a very small percentage of the adult population for this purpose. We want to know, then, the status which is being accorded to their reference services today by public libraries. We also ask whose interests are being appealed to and how community minded reference services are.

An examination of promotional materials put out by public libraries, news notes and articles in the professional literature, and the *Report from the States,* issued by the New York State Library, give us some indication of the status of reference practice today.[21]

Many public libraries are engaged in public awareness campaigns which include imaginative marketing of reference service and there are statewide promotional campaigns in a number of states. But probably most public libraries are not in these budget-tight times considering major expansion of their reference services. Indeed, libraries which have suffered severe financial setbacks and those in rapidly growing communities, may even hesitate to advertise their services for fear of further taxing already overloaded services. Certainly there does not seem to be a major drive in the profession to reorient the public to think of public libraries as information centers despite the leadership of some libraries and a push for such a reorientation by Lowell Martin and others.*

But some libraries are offering new reference related services including prominently specialized health, job and career, and legal information services. Service to business and local government forms part of the public library's service equation. Some libraries are strengthening these services in response to their city's economic plight.

Libraries have varying degrees of community involvement not necessarily focused on reference services per se including special programs for ethnic groups and for handicapped people. While many libraries participate in community affairs, as Mary Lee Bundy found earlier, few are using the library as a forum for the discussion of controversial issues.[2] Few were found to be promoting environmental information. The thrust of effort is still toward helping people on an individual basis.

This era has seen what would probably be considered the major reference development vis-a-vis the community and that is the organized I and R services now offered by at least half of major

---

*See his study of the Philadelphia Public Library for one model of the library as a community information resource.[14]

libraries with other libraries employing a range of tools to give some of the same service.

I and R has the potential of encouraging citizen participation in local affairs by linking people to groups engaged in civic action. But as it is presently conceived by librarians it is primarily a means whereby people with personal needs can be directed to possible sources of assistance. It is thus being delivered as a coping service particularly for those in economic need.

As one would expect, there are important computer related reference trends. Undoubtedly, more and more libraries will be subscribing to online data base services, some of which have interest for civic groups and others concerned with community problems. Public libraries are increasingly becoming involved with computer use for networking efforts which have direct interlibrary loan and reference service provisions. We are also already seeing the beginning of public library service to home computer users.

We find, then, that while the *status quo* of reference probably remains basically unchanged, many public libraries are responding to trends in society in their reference service and more and more are applying advanced technology to improve their ability to link people with information.

Inevitably, we come again to the critical question of who gets served. Technology may, unless consciously redirected, go primarily to advantage the well-off rather than to equalize the information situation. In looking at the evaluation practices of public libraries today we are particularly interested in whether they are concerning themselves with the troubling question of who they serve.

CURRENT EVALUATION PRACTICES

The majority of the 50 public libraries who cooperated in the survey serve populations under 300,000, 37 of them. Only three—Milwaukee, Houston, and Philadelphia—serve populations over one million. These city, county and regional libraries are located in 28 states.

When the responses of these libraries were tabulated, they revealed a not surprising picture.

Those evaluation related activities which may be said to constitute current practice (engaged in by three-fourths or more currently or in the last five years) are: *Maintain a count of reference requests (regularly or on a sample basis)* 94 percent, and *Evaluation of reference collections,* 82 percent.

It is fairly common practice to at least partially (for some questions) *keep a record of requests by content either regularly or on a sample basis.* One-half reported this activity while 42 percent reported *Study of information needs of library users.*

Related to evaluation, 66 percent reported having a written reference policy (statements of objectives, standards, approved practice) or having reference policy in larger statements.*

These were the only activities engaged in by more than 36 percent of the responding libraries. Six activities were reported by about one-third, namely, *Study of reference user satisfaction (more than informal feedback),* 36 percent; *Study of characteristics of library reference users (age, occupation, etc.),* 36 percent; *Study of community information needs (users and non-users or of particular elements such as senior citizens),* 32 percent. *Evaluation of time spent answering reference inquiries or other management efficiency analyses,* 32 percent; *Follow-up on referrals made to other libraries, government agencies, and/or to sources of personal assistance (I and R),* 30 percent; *Study of staff assessment of success in answering questions and reasons for failure,* 30 percent.

Ranking at the very bottom, reported by less than 20 percent, were: *Study of public awareness and/or public interest in reference services,* 18 percent; *Study of organization use of reference (by business, government agencies, civic and other private organizations and services),* 16 percent; and *Unobtrusive measures (calling and/or visiting a library and purporting to be a patron),* 8 percent.

Several libraries added comments indicating considerable interest in doing more evaluation, particularly as to the quality of the reference service given by librarians. The chief reason cited for not doing more at the present time was lack of manpower. As one put it, " . . . at present we can barely keep up with our desk work and the reference collection's maintenance and development."

At least a few libraries have had or plan to have reference studied as part of a more general library study, including Pasadena Public Library's recent involvement with an extensive study of the Pasadena community and its information needs.[18]

While only the two evaluation related activities were engaged in

---

*This is compared with the findings of Bernard Vavrek's survey of small rural libraries in Pennsylvania, that 73 percent used no written reference policy statement.[23]

by most, this is not to say that most libraries engage in only this minimal effort. Only 30 percent reported three activities or less, while 48 percent reported between four and seven. We do not, from this analysis, know how extensive the activities reported are.

As for those activities particularly community related, we see that the vast majority make no formal effort to determine the characteristics of reference users or to learn about community information needs. Even fewer examine organization use of reference or engage in public awareness research.

These libraries are, nevertheless, in terms of numbers of inquiries, lending considerable reference assistance. The reference inquiries handled, other than directional, over a one-year period by the 37 libraries supplying figures ranged from 13,352 to 2,868,328.

No. of Inquiries	*No. of Libraries*
10,000-50,000	8
50,001-100,000	9
100,001-200,000	10
200,001-500,000	4
over 500,000	6

Impressively, altogether, they handled over 11 million reference inquiries in a year's time.*

We have identified foregoing aspects of current reference use and practice of most significance to the development of public library reference service as a community information resource. The most important consideration is the nature of the reference commitment vis-a-vis the library's community. Following we propose what such a commitment might entail.

A COMMUNITY APPROACH TO REFERENCE PLANNING*

A community approach to reference planning begins with accepting responsibility for meeting the information needs of the commu-

---

*Figures are an approximation. Some libraries provided information on a fiscal year basis rather than for the calendar year 1982 requested. A few were able to give only a partial total.

*For a further discussion of these potentials, see Mary Lee Bundy, *Helping People Take Control: The Public Library's Mission in a Democracy.*[3]

nity served by the library. This commitment involves several related commitments.

The library is committed to meeting the information needs of *all* elements in its community. It is thus committed to reference outreach to encourage non-traditional reference users to call on this service and the related services of the library.

A community approach involves concern for putting information to work to meet the developmental needs of the community, including most importantly information support for solving its most pressing environmental, economic and other social problems.

The central means for realizing this commitment is support for citizen participation in public affairs of the community and in broader state and national affairs. This commitment involves, importantly, support for citizen groups working on one or another community problem or project.

These statements have vast implications for those libraries working seriously to realize them as goals of service. Clearly a key change in the reference role is a shift from a passive instrument, there to be called upon, to an active force in both building information resources for the community and in encouraging use of them and of reference assistance. Among the library's activities, reference would assume a most prominent role.

The social imperative. The rationale for this definition of the public library's community role lies in the real world in which we live. This is a world in which many millions of people are living without basic life necessities, and will continue to be, unless there is concerted public outcry. American communities have major environmental and social problems which must be addressed by a concerned and informed citizenry. As never before we need a government made responsive to people's interests and to moral conscience of the highest order.

These are the reasons why we believe helping to educate, inform and alert and otherwise assist citizens in information terms in solving the social problems of our times is not one worthwhile task for the public library. It is the paramount one.

In pursuing this goal, public libraries have a great social contribution to make, for information access and dissemination is central to every organized effort to improve conditions for people. Major problems confront citizen groups and citizens in getting information bearing on their most vital interests. Aware, skilled and responsive public libraries can be of valuable assistance in solving those information problems and in keeping the information situation in the U.S. from becoming more closed.

DYNAMIC EVALUATION

Given the *status quo* of reference service, when we talk about community oriented reference we are clearly talking about change in reference policy and practice. Even more, we are talking about changing library priorities.

Evaluation would come into play *only* after the library has defined its goals in change terms and decided on the actions to take to realize them. Evaluation *then* becomes the means by which it apprises itself as to how well it is doing.

While each library would have its own unique action goals, we can identify general community reference change goals for public libraries so as to allow them to achieve the general goal of obtaining, organizing, and disseminating information to a maximum number of people and groups bearing on their vital community interests.

In effecting a community change oriented reference service, the following would be involved:

1. Systematically acquire and organize for ready access, or know the whereabouts of, published and unpublished information in all areas of public concern, including child care, education, employment, energy, environment, food, handicapped, health care, housing, the justice system (police, courts and prisons), mental health care, public assistance, and transportation. In particular look to private groups active in community affairs and relevant national groups for information as well as collect information from government sources.
2. Set up a network whereby concerned people and groups working on community problems so as to effect change can get in touch with one or another.
3. Educate, through in-service training, community involvements and other ways, *all* staff involved in selecting or giving out information, regarding the community, its problems, the groups working on these problems, the direction of their effort, and the information resources and sources bearing on these problems.
4. Allocate staff and other resources and plan and carry out the

provision of reference service so as to maximize both its quality and its community relevancy.

5. Make all sectors of the community and community groups and leaders aware of the library as a valuable community information resource.
6. Consider the need, feasibility, and ways of directly disseminating information to groups and the public on the library's own initiative, and initiate selected activities. This would include sponsoring programs or public meetings on community issues or the use of cable TV to inform the community on matters affecting them.
7. Involve community members and community leaders in all phases of planning and implementing services.
8. Develop measurable action goals in each of these areas and a plan to evaluate how well the library is succeeding in achieving these goals.

The foregoing is not a total reference plan. It is not a plan to exclude services to business and local government or service on an individual basis. Those are part of community service.

But we are proposing a community thrust as the next major development for public libraries which has for its central ingredient lending information support to citizens and to groups active in community development. This thrust calls for particular actions on the part of the library and for supportive evaluation. Types of analysis to be called upon include the following:

Community analysis. A staff conducted study of the library's community can reap unique and valuable rewards including a greatly increased knowledgeability and commitment to serving the community on the part of the staff.

Lending information support toward solving community problems dictates a problem solving focus for the study whereby community needs are identified in every major social area. Additionally, it would identify groups working on the problem and what is being proposed to alleviate situations. In the area of homelessness, for instance, the analysis would look into the nature and extent of the problem (how many homeless people there are, who they are, and what is presently available for them in the way of food, shelter and medical care and assistance in getting work or financial assistance). But also what advocate groups are calling for to begin to meet the needs of people who have nowhere to live.

The library cannot necessarily conduct original investigations as, say, to determine the extent of overcrowding in a local jail and what can be done about it, or about juveniles being housed in the adult jail. But it can learn from available studies and community experts what the situation is and what alternatives to incarceration are being proposed as remedies. While learning, the library will naturally obtain studies, documents, proposals, names of groups, and other information for the library.

The survey would look into neighborhood concerns. It would look into particular needs of women and other social groups. In short, this people-oriented analysis would give attention to pressing needs in the community including those often overlooked or minimized. The survey would collect other vital information about the community and the people who live there. But reference program responsiveness is most linked to these community needs.

Using marketing research techniques. To gain a measure as to how its change efforts are succeeding, there are advertising and product research techniques to be employed. For instance, informal marketing research experiments can measure the effect of a promotion campaign effort. Attitude change and/or change in behavior, i.e., library use, can be determined by "before-and-after" research and attitudes and behavior related to socioeconomic characteristics. Particular target groups can be studied separately. Using various techniques, at all decisional stages of planning and launching a new dissemination service or other new library program, libraries can collect helpful information about consumer attitudes and reactions.

Needless to say, marketing surveys must involve more than collecting testimonials from well-meaning citizens and librarians should be aware that simply asking people to indicate their interest in possible library services has low predictive value—may not serve to identify the actual use which would be made of services, particularly when respondents have no past experience with the services.

Evaluating non-conventional collections. To any library just getting started in building its community collections and data bases, community specialists can lend valuable help, particularly where conventional indexing and selection and reviewing media fall down. Experts in one or another area can supply expertise for evaluating the library's collections, and its acquisitions practices. Reading lists put out by local and national organizations are another important evaluative tool.

Collections are a most dynamic aspect of the library's program. It is essential, therefore, to set in motion arrangements to learn of new publications and new information, particularly about forthcoming events, that is, not to wait for periodic evaluations to keep the collection up to date and relevant. Evaluation itself is a continuous process whereby every user inquiry becomes the opportunity to test the library's collection against user needs so as to fill gaps.

Answering the who and why questions. Without benefit of major research, libraries can learn who their patrons are and why they sought information from the library. Employing samples and with brief forms or interview schedules, inquirers can be asked what they intend to do with the information, i.e., the context in which they seek information. If properly explained, they may also be asked for personal information about themselves so as to identify them by social class or other characteristic. Those seeking information for organization purposes may also be asked in general terms about their group and its activities.

This information is vital at several levels. At the operating level it allows reference librarians to know who their customers are and what their needs are. It tells the library what types of groups and people it is serving and how. This is, of course, the critical intelligence it needs to learn if it is succeeding in extending its service base and its contribution to solving community problems.

Evaluating referrals. In the writers' unobtrusive study of how libraries respond when asked questions about draft registration, a principal failure was inappropriate referrals, some even amounting to little more than a way to get rid of the caller. Inquirers were referred to both government agencies and to private groups which did not have the information wanted by the patron. Anyone who has ever sought information from a government agency knows how people can be referred from one agency to another without ever getting their question answered. Further, it frequently takes an advocate just to get government agencies to divulge information wanted by citizens.

Referrals are important because much needed information in the government's hands is in unpublished form, that is, the agency itself must supply the information. And, the library's goal of putting people and community groups in touch with one another rests heavily on referrals.

Particularly, the first time an agency or group is to be called it is wise for the librarian to make the call so as to check out her judgment as to the appropriateness of the referral and to learn of any problems in clients getting the information they seek. A second, customary method for evaluating referrals is to ask clients to give the library feedback. A third is for the library at periodic intervals to do a study of how well the library does in this respect. For this analysis, libraries may consider using unobtrusive measures but only if the study is conducted so as not to threaten staff morale.

Measuring quality. In general, a library can assess how well it responds to inquiries by obtaining regular gauges of user satisfaction which probe the reasons for dissatisfaction and by at intervals investigating whether librarians are providing adequate answers to questions.

Quality has been discussed last here but its importance in achieving community service goals cannot be overstated. The library's contribution to its community, its ability to greatly increase the number of people and groups who turn to it for information rests ultimately on its demonstrated ability to deliver wanted information. Whether its librarians can and do provide ready access to strategic community information should be a particular focus for study.

Cautions. Too frequently, new developments are evaluated before they have had a chance to prove themselves. As a consequence, good programs can get abandoned, particularly when the institutional commitment to them was weak in the first place. This was the case with many of the outreach programs of the sixties. To the profession's discredit, these programs faced near hostile institutional and funding evaluations. Any early evaluation should be for the purpose of *helping* a program to work, *not judging it.*

Be hesitant to become involved in cost analysis during this period of change and flux. The poor showing of libraries in the unobtrusive measures research was probably due in great measure to librarians doing hit-and-run reference to cut down on the time spent with the individual inquirer. Rather, libraries might better experiment with creative—and even more time consuming—methods such as the concept of team reference to borrow on the medical profession model. Libraries may wish to revive the notion of the community information specialist working largely out in the community under virtually unsupervised circumstances. They may want to have central staff specialize in one or another area of community expertise such as housing. That is to say, experts will be faster and better.

We have sketched here evaluation and research options for an institution which is striving to reach and maintain a high level of information service while at the same time propel itself toward realizing goals which will considerably change its user composition and the nature of its community service. Although of necessity speculative, we believe these options offer promise in these challenging circumstances.

CONCLUDING REMARKS

Institutions today in a time of social crisis, hesitant before the seemingly unlimited power of the computer, need a very clear sense of and commitment to their social mission. That is why this article has been concerned not so much with *how* to evaluate, as with the more crucial question of *what* to evaluate. Should the profession be evaluating an institution which without much reexamination of its basic goals or concern for reaching its non-reference users, is nevertheless supplying information services and resources to many people—or evaluating an institution which is consciously seeking to change so as to expand its influence as an information institution inextricably linked to the future well being of its community and all of its citizens?

It is this fundamental reassessment of how to realize its commitment to people that we believe the public library profession is called upon to make, not for a failing, but rather for a viable social institution.

REFERENCES

1. Bundy, Mary Lee, Amy Bridgman and Laura Keltie, "Public Library Reference Service: Myth and Reality," *Public Library Quarterly*, V. 3, no. 3, Fall 1982, pp. 11-22.

2. Bundy, Mary Lee, "An Advocacy Perspective: The Public Library and The Poor," *Catholic Library World*, V. 53, No. 9, April 1982, pp. 380-384.

3. Bundy, Mary Lee, *Helping People Take Control: The Public Library's Mission in a Democracy*, Urban Information Interpreters, Inc., College Park, Maryland, 1980.

4. Chen, Ching-chih, and Peter Hernon, "Library Effectiveness in Meeting Information Consumer's Needs," in *Library Effectiveness: A State of the Art*, American Library Association, Library Administration and Management Association, Chicago, Illinois, pp. 50-62, 1980.

5. Chen, Ching-chih, and Peter Hernon, *Information Seeking: Assessing and Anticipating User Needs*, Neal-Schuman Publishers, Inc., New York, 1982.

6. Childers, Thomas, *The Effectiveness of Information Service in Public Libraries: Suffolk County, Final Report*, Drexel University, Philadelphia, Pennsylvania, 1978.

7. Childers, Thomas, "Telephone Information Service in Public Libraries," in *Information Service in Public Libraries, Two Studies*, Scarecrow Press, Inc., Metuchen, New Jersey, 1971, pp. 73-204.

8. Crowley, Terence, "The Effectiveness of Information Service in Medium Size Public Libraries," in *Information Service in Public Libraries, Two Studies,* Scarecrow Press, Inc., Metuchen, New Jersey, 1971, pp. 1-71.

9. Durance, Joan Coachman, *Citizens Groups and the Transfer of Public Policy Information in a Community,* Ph.D. Dissertation, University of Michigan, 1980.

10. House, David E, "Reference Efficiency or Reference Deficiency," in *Library Association Record,* V. 76, No. 11, November 1974, pp. 222-223.

11. Jirgees, Jassim Muhammed, *The Accuracy of Selected Northeastern College Library Reference/Information Telephone Services in Responding to Factual Inquiries,* Ph.D. Dissertation, Rutgers University, 1981.

12. King, G. B., and L. R. Berry, *Evaluation of the University of Minnesota Libraries Reference Department Telephone Information Service, Pilot Study,* Minneapolis, University of Minnesota Library School, 1973.

13. Lancaster, F. W. *The Measurement and Evaluation of Library Services,* Information Resources Press, Washington, D.C., 1977.

14. Martin, Lowell, et al., *The Free Library and the Revitalization of Philadelphia, A Program for the 1980's,* 1981.

15. McClure, Charles R., and Peter Hernon. *Improving the Quality of Reference Service for Government Publications,* Chicago, Illinois, American Library Association, 1983.

16. Myers, Marcia J., "The Accuracy of Telephone Reference Services in the Southeast. A Case for Quantitative Standards," in *Library Effectiveness: A State of the Art,* American Library Association, Library Administration and Management Association, Chicago, Illinois, 1980, pp. 220-234.

17. Myers, Marcia J., and Jassim M. Jirjees, *The Accuracy of Telephone Reference/Information Services in Academic Libraries: Two Studies,* Metuchen, New Jersey, Scarecrow Press, 1981.

18. *The Pasadena Community and Its Information Needs: A Program for Pasadena Public Library Services,* Pasadena Public Library, Pasadena, California, 1983.

19. Peat, Marwick, Mitchell and Co., *California Public Library Systems, A Comprehensive Review with Guidelines for the Next Decade,* Los Angeles, The Co., 1975.

20. Ramsden, Michael J., *Performance Measurement of Some Melbourne Public Libraries, A Report to the Library Council of Victoria,* Melbourne, Library Council of Victoria, 1978.

21. *Report from the States, White House Conference on Library and Information Services, Follow-up Inquiry,* 1981, 1982, 1983, New York State Library, Albany, New York.

22. Schmidt, Janine, "Evaluation of Reference Service in College Libraries in New South Wales, Australia," in *Library Effectiveness, A State of the Art,* American Library Association, Library Administration and Management Association, Chicago, Illinois, 1980, pp. 266-294.

23. Vavrek, Bernard, "A Struggle for Survival: Reference Services in the Small Public Library," *Library Journal,* May 15, 1983, pp. 966-969.

24. Weech, Terry L, and Herbert Goldhor, "Obtrusive Versus Unobtrusive Evaluation of Reference Service in Five Illinois Public Libraries: A Pilot Study," *The Library Quarterly,* V. 52, No. 4, October 1982, pp. 305-324.

25. Wilson, Pauline Christine, *Information-Seeking Activity of Selected Members of Community Groups Seeking Social Change,* Ph.D. Dissertation, University of Michigan, 1972.

26. Zweizig, Douglas, and Brenda Dervin, "Public Library Use, Users, Uses: Advances in Knowledge of the Characteristics and Needs of the Adult Clientele of American Public Libraries," in *Advances in Librarianship,* Academic Press, V. 7, 1977, pp. 231-255.

27. Zweizig, Douglas, and Eleanor Jo Rodger, *Output Measures for Public Libraries: A Manual of Standardized Procedures,* Chicago, Illinois, American Library Association, 1982.

Evaluating Reference Service
From the Patron Point of View:
Some Interim National Survey Results

Marjorie Murfin
Charles Bunge

Many of those who participated in the recent field-test of computer scannable reference survey forms, and also others who were unable to participate, expressed a strong interest in an overall report of results. This article will attempt to bring interested persons up-to-date (early 1984) on exactly what this project is, and how it has turned out.

For those who are not familiar with the project, it is described in the following news release:

> A survey instrument designed to collect reference transaction data on computer scannable sheets, was introduced and distributed to interested libraries at the conclusion of the LAMA Statistics for Reference Services Committee program in Los Angeles. This survey, a special project of Marjorie Murfin and Charles Bunge, has been approved for field-testing in academic libraries by LAMA, in order to determine if such a survey is feasible and useful.
>
> Tentative data may be obtained, by use of this one-day survey, to compare a library's reference service with reference services in other libraries of the same size and type in regard to (1) subject and type of questions and by whom asked, (2) type of personnel responding, type of response, search patterns and problems encountered, (3) success of this response in terms of

Ms. Murfin will be found in the Reference Department of Ohio State University Library, 1858 Neail Ave., Columbus, OH 43210. Professor Bunge is at the Library School, University of Wisconsin, Madison, WI 53706.

© 1984 by The Haworth Press, Inc. All rights reserved.

175

patron and librarian rating, (4) patron report of amount learned in connection with the transaction.

Interested academic libraries may obtain a packet of forms and materials free of charge for examination and consideration, without obligation to do the survey. All that is asked is that packets be returned if not used.

This news release was published in major library publications, and a waiting list of over 100 academic libraries has accumulated, including libraries in Great Britain, Canada, Australia, and Latin America.

Results were presented to participants in the form of statistical profiles, designed for easy comparison and interpretation. The entire form for these statistical profiles, with accompanying norms, cannot be reproduced here, but it is hoped that it can be made available in some form in the literature at a later date.

DATA ANALYSIS

Much data analysis, however, remains to be done when computer programming for this can be completed. Goals for the project at the present time are to seek a grant to complete final programming, to make changes and improvements suggested by participants, and to make forms available to those on the waiting list for further field-testing. Though forms are not available at the present time, expressions of interest are encouraged. If a grant is received, this situation might change within a relatively short time, and forms could then be made available.

As of early 1984, eighteen academic libraries from all parts of the country have performed the one-day survey and sent in completed forms. This includes five libraries with collection sizes under 500,000 volumes (one public and four private), five libraries with collection sizes of 500,000 to 1,000,000 (one private and four public), and six libraries with collection sizes over 1,000,000 volumes (two private and four public). Also participating were a large undergraduate library and a large public library, bringing the total to eighteen.

The basic design of the survey appeared, overall, to be workable, by evidence that eighteen libraries were able to complete it satisfactorily. Some participants reported no major difficulties. "On the whole, it went well." One library, where forms were completed after each question, rather than batched for completion off the desk, reported interference with reference service. Most librarians reported the need for the librarian form to be shortened. Participants sent in many other excellent suggestions, all of which are being carefully considered for future implementation.

VALIDITY

Face validity of the data appears good. Internal validity can be determined by matching patron and librarian responses on the same or similar questions. One example of this is the correspondence between the librarian's report of the amount of time spent and the patron's report of the adequacy of time received. Almost all of the patron reports of "not enough time" occurred when the librarian reported that 0-2 minutes were spent. Only once did this occur when 5-15 minutes were spent. Final determination of validity of the data remains to be determined after computer programming for data analysis is complete.

Some preliminary results of this survey of sixteen libraries will be given here. Final results must, of course, wait for completion of computer programming.

The overall percentage of academic library patrons reporting that they found *exactly* what was wanted varied from a low of 42 percent to a high of 70 percent. By examining norms, it can be seen that the

PERCENTAGE OF PATRONS WHO FOUND

EXACTLY WHAT WAS WANTED

Small Libraries (Under 500,000 v.)	Medium Libraries (500,000 to 1,000,000 v.)	Large Libraries (Over 1,000,000 v.)
52.5	55.2	58.0

PERCENTAGE OF PATRONS WHO FOUND

APPROXIMATELY WHAT WAS WANTED

Small Libraries (Under 500,000 v.)	Medium Libraries (500,000 to 1,000,000 v.)	Large Libraries (Over 1,000,000 v.)
67.5	72.0	73.5

percentage of those who found *exactly* what was wanted increased with the size of the library, as did the percentage of those who found *approximately* what was wanted.

Much of the patron data (for example, what types of patrons asked what type of questions in what subject areas) remains on tape, waiting for the programming required for complete data analysis. Some patron data is available, however, and is given here.

If we examine the reference clientele in the small library, we see an almost equal division between underclass and upperclass students, with a sprinkling of graduates. In the large library, some of the underclass students have been displaced by upperclass students (now forming a clear majority). Also, the proportion of graduates has doubled.

In regard to success by class, we see that success of underclass students remains relatively stable across library size.

It appears that in this sample, small libraries could be as satisfactory as the larger ones in reference service to underclass students. Upperclass students show somewhat increased success in the medium and large libraries. Graduates, however, report a clear increase in success, as the size of library increases. The difficulties of doing graduate reference work with the smaller collection are strongly suggested here.

ADVERSE FACTORS UNDERMINING
REFERENCE SERVICE

Two factors emerged in this study which appeared to undermine reference service seriously. One factor was that of the librarian being too busy, and the other was the librarian's practice, or necessity, of directing and suggesting only, rather than helping search.

Results of five libraries in this survey were selected to be studied in regard to the performance of professional reference librarians under these adverse conditions. It was found that the factor which *most* lowered patron success in these libraries was the librarian's report of being busy.

The average patron success score when the librarian was *not* busy and helped the patron search was 69 percent. If the librarian was busy while helping the patron search, success dropped to 47 percent, a loss of 22 percentage points.

REFERENCE CLIENTELE BY SIZE OF LIBRARY

	Small Library (%)	Large Library (%)
Underclass	46	33
Upperclass	49	55
Graduates	5	12

PATRONS WHO FOUND EXACTLY WHAT
WAS WANTED BY CLASS

	Small Library (%)	Medium Library (%)	Large Library (%)
Underclass	60.25	61.00	60.80
Upperclass	48.75	56.90	52.80
Graduates	16.50	47.70	57.50

PATRONS WHO FOUND EXACTLY
WHAT WAS WANTED

Librarian Reports Busy and Helps Search   47%)
)   22 points
Librarian Reports Not Busy and Helps Search   69%)

Librarian Reports Not Busy and Directs   59%)
)   10 points
Librarian Reports Not Busy and Helps Search   69%)

Directing, on the other hand, caused only a ten point drop overall, from 59 percent to 69 percent.

As would be expected, when these two adverse conditions were combined, reference librarians' success in helping patrons sank to an average of 22 percent in these five libraries. In other words, if a librarian was busy and directed a patron, the chances of success were 22 percent. The highest score obtained by any of these libraries when both of these adverse conditions were present was 38 percent.

On the other hand, under the most favorable conditions of *not* being busy and helping search, reference librarians in two of the five libraries obtained scores of 75 percent and 80 percent. These scores are substantially above even that of the top scoring academic library in this survey. This suggests the possible extent to which these two factors may operate to undermine reference performance.

It would appear that the librarians in these two libraries were extremely competent. It suggests that the conditions of being busy must have been very severe in these libraries to have caused such a loss of success on the part of such competent staff.

It also suggests that the practice, policy, or necessity of directing rather than helping search also was a factor in causing these librarians to perform far below their actual potential. This is clearly substantiated by the fact that the percentage of questions which were reported as being handled by direction in these libraries was 41 percent and 42 percent, as opposed to averages of 37 percent and 24 percent for medium- and large-sized libraries.

In studying these two adverse factors, it appeared that, in order to gain an estimate of the upper level of performance of which reference librarians were capable, it was necessary to separate the two adverse factors. For example, in the case of the two libraries previously mentioned, patron success scores appeared to be 57 percent and 69 percent *before* adverse factors were separated. After adverse factors were separated, success scores rose to 75 percent and 80 percent. For example, in the case of these libraries, optimum performance at *non-busy* times was lowered by too-frequent directing. Success when searching was lowered by being too busy. Thus, it was not possible to assess optimum potential until the effect of these adverse factors could be separately examined.

The following table illustrates how these factors were separated into four different conditions.

This preliminary analysis indicates that large research libraries' loss through being busy is twice that of the smaller libraries, in view of upper level potential. The loss due to directing is less in terms of percentage points, but even greater in proportion to the loss in the smaller library. This is logical in view of the complexity of the large library where direction may work less well.

How do these adverse factors affect the performance of nonprofessional reference personnel? The success of nonprofessionals in these same five libraries was studied and results will be presented only in overall terms since the number of examples was small.

In evaluating the upper level scores, we must take into consideration that some consulting was done, and that easier questions may have gravitated to the nonprofessionals.

It can be seen that nonprofessional personnel in these libraries ap-

THE EFFECT ON SUCCESS OF PROFESSIONAL REFERENCE
LIBRARIANS UNDER FOUR DIFFERENT CONDITIONS

	Medium-Sized Libraries Success (%)		Large Libraries Success (%)	
Busy and Direct	20		23	
Busy and Search	50		44	
Not Busy and Direct	63		57	
Not Busy and Search	64		72	
Busy and Search	50	)	44	)
Not Busy and Search	64	) 14 points	72	) 28 points
Direct	63	)	57	)
Search	64	) 1 point	72	) 15 points

PATRONS WHO FOUND EXACTLY WHAT WAS WANTED WHEN
HELPED BY NONPROFESSIONAL PERSONNEL
(BASED ON ANALYSIS OF FIVE LIBRARIES ONLY)

Busy and Search	50%	)
Not Busy and Search	78%	) 28 points
Direct and Not Busy	25%	)
Search and Not Busy	78%	) 53 points

peared to be affected to an even greater extent by these adverse factors, losing twenty-eight points to twenty-two for professional librarians, due to being busy. The greatest effect is seen in directing versus giving help in searching. Here the nonprofessionals in these libraries lost fifty-three points when directing, in contrast to losses of ten points for professionals.

The data presented in this article are but a small portion of the total data which will eventually be available from this field-test. We hope that work on a computer scannable reference survey instrument can continue. If this type of instrument proves valid and useful, it is hoped that it can be made available, in the future, on an on-going basis, perhaps under the sponsorship of professional associations. A Center for Reference Measurement and Evaluation might eventually be established to provide a variety of services, utilizing both methods now available and those yet to be developed.

Analyzing Success in Meeting Reference Department Management Objectives Using a Computerized Statistical Package

Margaret A. Joseph

The purpose of this study was to develop a methodology for a reference department to evaluate its success in using staff efficiently to serve appropriate patrons. A method of data collection and analysis was desired that would meet the following criteria: 1) require no equipment other than that already available in the library or accessible to librarians on campus, 2) require little or no clerical support staff time to use, and 3) be simple to use so that reference staff could collect the data while on duty at the desk. Obviously many important goals of a reference department (particularly those relating to accuracy of information provided, patron satisfaction, and ultimate value of the service to individuals) cannot be measured by simple, inexpensive means. However certain management objectives relating to staff utilization and effectiveness are amenable to such measurement. At present, it is still a rare library that has an accurate statistical description of its reference department's quantitative input, throughput, or output, let alone its qualitative output. Therefore, such steps as can be made in the direction of more thorough evaluation of the reference process are rightly viewed as progress. In the present study the following objectives from one library's service plan were considered to be amenable to relatively inexpensive measurement under the criteria outlined above:

Ms. Joseph is Assistant Director for Public Services, University of Texas at San Antonio, 78228.

183

OBJECTIVES

1. To provide brief assistance to a relatively large number of patrons rather than to provide in-depth assistance to relatively few patrons.
2. To emphasize service to students over service to faculty and staff with an established criterion that 80% of service to institutionally-affiliated patrons be provided to students.
3. To provide service to noninstitutionally-affiliated patrons on a secondary basis using a criterion that 80% go to institutionally-affiliated and 20% to others.
4. To use reference staff optimally when possible by having non-professional staff handle directional questions and professional staff handle reference questions.
5. To provide "egalitarian" reference service, i.e., to base the decision as to level of staff assigned to provide service not on patron status but on patron need, staff skill, and staff availability.
6. To have professional staff handle more complex, time-consuming questions and nonprofessional staff handle relatively less complex, quick answer questions.
7. To handle directional transactions as quickly as possible.

Some of these objectives could be assessed using simple frequency counts of number of individuals served in each category of interest. Others could more appropriately be studied through classical statistical measures of association.

METHODOLOGY—THE DATA COLLECTION INSTRUMENT

The survey instrument, called the Library Survey Form, was developed through much trial and error under conditions not atypical in library studies, namely minimal funds to support library research, lack of clerical staff to assist in collecting and coding data, and resistance to anything which would increase the work load of an already busy reference staff. Since these conditions are so common in academic reference departments, a somewhat detailed review of the data collection instrument may be useful to others interested in measuring library effectiveness. A very strong case has been made in recent years for the use of machine-readable forms in collecting data for analysis of reference desk service.[1] And, if the means are at hand to use them, machine-readable forms are the logical choice. Unfortunately optical scan forms are expensive to develop and print and equipment to read them is often unavailable. Therefore, the Library Survey Form presented here (Figure 1) was developed as a reasonable alternative to the optical scan format.

As can be seen in Figure 1, all recording on the form (other than comments) is numerical and can be entered easily (blanks being interpreted as zeros by the computer). The hour was recorded in military time for easy computer interpretation. Each library staff member was assigned a numerical identification code. "General question type" and "Subject code" were the only two data cells that were not recorded at the reference desk; these were added later as the form was checked and edited by the researcher. Subject information was noted in the "Subject/other comments" section. Since data were being recorded at a busy service desk, it was only to be expected that codes would occasionally be recorded in the wrong slot. In fact, surprisingly few transactions were garbled beyond reconstruction. The "Subject/other comments" part of the form served to refresh the staff's memory about a particular transaction if the codes assigned seemed illogical or otherwise problematic. For "Length of help," "short" was arbitrarily defined as "less than 3 minutes" and "long" as "3 minutes or more" on the basis of earlier in-house studies of typical duration of help given. Directional and reference transactions were counted based on the standard definitions developed within the American Library Association.[2] Each line on the form represented one transaction. The multidimensional quality of some transactions was captured by recording every relevant category whether directional or reference for each transaction. The "General question type" code provided the count of directional and reference transactions. The subcategories of reference transactions are based on those in the *Library Data Collection Handbook*.[3]

To demonstrate how transactions were translated into codes, five sample transactions are presented corresponding to the first five lines of data recorded on the form shown in Figure 1.

1. 8:25 a.m.—"Where is Buros [Mental Measurements Yearbook]?" University graduate student. Librarian accompanies her to the shelf and explains the index. Elapsed time, 5 minutes.
2. 11:59 a.m.—"What is the annual rainfall on the plain in

Spain?'' Question is phoned in by someone classifiable only as general public. Elapsed time 3 minutes.
3. 1:15 p.m.—Librarian shows a faculty member how to look for journals he has not found in the library in the local consortium's union list and explains how to get to the library that owns the wanted titles. Elapsed time, 6 minutes.
4. 3:02 p.m.—''What are your weekend hours?'' Freshman. Elapsed time, less than 1 minute.
5. 8:49 p.m.—''What does this mean?'' (pointing to part of an entry in *Biological Abstracts*) Sophomore. Elapsed time, 2 minutes.

PROCEDURE

Data were collected during a ''typical week'' in the Fall and Spring semesters and first summer session as defined for HEGIS (and LIBGIS) to avoid the inconvenience of doing more than one survey. The data were checked briefly by the researcher as Library Survey Forms were turned in and were later input directly to an online computer file from a CRT. Editing and inputting data took approximately 5 and 8-10 hours, respectively, each semester. The data presented here were collected during Fall 1981 through Fall 1982. Each semester's data were analyzed separately using the frequency counts and cross-table routines of the Statistical Package for the Social Sciences (SPSS) program library. This package is almost universally available on college/university computer systems. The Chi-square test of significance and the Gamma statistic, as proposed in the recent article by White[4] for use in library research, were used to evaluate the results. Briefly, Gamma is a measure of degree and direction of correlation applicable to pairs of ordinal variables arranged in a 2 × 2 table. As explained by Norusis, ''Gamma can be thought of as the probability that a random pair of observations is concordant minus the probability that the pair is discordant, assuming the absence of ties. The absolute value of Gamma is the proportional reduction in error between guessing concordant and discordant ranking of each pair depending on which occurs more often and guessing rank according to the outcome of a toss of a fair coin. Gamma is 1 if all observations are concentrated in

Figure 1. Library Survey Form

STAFF MEMBER: 04

DATE: 09-29-82

REFERENCE

DIRECTIONAL

UTSA   NON-UTSA

UTSA: FRESH=1, SOPH=2, JUNIOR=3, SENIOR=4, GRAD=5, STAFF=6, FACULTY=7, OTHER=8
NON-UTSA: CORAL=1, UTHSC=2, GEN PUB=3, HS=4, OTHER/UNKNOWN=5

IN PERSON=1, BY TELEPHONE=2, IN WRITING=3

DIRECTIONAL: PATRON HAS CALL#; MACHINES; POLICIES; CORAL CARDS; KEYS; ROUTING; PHONE CALLS; ETC.

Column headers: DATE | HOUR | LIBRARIAN | IN PERSON/BY TELEPHONE/IN WRITING | UTSA | NON-UTSA | QUESTION TYPE | SUBJECT CODE | GENERAL | LENGTH OF HELP? SPENT LESS? | CATALOG INFO. | FACT-FINDING | READER'S ADVISORY | REFERRAL | LITERATURE SEARCH | OTHER REFERENCE | SUBJECT/OTHER COMMENTS

Data rows (HOUR):
- 08.04 | 1 | 5 | | 2 | | | | | 1 | 1 | | | Bucos MMY – Education
- 11.04 | 2 | | 2 | 3 | | 2 | 3 | | 1 | 1 | 1 | | ren in Spain
- 13.04 | 1 | 7 | 2 | 1 | | 2 | | | 1 | | | | union list – refer to other library
- 15.04 | 1 | 2 | 1 | 2 | | 1 | 1 | | | | | | hours
- 20.04 | 1 | | 1 | 4 | | 1 | | | 1 | | | | explain Bio Abs. entry

187

the upper-left to lower-right diagonal of the table. In the case of independence, Gamma is 0."[5] The rationale for using Gamma as a test statistic is that information is lost by using only Chi-square when the data are ordinal. Gamma is a more sensitive statistic and a more powerful measure of degree and direction of association.

RESULTS AND DISCUSSION

Success in meeting the first three management objectives was assessed through examination of simple frequency counts.

Success in meeting the first objective (namely, to provide brief assistance to a relatively large number of patrons rather than to provide in-depth assistance to relatively few patrons) could be assessed only for the Fall 1982 semester since earlier data were unavailable. Output from frequency analysis of nearly 1400 transactions is shown in Table 1. The adjustment in the third column is for the 8 cases that were "missing." This code was assigned when the researcher was unable to classify the length of help.[6]

For the present study, the first objective appears to have been met for Fall 1982 with about three-fourths of the transactions having a "short" duration.

Success in meeting the second objective (to emphasize service to students over service to faculty and staff with an established criterion that at least 80% of services to institutionally-affiliated patrons be provided to students) could be measured for four semesters and is reported in Table 2.

The second objective appears to have been met with the percentage of transactions with students never falling below 81%. Should the percentage drop below 80% and the absolute frequency of transactions with students also drop, it would be a signal that the library might need to increase the marketing of reference services to students.

The third objective (to provide service to non-institutionally affiliated patrons on a secondary basis using a criterion that 80% go to institutionally-affiliated patrons and 20% to others) could also be measured for all four semesters and is reported in Table 3. Using the criterion of 80 to 20 it is apparent that this objective was met in only one out of four semesters (Summer 1982). Furthermore, the discrepancy in the Spring 1982 semester was quite substantial. Examination of the detailed patron data for Spring 1982 revealed both

Table 1. Length of Help (Fall 1982)

	Number of Transactions	% of Transactions	Adjusted % of Transactions
Short	1046	75.1	75.5
Long	339	24.3	24.5
Missing	8	.6	missing
	1393	100.0	100.0

Table 2. Transactions with Patrons Affiliated with the Institution

Semester	Students	Faculty/Staff
Fall 1981	89.1(901)[7]	10.9(110)
Spring 1982	81.3(670)	18.7(154)
Summer 1982	86.7(738)	13.3(113)
Fall 1982	86.6(954)	13.4(147)

Table 3. Transactions with Patrons

Semester	Affiliated with Institution	Not Affiliated with Institution
Fall 1981	78.6(1024)	21.5(280)
Spring 1982	69.6(826)	30.5(363)
Summer 1982	80.8(874)	19.1(206)
Fall 1982	79.1(1102)	20.9(291)

an increase of 29% (75 transactions) in the combined categories of general public and high school students and a decrease of 35% (261 transactions) in the undergraduate category (over the Fall 1981 data). The library may need to consider ways to reduce service to nonaffiliated patrons and/or increase service to its primary clientele.

Cross tabulations were used to look for associations among some of the factors of interest in the study. Results of the crosstabulation of the variable "General question type" with the variable "Staff type" (professional versus nonprofessional) are reported in Table 4. This cross tabulation measures the extent to which objective 4 (to use reference staff optimally when possible by having nonprofessional staff handle directional questions and professional staff handle reference questions) is achieved.

As noted before, the Gamma indicates the degree and direction of association between "Staff type" and "General question type."

Table 4. Staff Type Correlated with General Question type

	Directional	Reference	χ^2	p	Gamma
Fall 1981					
Nonprofessional	52.1(170)	47.9(156)			
Professional	43.3(413)	56.7(540)	7.25	.007	.175
Spring 1982					
Nonprofessional	57.0(224)	43.0(169)			
Professional	46.0(362)	53.6(419)	11.43	.001	.211
Summer 1982					
Nonprofessional	43.9(129)	56.1(165)			
Professional	38.7(300)	61.3(475)	2.16	.142	.106
Fall 1982					
Nonprofessional	50.9(237)	49.1(229)			
Professional	42.8(395)	57.2(528)	7.80	.005	.161

The Chi-square (χ^2) and probably (p) values indicate the statistical association observed is greater than would be expected by chance. There was a low, positive, statistically significant correlation between "Staff type" and "General question type," with Gamma ranging from .161 to .211 for the Fall and Spring Semesters indicating that professional staff were slightly more likely to answer reference questions and nonprofessional staff were slightly more likely to answer directional questions. Results for Summer 1982 do not indicate a statistically different answering pattern. It is possible that Gamma is artificially low because at times only nonprofessional staff are on duty as opposed to the system of referring reference questions not working very well. However the data and statistical analysis do not provide information as to which of these explanations is correct.

Results of the cross tabulation of the variable "Staff type" with "Affiliated patron type" and "Student level" were used as tests of success in meeting objective 5 (to provide "egalitarian" reference service, i.e., to base the decision as to appropriate level of staff on patron need, staff skill, and staff availability rather than on patron status). These results are reported in Tables 5 and 6, respectively. The library's objective in providing "egalitarian" service between faculty and students was apparently being met during this period of time, since statistically significant differences were observed in correlating "Staff type" with "Affiliated patron types" as indicated in Table 5. Although the Gamma scores were highly inconsistent across semesters ranging from −.129 to .205 none were statistically significant and hence can be assumed not to differ from zero association except by chance. However, interestingly enough, Table 6

Table 5. Affiliated Patron Type Correlated with Staff Type

	Student	Faculty/Staff	χ^2	p	Gamma
Fall 1981					
Nonprofessional	91.9(227)	8.1(20)			
Professional	88.2(674)	11.8(90)	2.24	.134	.205
Spring 1982					
Nonprofessional	78.5(201)	21.5(55)			
Professional	82.6(469)	17.4(99)	1.65	.199	-.129
Summer 1982					
Nonprofessional	89.4(202)	10.6(24)			
Professional	85.8(536)	14.2(89)	1.59	.208	.166
Fall 1982					
Nonprofessional	87.9(313)	12.1(43)			
Professional	86.1(642)	13.9(104)	.57	.450	.082

Table 6. Student Level Correlated with Staff Type

	Undergrad	Grad	χ^2	p	Gamma
Fall 1981					
Nonprofessional	71.8(163)	28.2(64)			
Professional	85.9(579)	14.1(95)	22.27	.000	-.410
Spring 1982					
Nonprofessional	64.7(130)	35.3(71)			
Professional	74.8(351)	25.2(118)	6.68	.010	-.288
Summer 1982					
Nonprofessional	75.2(152)	24.8(50)			
Professional	76.5(410)	23.5(126)	.066	.797	-.034
Fall 1982					
Nonprofessional	75.6(232)	24.4(75)			
Professional	84.9(533)	15.1(95)	11.38	.001	-.289

shows that for the Fall and Spring semesters a moderately negative correlation, significant at .010, was found between undergraduate and graduate students indicating that professional staff were actually somewhat more likely to help the patrons with the lowest academic status. Direct observation of reference desk service does not suggest the interpretation of this phenomenon as the result of reverse discrimination against graduate students. Differences in service more likely reflected actual differences in the needs of graduate and undergraduate students as expressed to reference staff. The correlation for Summer 1982 in Table 6, although also resulting in a negative Gamma ($-.034$), did not indicate any statistically significant difference between graduate and undergraduate students. The explanation for this finding is not immediately apparent.

Data to assess the library's success in meeting the sixth objective (to have professional staff handle relatively more complex, time-consuming questions and nonprofessional staff handle relatively less complex, quick-answer questions) was available only for the Fall 1982 semester. It is reported in Table 7. These results do not support the hypothesis that professional staff handled relatively more long questions and nonprofessional relatively more short questions. A χ^2 of 7.31, significant at .007, and a Gamma of $-.177$ argues the opposite. The results of this cross tabulation forced a re-examination of the assumption that "Length of help" was a simple function of question complexity. It seems likely that other factors such as staff skill[8] or even amount of traffic at the reference desk may well be more strongly related to "Length of help" than question complexity.

Success in meeting the seventh objective (to handle directional transactions quickly) was measured only for Fall 1982 by cross tabulating "General question type" with "Length of help." Results are reported in Table 8. The Gamma score of .779 shows a very strong positive association between the two variables. Clearly, the pattern of service at the reference desk was overwhelmingly oriented to brief assistance and purely directional transactions rarely required longer assistance.

Table 7. Staff Level Correlated with Length of Help (Fall 1982)

	Short	Long	χ^2	p	Gamma
Nonprofessional	71.0(331)	29.0(135)			
Professional	77.8(715)	22.2(204)	7.31	.007	-.177

Table 8. General Question Type Correlated with Length of Help (Fall 1982)

	Short	Long	χ^2	p	Gamma
Directional	92.7(584)	7.3(46)			
Reference	61.2(461)	38.8(292)	182.33	.000	.779

CONCLUSION

The gathering and analyzing of data descriptive of some aspects of reference desk service can be made efficient enough to justify its widespread use given access to a "user-friendly" computerized statistical package. Data thus analyzed are suitable as a measure of success in meeting some objectives of a reference department. The variable "Length of help" is the only one used in this study which seems of questionable utility. So many factors can affect it that interpretation of the results seems equivocal. Although not many of the correlations found in this study were substantial, Gamma scores were certainly more helpful than Chi-squares alone since they communicate both the strength and direction of the observed association.

REFERENCES

1. Hallman, Clark N. "Designing Optical Mark Scan Forms for Reference Statistics," *RQ* 20( ): 257-264 (Spring 1981); and two presentations made at ALA's Annual Conference in Los Angeles at the LAMA SS Statistics for Reference Services Committee's program, "Computer Analysis of Reference Services," June 27, 1983: Halperin, Michael, "Packaged Computer Programs for Libraries," and Smith, Dana E. "Adaption of Optical Mark Scan Sheets for Microcomputer Use."

2. Emerson, Katherine. "National Reporting on Reference Transactions, 1976-78," *RQ* 16(3):199-207 (Spring 1977).

3. *Library Data Collection Handbook,* edited by Mary Jo Lynch. Chicago: Office for Research, American Library Association, 1981.

4. White, Howard D. "Measurement at the Reference Desk," *Drexel Library Quarterly* 17(1):3-35 (Winter 1981). For further discussion of Gamma see White, p.17; Norusis, Marija. *SPSS^x Introductory Statistics Guide.* New York: McGraw-Hill, 1983, pp. 57-58; and Davis, James A. *Elementary Survey Analysis.* Englewood Cliffs, N. J.: Prentice-Hall, 1971, pp. 72-80.

5. Norusis, p. 58.

6. Data in Table 1 are taken from a typical SPSS printout. Corresponding column headings in SPSS are labelled "Absolute Frequency," "Relative Frequency," and "Adjusted Frequency."

7. Numbers in parentheses indicate actual transactions.

8. Bunge, Charles A. "Library Education and Reference Performance," *LJ* 92:580 (April 15, 1967).

OTHER APPROACHES

Performance Standards for Accuracy in Reference and Information Services: The Impact of Unobtrusive Measurement Methodology

Alvin M. Schrader

At the end of the 1960s, Terrence Crowley and Thomas Childers developed and applied the first systematic methodology for unobtrusively measuring the accuracy of reference and information services in public libraries. This innovative work was the outcome of their respective doctoral dissertations. In 1971, this methodology was presented for consideration to a wider professional audience through publication in a joint research monograph. There is no published evidence that unobtrusive measures were adopted by the profession as an immediate response to the publication of the 1971 monograph.

More than ten years have since elapsed. It seems timely, therefore, to determine whether this methodology has been given further consideration by the profession, during the ensuing period of time. Such a determination would identify any effect of this particular research on the profession's principles and practices. Perhaps more importantly, it would also contribute to the investigation of another problem, namely, the place of doctoral research in library and information science; factors pertinent to this investigation would include the time lag between research activity, dissemination, acceptance, and eventual adoption, together with the patterns of possible modification and adaptation and of possible influences on other areas of the discipline.

Accordingly, the present report had two objectives. The first objective was to trace any citations in the professional literature to the

Professor Schrader is on the Faculty of Library Science, University of Alberta, Edmonton, Canada T6G 2J4.

The author wishes to acknowledge the important contributions made to this paper by his research assistant, Keith Walker, and by his faculty colleague, Professor Gloria Strathern.

197

seminal work of Crowley and Childers. A citation study would identify who had cited it, when, and in what contexts. If no citations or only a small number of citations were to be found, one could presumably conclude that there had been virtually no impact on the profession.

Since citations were identified, however, it was possible to proceed to a second objective of the present report—more ambitious, and so more tentative, than the first. This objective was to assess the nature of any subsequent impact of the research of Crowley and Childers on the discipline of library and information science. Such disciplinary impact must be related to at least three areas: research, education, and professional practice. As a rule, impact will differ from area to area. The impact on the research front would likely consist of replication and extension of the concepts and methodology of the seminal work. The impact on education would likely take the form of textbook references and descriptions, and of citations on course reading lists. The impact on professional practice would likely result in changes to recommended procedures for evaluating and monitoring the accuracy of library reference and information services. Selected indicators of impact will be examined after the citation history has been set forth.

CITATION STUDY

In order to ascertain the full range of citations to Crowley and Childers' early work, citation searches were undertaken on four source documents. These were:

1. the unpublished doctoral dissertation by Crowley (1968);
2. the unpublished doctoral dissertation by Childers (1970);
3. the joint research monograph by Crowley and Childers (1971) which made available their doctoral work to a wider audience; and,
4. a journal report of their doctoral work by Childers (1972).

Journal article citations were obtained primarily through the online version of *Social Sciences Citation Index (SSCI)*. A number of unfortunate citation anomalies rendered the search somewhat laborious. These consisted of the appearance in *SSCI* of cited references to: "Crowley T, 1970", "Crowley T, 1971, v6, p51", "Childers T, 1971, v96, p2727", "Childers T, 1972, v3, p53", and

''Childers T, 1972, v3, p613''; all of these referred to other authors or titles. There were also two cited references in which the journal volume number to the 1972 Childers article was incorrect. A further impediment was the absence from *SSCI* of citations to *Advances in Librarianship* and to the indispensable scholarly journal *Library Research,* now retitled *Library and Information Science Research.* These had to be searched manually, article by article.

Despite the problems described above, journal article citations are still relatively easy to retrieve through *SSCI.* However, the effort required to locate citations in the monograph and technical report literature is a genuine instance of the law of diminishing returns. What follows, then, is at best a partial listing from such literature, constructed by checking the bibliographic references in such research monographs as those by Myers and Jirjees (1983) and by McClure and Hernon (1983); doctoral dissertations produced after 1972 which were indexed under the heading ''Reference Service'' in the Davis (1980) compilation were also checked.

Table 1 lists those authors who cited all or any one of the four source documents produced between 1968 and 1972 by Crowley and Childers. It should be noted that the number of source documents cited in any one publication did not affect the citation count. That is to say, citations to more than one source document in a given publication did not yield multiple counts. It is the seminal concept of unobtrusive testing as represented by the whole set of documents that we wish to examine in this analysis.

This table shows that since 1968 Crowley and Childers' seminal research has been cited by 58 authors, including a small number of self-citations. (And, for the reasons given earlier, this figure presumably understates the total count in some unknown degree.) Of the 58 known citing authors, exactly half were published in the journal literature. The first citation in the journal literature appeared in 1972. The first citation in a research report was a year later. Except for a self-citation in 1975, no annual review cited their work until 1981.

An additional six authors of doctoral dissertations have also cited them, together with seven authors of research reports, research monographs, and conference papers. Their work has also been cited by nine textbook authors, by two authors of handbooks, and by two authors of articles in the *Encyclopedia of Library and Information Science.*

Of the thirteen journals which yielded citations to the work of

TABLE 1

Citations to Crowley and Childers' Seminal Research, 1968-1984

Citing Author	Year	Doctoral Dissertations	Reports, Monographs, Conf Papers	Journals	Annual Reviews	Textbooks	Readings, Handbooks, Encyclopedias
Wilkinson	1971	*					
Peele	1972			*			
De Prospo et al.	1973		*				
Neill	1973			*			
Orr	1973			*			
Beeler et al.	1974						*
Hamburg et al.	1974					*	
Katz	1974					*	
Weech	1974			*			
Childers	1975	*					
Figueiredo	1975			*			
Swartz	1975				*		
Childers	1976			*			
Martin	1976			*			
Orgren and Olson	1976			*			
Powell	1976	*					
Williams & Dunatov	1976			*			
Bunge	1977		*				
Lancaster	1977					*	
Murfin & Wynar	1977						*
Rothstein	1977			*			
Whitbeck & Hernon	1977			*			
Childers	1978			*			
Freiband	1978			*			
Calvin	1978						
Harter and Fields	1978			*		*	
Katz	1978						*
Lancaster & McCutcheon	1978		*				
Murphy	1978	*					
Powell	1978			*			
Ramsden	1978		*				
Rebenack	1978						*

TABLE 1, continued

Citations to Crowley and Childers' Seminal Research, 1968-1984

Citing Author	Year	Doctoral Dissertations	Reports, Monographs, Conf Papers	Journals	Annual Reviews	Textbooks	Readings, Handbooks, Encyclopedias
Freides & Vavrek	1979	*					
Myers	1979			*			
Vavrek	1979			*			
Busha & Harter	1980					*	
Childers	1980			*			
Jahoda & Braunagel	1980					*	
Jirjees	1980	*					
Myers	1980		*				
Schmidt	1980		*				
Schrader	1980			*			
Bates	1981				*		
Kantor	1981			*			
Martin & Lancaster	1981					*	
White	1981			*			
Cronin	1982			*			
Cronin	1982			*			
Hernon	1982			*			
Hernon & McClure	1982			*			
Kantor	1982				*		
Katz	1982					*	
Rothstein	1982			*			
Weech & Goldhor	1982			*			
Lee	1983			*			
Lynch *	1983					*	
McClure & Hernon	1983		*				
Myers & Jirjees	1983		*				
Olson	1984			*			
TOTALS		6	8	29	3	9	4

* A slightly troublesome citation--the author discusses the Crowley and Childers seminal work and even mentions their dissertations, but does not cite these or any of the other source documents on which the present article is based; her citations are to later research reports only.

Crowley and Childers, three were more heavily represented than others. They were: *RQ, Library Quarterly,* and *Library Trends.* The full set of citing journals have been ranked in Table 2.

Graph 1 shows the frequency of citation to the work of Crowley and Childers since 1968.

The graph reveals that their work has been cited approximately four times per year since 1971. The median year of citing activity has been (so far) 1978.

One might hope that it is premature to infer from the patterns revealed here that the citing activity has already peaked. Moreover, citation in certain forms of the professional literature, such as textbooks and handbooks, may well increase in the future. Such an increase might be anticipated if the educational and practitioner sectors of library and information science begin to transform the Crowley and Childers methodology into forms appropriate to the evaluation of performance in social practice.

Further analysis of citing patterns has not been attempted here,

TABLE 2

Journals Citing Crowley and Childers' Seminal Research, 1972-1984

	Number of Citations	Rank
RQ	6	1
Library Quarterly	5	2
Library Trends	4	3
Aslib	2	___
Drexel Library Quarterly	2	
Government Publications Review	2	
Library Journal	2	
Canadian Library Journal	1	
Journal of Academic Librarianship	1	
Journal of Documentation	1	
Journal of Education for Librarianship	1	
Library Research	1	
Unesco Bulletin for Libraries	1	
Total	29	

Graph 1.

Frequency of Citations to Crowley and Childers' Seminal Research, 1968-1984

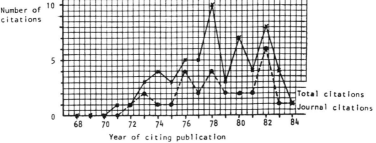

but fruitful insights could be gained through citation context analysis.

EVIDENCE OF IMPACT

Evidence of impact in the professional literature can be considered from two points of view. The first considers the presence of in-depth treatments in the professional literature.

The second focuses on the absence of such treatment and on the absence of bibliographic acknowledgment in that subset of the professional literature where citation could reasonably be expected. In other words, the questions are: Where has the Crowley and Childers work been used in some fashion or other, and where has it not been used at all?

These two dichotomous points of view, coverage and omission,
· can be taken as complementary reflections of the importance attached to a particular concept or work by the professional community of researchers, educators, and practitioners. The status of Crowley and Childers' seminal research in each sector of this community will be examined below, in the light of this perspective.

1. Researchers

The following researchers have replicated and extended the unobtrusive procedures developed by Crowley and Childers for measuring and evaluating library reference and information service accuracy:

1978—Ramsden, conference report
1979—Myers, doctoral dissertation
1980—Jirjees, doctoral dissertation
1980—Schmidt, conference report
1982—Weech and Goldhor, journal report
1983—McClure and Hernon, research monograph
1983—Myers and Jirjees, research monograph

The two dissertations and the research monograph reporting on them by Myers and Jirjees are major extensions to academic libraries of the Crowley and Childers methodology; the research monograph by McClure and Hernon is a major extension to academic depository libraries charged with the provision of U.S. government information service. Together, these investigations represent the most important advances to date, just slightly more than a decade following the seminal contributions by Crowley and Childers.

Other researchers who have used an unobtrusive procedure but who did not cite Crowley and Childers are:

1972—Tri-County Regional Planning Commission and Blasingame, technical report
1973—King and Berry, technical report
1974—House, journal report
1975—Peat, Marwick, Mitchell and Company, technical report
1978—Childers, technical report.

With the exception of House (1974), these researchers were functioning in the capacity of social planning consultants.

2. Educators

Few educators, or more precisely, few educational textbook authors have paid much attention to Crowley and Childers. Only the following texts have provided in-depth treatment of their work:

1974
1978
1977—Lancaster

1980—Jahoda and Braunagel
1981—Martyn and Lancaster.
1982—Katz

The research methods text for library and information science by Busha and Harter (1980) provided a bibliographic reference to Crowley and Childers, but no discussion of their work or its importance. Hamburg et al. (1974) described briefly their research, but did not build it into their own model library program. The Davis and Rush (1979) guide to information storage and retrieval systems did not mention them. Other similar monographs, even the more theoretical ones such as Kochen's (1974) *Principles of Information Retrieval,* have not mentioned them either. Lancaster's (1977) description of their work is still the most detailed treatment in a textbook, calling their work an unobtrusive evaluation the most important to date.

3. Practitioners

This sector of the community is presumed to be at least loosely concerned not only with the library policy and planning literature, but as well with collected readings, handbooks, guides, and encyclopedias. (This literature may also be of interest to the research and educational sectors, and so the categorization is not intended to be "prescriptive" and "exclusionary.)

Over the past decade, the following committees, conferences, and institutes have dealt with issues relevant to reference and information services:

1974—*Symposium on Measurement of Reference,* sponsored by the Committee on Statistics for Reference Services of the ALA (ed. Katherine Emerson)
1975—NATO Advanced Study Institute on the *Evaluation and Scientific Management of Libraries and Information Centres* (Proceedings published 1977, eds. F.W. Lancaster and C.W. Cleverdon)
1976—Program on *The Purposes of Reference Measurement,* sponsored by the above-named Committee (ed. Candace Morgan)
1977—Institute on *Quantitative Measurement and Dynamic Library Service* (published 1978, ed. Ching-Chih Chen)

1980—ALA preconference on *Library Effectiveness: A State of the Art.*

Although some of the papers read at these meetings cited Crowley and Childers, only the 1980 ALA preconference on library effectiveness included papers that treated their procedures in-depth. These papers were by Myers and by Schmidt.

Similarly, a number of collected readings, handbooks, guides, and other professional reference tools revealed some but rather limited interest in Crowley and Childers. The following works did not acknowledge them at all, however:

1976 to
1983—*ALA Yearbooks*
1978—Katz and Tarr, collected readings
1980—Bunge in *ALA World Encyclopedia of Library and Information Services*
1982—Katz and Clifford, reference and online services handbook of guidelines, policies, and procedures.

The works listed below included bibliographic citations to Crowley and Childers, and in a small number of instances gave their research additional treatment in the text:

1974—Beeler et al., reprint of one chapter from Crowley and Childers (1971)
1977—Rowland, inclusion of Childers (1972) in suggested additional readings
1977—Murfin and Wynar, annotations to all four source documents being studied here
1978—King, reprint of the well-known Orr (1973) paper on measuring library goodness, in which Childers (1972) is cited
1978—Separate articles by Galvin and by Rebenack in the *Encyclopedia of Library and Information Science,* citations to Crowley and Childers (1971) and to Childers (1972), respectively
1979—Grogan, practical reference work, including a citation to and brief description of Crowley and Childers (1971).
1983—Lee, citation to Crowley and Childers (1971) in bibliography.

With respect to public library reference services, there has been considerable interest over the past decade in developing quantitative performance measures. The major works are as follows:

1973— *Performance Measures for Public Libraries,* by De Prospo et al.
1974— *Measuring the Effectiveness of Basic Municipal Services,* by The Urban Institute and the International City Management Association
1976— ''A Commitment to Information Services: Developmental Guidelines'', by the Standards Committee of the Reference and Adult Services Division, ALA
1976— *A Data Gathering and Instructional Manual for Performance Measures in Public Libraries,* by Altman et al.
1977— *How Effective are Your Community Services? Procedures for Monitoring the Effectiveness of Municipal Services,* by Hatry et al., for The Urban Institute and the International City Management Association
1980— *Do We Really Need Libraries? An Assessment of Approaches to the Evaluation of the Performance of Libraries,* by Blagden
1981— *A Planning Process for Public Libraries,* by Palmour et al.
1982— *Output Measures for Public Libraries,* by Zweizig and Rodger.

With the exception of the 1973 report by de Prospo et al., however, none of the other documents listed above cited Crowley and Childers. Moreover, the 1973 report did not seek to incorporate the unobtrusive method into the recommended approaches to public library performance measurement. Rather, the researchers concluded that, although ingenius, the unobtrusive approach was administratively impractical and consequently of limited utility; user satisfaction was the preferred focus (p. 14).

With respect to quantitative measurement of academic library reference services, much less progress has been reported in the literature. This situation is reflected in the omission of references to unobtrusive techniques from two documents: a) the MRAP (management review and analysis program) self-studies (see Webster, 1974, for a description); and, b) the 1981 ''SPEC Kit'' on user surveys and evaluation of library services, compiled by the Office of Management Studies of the Association of Research Libraries.

However, just published is a paper by Olson (1984) in which she has developed a model for the evaluation of reference services in medium-sized academic libraries. This highly practical model builds on the research methodologies and findings of a number of works, including those of Crowley and Childers. The model calls for the collection of data on the real quality of reference services, with a view to facilitating performance improvement through mutually supportive efforts of both library management and library reference staff.

SUMMARY AND CONCLUSIONS

In summary, if we were to highlight the "flow" of contributions issuing from the work by Crowley and Childers over the past decade and a half, the following tentative time line might be contemplated (Table 3).

This table suggests a surprising pattern of major contributions to the literature issuing from the seminal research by Crowley and Childers at the end of the 1960s. The contributions range from educational textbooks to doctoral dissertations, research monographs, and most recently, a journal article describing a performance evaluation model for use in professional practice. This pattern of knowledge dissemination and cumulation does not conform to what is believed to be the conventional model for the aging and compaction of knowledge in scientific fields. In this model, doctoral dissertations, research monographs, and conference research papers are followed by journal articles, annual reviews, textbooks, handbooks for practice, and encyclopedia articles (see Houser and Schrader, 1978, and Garvey, 1979).

What can be concluded from the present study—in spite of the difficulties involved in trying to estimate the impact of ideas on a professional community of researchers, educators, and practitioners—is that Crowley and Childers' unobtrusive procedures have not yet become a component of the standard methods for evaluating library and information service performance. To date, their procedures have remained in the realm of methodological tools for research. Olson's (1984) model-building is the most promising adaptation and refinement so far devised for meeting the needs of professional practice. In Olson's work, the research methodology has been transformed into a professional tool for performance evaluation and performance improvement.

It is in this kind of transformation that the fruits of research are

TABLE 3

Major Contributions to the Literature Issuing
from the Seminal Research of Crowley and Childers, 1968-1984

1968	Crowley	Seminal doctoral research
1969	Childers	Seminal doctoral research
1971	Crowley and Childers	Research monograph publication of seminal work
1972	Childers	Journal report of seminal work
1974	Katz	Textbook on reference services
1977	Lancaster	Textbook on measurement of library services
1979	Myers	Doctoral research replicating seminal work
1980	Jirjees	Doctoral research replicating seminal work
1981	Martyn and Lancaster	Textbook on research methods
1983	McClure and Hernon	Research monograph replicating seminal work
	Myers and Jirjees	Research monograph publication of doctoral work
1984	Olson	Journal report of a model for reference service

ultimately realized, when professional practice is able to demonstrate enhanced accountability to the society it is trying to serve. Shaughnessy (1976) has observed:

> The main problem confronting the profession with regard to research does not appear to be *what* to do, but rather how to communicate the results of research to the field in meaningful ways. Dealing with this issue will require not only additional effort on the part of researchers, but an extraordinary commitment on the part of the profession to continuing education programs which, hopefully, will enable us to become more appreciative, and at the same time, more discriminating in our use of research results. (p. 52).

Shearer (1979) concluded from his investigation of the limited impact of research on the practice of librarianship that two failures could be identified. He wrote:

> [Librarianship] often fails to teach the ramifications of sound research in library education and to implement carefully researched recommendations. One method to help remedy the first defect is for the Committee on Accreditation at A.L.A. to explicitly examine how research findings are incorporated in library science curricula.
>
> A method to help remedy the second defect is the A.L.A.'s research committees, Library Research Round Table and Office for Research to assume responsibility for the identification and interpretation of the implications of research more completely than is now done. (p. 126)

Nonetheless, in spite of these remedial solutions, there remains one fundamental problem that has not been addressed: the lack of professional will. The "ethics of service" statement added in 1979 to the ALA's developmental guidelines for reference and information services begins with the following: "Information provided the user in response to any inquiry must be the most accurate possible" (p. 277). It is in itself a comment on prevailing professional attitudes that such a statement is required at all.

The problem of the lack of professional commitment to reference service excellence will neither go away nor be resolved by the kind of passive approach which has so far characterized our efforts. Researchers, educators, and practitioners must, first and foremost, acknowledge the existence of problems with respect to reference service accuracy. This acknowledgement has not yet occurred on a wide scale. Until it does, until our community is prepared to take seriously the call for reference service accuracy, unobtrusive performance measurement will remain as the next frontier for library and information services. As of now, we are still in the age of misinformation.

BIBLIOGRAPHY

Altman, Ellen, et al. *A Data Gathering and Instructional Manual for Performance Measures in Public Libraries.* Chicago: Oberon Press, 1976.

American Library Association, "A Commitment to Information Services: Developmental

Guidelines." *RQ* 18 (Spring, 1979): 275-278. (Adopted January, 1976; revised January, 1979)

American Library Association. *ALA Yearbook: A Review of Library Events.* Chicago: American Library Association. Yearbooks for 1975-1983.

Association of Research Libraries. *User Surveys and Evaluation of Library Services.* Washington, D.C.: Association of Research Libraries, SPEC Kit #71, 1981.

Bates, M.J. "Search Techniques." *Annual Review of Information Science and Technology* 16(1981): 139-169.

Beeler, M.G., Fancher et al., eds. *Measuring the Quality of Library Service: A Handbook.* Metuchen: Scarecrow Press, 1974.

Blagden, John Frederick. *Do We Really Need Libraries? An Assessment of Approaches to the Evaluation of the Performance of Libraries.* London: Clive Bingley, 1980.

Bunge, Charles A. "Approaches to the Evaluation of Library Reference Services." In *Evaluation and Scientific Management of Libraries and Information Centres* (Proceedings of the NATO Advanced Study Institute, Bristol, August 17-19, 1975), eds. F.W. Lancaster and C.W. Cleverdon. Noordhoff: Leyden, 1977, pp. 41-71.

Bunge, Charles A. "Reference Services." In *ALA World Encyclopedia of Library and Information Services,* ed. R. Wedgeworth. Chicago: American Library Association, 1980, pp. 468-474.

Childers, T. *The Effectiveness of Information Service in Public Libraries: Suffolk County. Final Report.* Philadelphia: School of Library and Information Science, Drexel University, July 1, 1978.

Childers, T. "The Future of Reference and Information Service in the Public Library." *Library Quarterly* 48(1978): 463-475.

Childers, T. "Managing the Quality of Reference/Information Service." *Library Quarterly* 42(1972): 212-217.

Childers, T. "Neighborhood Information Center Project." *Library Quarterly* 46(1976): 271-289.

Childers, T. "Statistics that Describe Libraries and Library Service." *Advances in Librarianship* 5(1975):107-122.

Childers, T. "Telephone Information Service in Public Libraries: A Comparison of Performance and the Descriptive Statistics Collected by the State of New Jersey." Ph.D. dissertation. New Brunswick: Rutgers University, 1970.

Childers, T. "The Test of Reference." *Library Journal* 105 (April 15, 1980): 924-28.

Cronin, B. "Performance Measurement and Information Management." *Aslib Proceedings* 34(1982): 227-236.

Cronin, B. "Taking the Measure of Service." *Aslib Proceedings* 34(1982): 273-294.

Crowley, T. "The Effectiveness of Information Service in Medium Size Public Libraries." Ph.D. dissertation. New Brunswick: Rutgers University, 1968.

Crowley, T. and T. Childers. *Information Service in Public Libraries: Two Studies.* Metuchen: Scarecrow Press, 1971.

Davis, Charles H. *Library Science; A Dissertation Bibliography.* Ann Arbor: University Microfilms International, 1980.

Davis, Charles H. and James E. Rush. *Guide to Information Science.* Westport: Greenwood Press, 1979.

De Prospo, Ernest R. et al. *Performance Measures for Public Libraries.* Chicago: Public Library Association and American Library Association, 1973.

Emerson, Katherine, ed. *Proceedings of the Symposium on Measurement of Reference.* Chicago: American Library Association, 1974.

Freiband, S.J. "Reference Service in Colombian University Libraries." *Unesco Bulletin for Libraries* 32(1978): 92-95.

Freides, T. and B. Vavrek. "Report from Dallas—RASD Program." *RQ* 18(1979): 132-134.

Galvin, Thomas J. "Reference Services and Libraries." In *Encyclopedia of Library and Information Science.* New York: Marcel Dekker, vol. 25, 1978, pp. 210-226.

Garvey, William. *Communication: The Essence of Science.* London: Pergamon Press, 1979.

Grogan, Denis. *Practical Reference Work.* London: Clive Bingley, 1979.

Hamburg, Morris, et al. *Library Planning and Decision-Making Systems.* Cambridge: MIT Press, 1974.

Harter, S.P. and M.A.S. Fields. "Circulation, Reference, and the Evaluation of Public Library Service." *RQ* 18(Winter, 1978): 147-152.

Hatry, Harry P. et al. *How Effective are Your Community Services? Procedures for Monitoring the Effectiveness of Municipal Services.* Washington, D.C.: The Urban Institute and International City Management Association, 1977, ch. 5.

Hernon, P. "Documents Librarianship in the 1980s: Current Issues and Trends in Research." Government Publications Review 9(1982): 99-120.

Hernon, P. and C.R. McClure. "Referral Services in United States Academic Depository Libraries: Findings, Implications, and Research Needs." *RQ* 22(1982): 152-163.

House, D. E. "Reference Efficiency or Reference Deficiency." *Library Association Record,* 76 (1974): 222-223.

Houser, L. and Alvin M. Schrader. *The Search for a Scientific Profession: Library Science Education in the U.S. and Canada.* Metuchen: Scarecrow Press, 1978.

Jahoda, Gerald and Judith Schiek Braunagel. *The Reference Librarian and Reference Queries: A Systematic Approach.* New York: Academic Press, 1980.

Jirjees, Jassim M. "The Accuracy of Selected Northeastern College Library Reference/Information Telephone Services in Responding to Factual Inquiries." Ph.D. dissertation. New Brunswick: Rutgers University, 1980.

Kantor, P.B. "Evaluation of and Feedback in Information Storage and Retrieval Systems." *Annual Review of Information Science and Technology* 17(1982): 99-120.

Kantor, P.B. "Quantitative Evaluation of the Reference Process." *RQ* 21 (1981): 43-52.

Katz, William A. *Introduction to Reference Work. II. Reference Services and Reference Processes.* New York: McGraw-Hill, 1974. Also: 3rd ed., 1978, and 4th ed., 1982.

Katz, Bill and Anne Clifford. *Reference and Online Services Handbook: Guidelines, Policies, and Procedures for Libraries.* New York: Neal-Schuman Publishers, 1982.

Katz, Bill and Andrea Tarr, eds. *Reference and Information Services: A Reader.* Metuchen: Scarecrow Press, 1978.

King, Donald W., ed. *Key Papers in the Design and Evaluation of Information Systems.* White Plains: Knowledge Industry Publications. 1978.

King, Geraldine and Rachel Berry, *Evaluation of the University of Minnesota Libraries Reference Department Telephone Information Service, Pilot Study.* Minneapolis: University of Minnesota, Library School, 1973. ERIC Document ED 077 517.

Kochen, Manfred. *Principles of Information Retrieval.* Los Angeles: Melville Publishing, 1974.

Lancaster, F.W. *The Measurement and Evaluation of Library Services.* Washington: Information Resources Press, 1977.

Lancaster, F.W. and Deanne McCutcheon. "Some Achievements and Limitations of Quantitative Procedures Applied to the Evaluation of Library Services." In *Quantitative Measurement and Dynamic Library Service,* ed. Ching-Chih Chen. Phoenix: Oryx Press, 1978, pp. 12-30.

Lee, Sul H. *Reference Service: A Perspective.* Ann Arbor: Pierian Press, 1983.

Lynch, Mary Jo. "Research in Library Reference/Information Service." *Library Trends* 31 (Winter, 1983): 401-420.

Martin, L.A. "User Studies and Library Planning." *Library Trends* 24(1976): 483-495.

Martyn, John and F. Wilfrid Lancaster. *Investigative Methods in Library and Information Science: An Introduction.* Arlington: Information Resources Press, 1981.

McClure, C.R. and P. Hernon. *Improving the Quality of Reference Service for Government Publications.* Chicago: American Library Association, 1983.

Morgan, Candace, ed. *The Purposes of Reference Measurement.* Chicago: American Library Association, 1976.

Murfin, Margorie E. and Lubomyr R. Wynar. *Reference Service: An Annotated Bibliographic Guide.* Littleton: Libraries Unlimited. 1977.

Murphy, Marcy. "Criteria and Methodology for Evaluating the Effectiveness of Reference and Information Functions in Academic Libraries: A Regional Case Study." Ph.D. dissertation. Pittsburgh: University of Pittsburgh, 1978.

Myers, Marcia Jean. "The Accuracy of Telephone Reference Services in the Southeast: A Case For Quantitative Standards." In *Library Effectiveness: A State of the Art.* Chicago: American Library Association, 1980, pp. 220-233.

Myers, Marcia Jean. "The Effectiveness of Telephone Reference/Information Services in Academic Libraries in the Southeast." Ph.D. dissertation. Florida State University, 1979.

Myers, Marcia Jean and Jassim M. Jirjees. *The Accuracy of Telephone Reference/Information Services in Academic Libraries; Two Studies.* Metuchen: Scarecrow Press, 1983.

Neill, S.D. "Who Needs to go to a Graduate Library School?" *Journal of Education for Librarianship* 13(1973): 212-225.

Olson, Linda M. "Reference Service Evaluation in Medium-Sized Academic Libraries: A Model." *Journal of Academic Librarianship* 9(January, 1984): 322-329.

Orgren, C.F. and B.J. Olson. "Statewide Teletype Reference Service." *RQ* 15(1976): 203-209.

Orr, R.H. "Measuring the Goodness of Library Services: A General Framework for Considering Quantitative Measures." *Journal of Documentation* 29(1973): 315-332.

Palmour, Vernon E. et al. *A Planning Process for Public Libraries.* Chicago: American Library Association, 1981.

Peat, Marwick, Mitchell and Company. *California Public Library Systems: A Comprehensive Review with Guidelines for the Next Decade.* Los Angeles: Peat, Marwick, Mitchell and Company, 1975. ED 105 906.

Peele, D. "Evaluating Library Employees—Written Appraisals or Oral Assessments—Exploration of British and American Preferences." *Library Journal* 97(1972): 2803-2807.

Powell, R.R. "Investigation of Relationships between Quantifiable Reference Service Variables and Reference Performance in Public Libraries." *Library Quarterly* 48(1978): 1-19.

Powell, R.R. "An Investigation of the Relationship between Reference Collection Size and Other Reference Service Factors and Success in Answering Reference Questions." Ph.D. dissertation. Urbana-Champaign: University of Illinois at Urbana-Champaign, 1976.

Ramsden, Michael J. *Performance Measurement of Some Melbourne Public Libraries: A Report to the Library Council of Victoria.* Melbourne: Library Council of Victoria. Melbourne: Library Council of Victoria, 1978, pp. 51-79.

Rebenack, John H. "Contemporary Libraries in the United States." In *Encyclopedia of Library and Information Science.* New York: Marcel Dekker, vol. 24, 1978, pp. 291-339.

Rothstein, S. "Across the Desk—100 Years of Reference Encounters." *Canadian Library Journal* 34(1977): 391-399.

Rowland, Arthur Ray, ed. *The Librarian and Reference Service.* Hamden: Shoe String Press, 1977.

Schmidt, Janine. "Evaluation of Reference Service in College Libraries, in New South Wales, Australia." In *Library Effectiveness: A State of the Art.* Chicago: American Library Association, 1980, pp. 265-294.

Schrader, Alvin M. "Performance Measures for Public Libraries: Refinements in Methodology and Reporting." *Library Research* 2(1980-1981): 129-155.

Shaughnessy, Thomas W. "Library Research in the 70's: Problems and Prospects." *California Librarian* 37(July, 1976): 44-52.

Shearer, K. "The Impact of Research on Librarianship." *Journal of Education for Librarianship* 20(Fall, 1979): 114-128.

Swartz, R.G. "The Need for Cooperation among Libraries in the United States." *Library Trends* 24(1975): 215-227.

Thomas, Diana M., Ann T. Hinckley and Elizabeth R. Eisenbach. *The Effective Reference Librarian.* New York: Academic Press, 1981.

Tri-County Regional Planning Commission (Medina-Summit-Portage) and Ralph Blasingame. *Survey of Public Libraries: Summit County.* Akron, Ohio, 1972.

Urban Institute and International City Management Association. *Measuring the Effectiveness of Basic Municipal Services, Initial Report.* Washington, D.C.: Urban Institute and International City Management Association, 1974.

Vavrek, B. "Reference Evaluation: What the Guidelines don't Indicate." *RQ* 18(1979): 335-340.

Webster, Duane E. "The Management Review and Analysis Program: An Assisted Self-Study to Secure Constructive Change in the Management of Research Libraries." *College and Research Libraries* 35 (March, 1974): 114-125.

Weech, T.L. "Evaluation of Adult Reference Service." *Library Trends* 22 (1974): 315-335.

Weech, T.L. and H. Goldhor. "Obtrusive versus Unobtrusive Evaluation of Reference Service in Five Illinois Public Libraries," *Library Quarterly* 52(October 1982): 305-324.

Whitbeck, G.W. and P. Hernon. "Attitudes of Librarians toward Servicing and Use of Government Publications: Survey of Federal Depositories in Four Midwestern States." *Government Publications Review* 4(1977): 183-199.

White, H.D. "Measurement at the Reference Desk." *Drexel Library Quarterly* 17(1981): 3-35.

Wilkinson, Billy R. "Reference Services for Undergraduate Students: Four Case Studies." Ph.D. dissertation. New York: Columbia University, 1971.

Williams, M.E. and E.T. Dunatov. "Data-Bases for Coping with Human Needs." *Drexel Library Quarterly* 12(1976): 110-138.

Zweizig, Douglas and Eleanor Jo Rodger. *Output Measures for Public Libraries; A Manual of Standardized Procedures.* Chicago: American Library Association, 1982.

Output Measures, Unobtrusive Testing, and Assessing the Quality of Reference Services

Charles R. McClure

One common purpose of library/information services is "the provision of accurate, prompt, and up-to-date answers in response to clientele's reference questions." Such a goal gets at the heart of library/information services and suggests a primary mission for which libraries exist. Unfortunately, librarians frequently have little knowledge as to the overall quality of the reference services provided, nor do they engage in an ongoing program of assessment, training, and program development vis a vis reference services.

Increasingly, pressure from both within and outside the library is being brought to bear on libraries to assess the degree to which various aspects of reference services meet criteria of "quality." Perhaps the most important development in this area is the national attention being given to the use of output measures. Simply stated, output measures are indicators of the degree to which library performance meets the service needs and requirements of the library's clientele. This emphasis on *outputs,* or the services provided from the library to the clientele, is one that forces librarians and information specialists to view "quality" of reference services from the other side of the desk and not to equate "quality" with collection size or comprehensiveness.

Additionally, there has been renewed interest in the use of unobtrusive testing, refinement of unobtrusive methodologies, and innovative techniques of unobtrusive testing data analysis (McClure and Hernon, 1983; Weech and Goldhor, 1982; and Myers and Jirjees, 1983). Unobtrusive testing of reference is an evaluation methodology in which library staff members are not aware that they are being

---

Professor McClure is at the School of Library Science, The University of Oklahoma, Norman, OK 73019.

215

evaluated. Individuals who ask questions or request services are known as proxies, and they record the activities, services, and responses given in test situations. Later, these records are assessed against established criteria (such as the correct answers to questions, the method of question negotiation, interpersonal skills, etc.) and an overall assessment of the quality of the reference activity is made.

Against this background, this paper provides a brief overview of the importance and potential applications of output measures and unobtrusive testing to assess reference services. It is neither a comprehensive review of the literature on these topics nor a "how-to" manual for actually implementing these techniques. However, the paper provides specific examples and discusses practical applications and techniques to be considered when using output measures and unobtrusive evaluation techniques.

ESSENTIAL

After first discussing the importance of using reference service outputs as indicators of quality and presenting a sample of possible output measures to assess the "quality" of reference services, a rationale for the use of unobtrusive testing with output measures will be presented. Specific strategies for implementing an ongoing program of unobtrusive reference services evaluation will be suggested. An underlying theme is that regular evaluation of reference services, *in terms of outputs* and by use of *unobtrusive testing* is essential if libraries and information centers are to significantly improve the *quality* of reference services.

ASSESSING REFERENCE SERVICE OUTPUTS

To avoid confusion between the terms "performance measures," and "output measures," both will be defined. The term performance measure is the broader, more generic term and refers to any type of measure that assesses the efficiency (allocation of resources) or effectiveness (accomplishment of goals and objectives) of the library. Output measures, a type of performance measure, concentrate specifically on the effectiveness or quality of the *services or products* which a library offers its clientele. As an example, the library might have an excellent performance measure for accuracy of catalog card production, but a very poor output measure for the degree to which catalog cards successfully assist clientele obtain a desired information resource.

Records of reference transactions, number and type of reference questions, and amount of time per reference question are examples of traditional techniques to assess reference services. Unfortunately such procedures rarely meet criteria of reliability and validity (Carmines and Zeller, 1981), and thus, cannot be considered to be *measures* of service. Frequently, they lack reliability because different people record types of transactions differently; they fail to record activities at the time the service is provided; or they combine data taken from different branches which were collected under constraints and conditions not present at other locations.

These traditional techniques also lack validity because they do not measure *quality of services.* Instead, they provide a count of the number of times an activity occurred. As an indicator of how many times a reference librarian answered a question (or engaged in other activities or processes) such indicators do have some usefulness. However, as measures of the degree to which service objectives are accomplished, the degree to which clientele receive accurate and timely services, and the degree to which clientele information needs are, in fact, resolved, such traditional indicators are useless. Worse, continued dedication to maintaining such traditional measures oftentimes serves only to lull the librarian into a false sense of security.

UNANSWERED QUESTIONS

As an example, library X finds that during the month of May, 567 reference transactions took place—of which 34% were quick fact, 43% were directional, and 23% were bibliographic. The number of transactions is up 8% over the same month a year ago and the breakdown of transaction types is roughly the same. Having such data, one still does not know:

— the degree to which reference services meet stated objectives and service priorities—should the library concentrate on providing quick fact reference services or other services?
— the degree of accuracy with which staff respond to the questions—what percentage of all the quick fact reference questions answered correctly is acceptable?
— the relationship between the number of staff hours at the refer-

ence desk and services provided—how many staff hours per reference transaction was needed? For example, if 185 staff hours this month were dedicated to reference service but 260 were used for the same month a year ago, are reference staff now more productive?

—the amount of time necessary for the receipt of a correct versus incorrect response, or to produce a satisfied versus unsatisfied client—for instance, how much time is acceptable as a response time for a correct answer to a quick fact question?

These, and other key issues MUST be addressed if, in fact, there is to be reliable and valid assessment of reference services. Further, evaluation of reference services in terms of *outputs* is essential for a valid assessment of the degree to which information services actually resolve clientele information needs; successful completion of two or more reference service activities contribute to the accomplishment of organizational goals and objectives.

Assessing reference services in terms of outputs encourages a planning environment where written goals and objectives are developed, output measures are linked to objectives, and the degree to which objectives are accomplished is measured. Identifying the factors that contribute or detract from quality reference service forces agreement as to which reference services or activities are to be emphasized or given priority and provides trend data as to how various indicators of reference service change over time.

Since planning is not the focus of this paper, readers may wish to consult sources (Palmour, et al. 1980; and McClure, 1982) which discuss the importance of planning and its relationship to output measures. Suffice to say here that using *both* output measures for assessing reference services *and* an ongoing planning process to develop programs for the improvement of reference services is necessary if the quality of reference services is to be increased.

POSSIBLE REFERENCE SERVICE OUTPUT MEASURES

Before evaluation can be done and data collected to assess the quality of reference services, the librarian must have a sense of possible service activities where output measures can be used. Listed below are a number of such measures targeted at typical reference activities with a brief description of the data elements for each.

1. Correct Answer Fill Rate

This measure determines the degree to which reference staff provide correct answers to specific types of reference questions in a given period of time and is usually based on a sampling process. It is computed as follows:

$$\frac{\text{Number of Correct Answers Given}}{\text{Number of Questions Asked}}$$

Typically, pre-selected questions are developed and administered to the reference staff without their awareness that the questions comprise a "test." Although the primary objective is to assess the degree to which the question is answered correctly, the testing may also investigate the reference negotiation skills, knowledge of specific reference tools/indexes, communication skills, referral ability, and other variables related to reference services (Katz, 1982).

This measure can be computed for different types of reference questions; for specific types of clientele (students, faculty, juveniles), it can be administered either obtrusively or unobtrusively, by telephone or in-person, and it can be computed for certain times of the day, week, or month.

2. Correct Answers Per Reference Staff Hour

This measure provides an assessment of the reference staff's accuracy in answering questions during a specific period of time in terms of the total number of reference staff hours dedicated to answering reference questions during that same period of time. Either obtrusive or unobtrusive testing can be used to determine "number of correct answers given." It can be computed thusly:

$$\frac{\text{Number of Correct Answers Given}}{\text{Reference Staff Hours}}$$

For instance, if during the sample time period 200 correct answers were given and the total number of reference staff hours was 60, then the correct answer per reference staff hour would be 3.3. This level of performance can then be compared to other allocations of staff with the intent of obtaining the maximum number of correct answers with the least number of reference staff hours.

This measure could be easily modified to assess reference activities other than "correct answers" by substituting another activity such as "successful referrals" divided by the total amount of reference staff hours dedicated to that particular activity. Thus, such measures consider the impact of having greater or fewer reference staff hours on the overall accuracy of questions answered (or some other reference activity) and can, to some degree, be considered as an overall measure of reference staff productivity.

3. Reference Services Delivery Rate

A key indicator of the quality of reference service is the amount of time it takes to complete a reference service *successfully*—the correct answer fill rate is important, but knowing the amount of time required to obtain that correct answer is equally as important. The general format for computing measures of reference delivery rate is:

$$\frac{\text{Total Amount of Time for Successful Service Deliveries}}{\text{Total Number of Successful Service Deliveries}}$$

Typically, such measures require a sampling process where an estimate of (1) total time can be computed for successful service deliveries and (2) the total number of successful service deliveries is identified. If, for instance, total time for successful service deliveries is 400 hours (for a specific period of time) and the number of deliveries was 56, then the measure would indicate that the reference service delivery rate was approximately 7.1.

Such measures allow the librarian to know how long, on average, "successful" reference service delivery requires. Such delivery times could be correct answers to reference questions, production of bibliographies, identification of appropriate referral source, and other services unique to a particular library. Criteria must be established to determine "successful" regardless of the specific service being investigated, and techniques to measure the time between the initiation and completion of the service or activity also would be necessary.

4. Cost per Correct Reference Answer

This measure, which provides the library with a means of determining the cost of providing a "correct" reference answer, can be computed as follows:

Total Cost of Reference Services for Given Time Period
Number of Correct Answers in Same Time Period

The number of correct answers to reference questions can be obtained from the data in correct answer fill rate, described above. Further, the measure can be easily modified to assess the cost of other reference services by, for example, using "number of correct referrals" in the denominator of the equation, or other services as appropriate.

Costing out reference services can become a complicated business, but for in-house use, arbitrary definitions of items to be included as the "cost" basis for reference can, in fact, be made. For instance, standard categories such as personnel, collection, support services (such as online data base searching) and supplies can be estimated for an entire year. Two samplings would be necessary, the first to have an estimate of the total number of reference questions asked during a given period, and a second to determine the percentage of correct answers in the same time period. If the sampling period to determine correct answers is for one month, the annual cost should be divided by twelve.

Each of these four examples can be modified into use for additional measures or different aspects of a service. For example, it may be equally important to measure the *incorrect* answer fill rate, or the *unsuccessful* reference services delivery rate, or the cost per *incorrect* reference answer or unsuccessful service. In short, each of these measures can be modified and adapted to measure several different aspects of reference services.

These four output measures are suggested to stimulate greater interest in the use of output measures to assess the quality of reference services and are not suggested to be either a comprehensive list of such measures or appropriate for all library settings. Additional descriptions of performance measures, data collection techniques, and methods of analysis can be found elsewhere (Zweizig and Rodger, 1982; Oklahoma Department of Libraries, 1982; Illinois Library Association, 1982: and Kantor, 1984) each of these sources provide excellent models for how output measures can be applied and implemented in a library.

These measures are suggested, however, to be illustrative of the types of measures that can be developed. The selection of performance measures should be based on the service objectives of the library, the amount of time and resources available to collect and analyze the data necessary for the computation of the measures, and the likelihood that a specific service area is "actionable," i.e., has the potential to be changed and improved.

UNOBTRUSIVE TESTING

Because of the unique nature of the reference librarian-client relationship, reliable and valid assessment of the quality of such services requires a methodology that, as best as possible, duplicates that relationship during data collection. Unobtrusive testing has a number of advantages that makes it well-suited for this type of evaluation: observation of staff members takes place under operating conditions assumed to be normal; measurement can be made of the success with which staff members answer various types of questions; and the methodology provides a means by which one can conjecture as to why certain types of questions were answered incorrectly (Lancaster, 1977, p. 108).

Unobtrusive testing does have disadvantages, however. To use the approach effectively and correctly, some preliminary planning is required, test instruments must be carefully developed, the specific measures to be used must be clearly defined and understood by the participants, and a long term commitment on the part of the reference staff and library administration is necessary to analyze, report, and maintain the data. Moreover, its effectiveness is limited if the library does not have written goals and objectives or fails to develop strategies to *improve* reference services (if necessary) as a result of the process.

To date, the use of unobtrusive testing has been limited to assessing the percentage of correct answers that are given to a preselected list of questions, usually administered by proxies. Within this context, Table 1 provides a listing of selected studies which investigated correctness of answers provided to preselected questions, administered unobtrusively. One must be careful in making direct comparisons among these findings as some studies include questions administered over the telephone, some were done in an academic versus a public library, and in some cases, the methods of administration were different. In general, however, it can be suggested that the accuracy of answers given in response to such studies is around 50%.

One recent study of government documents reference staff in academic U.S. government depository libraries found that, on aver-

TABLE 1

PERCENTAGE OF CORRECT ANSWERS IN SELECTED UNOBTRUSIVE
EVALUATION OF REFERENCE SERVICE

Year	Author	Library Type	Percent Correct
1968	Crowley[a]	Public	54
1971	Childers[a]	Public	55
1973	King and Berry[b]	Academic	60
1974	House[c]	Public	40
1975	Peat, Marwick, Mitchell & Co.[d]	Public	40
1978	Childers[e]	Public	47
1980	Myers[f]	Academic	50
1981	Jirjees[g]	Academic	56
1981	Weech and Goldhor[h]	Public	70
1982	McClure and Hernon[i]	Academic	37

Sources

a. Thomas Childers and Terence Crowley, Information Service in Public Libraries: Two Studies (Metuchen, NJ: Scarecrow Press, 1971).
b. G.B. King and L. R. Berry, Evaluation of the University of Minnesota Libraries Reference Department Telephone Information Service, Pilot Study (Minneapolis: University of Minnesota Library School, 1973). ED 077 517.
c. David E. House, "Reference Efficiency of Reference Deficiency." Library Association Record, 76 (November 1974): 222-23.
d. Peat, Marwick, Mitchell and Co., California Public Library Systems: A Comprehensive Review with Guidelines For the Next Decade (Los Angeles, CA: Peat, Marwick, Mitchell and Co., 1975). ED 105 906.
e. Thomas A. Childers, "The Test of Reference," Library Journal, 105 (April 15, 1980): 924-28.
f. Marcia J. Myers, "The Accuracy of Telephone Reference Services in the Southeast: A Case For Quantitative Standards," in Library Effectiveness: A State of the Art (Chicago: American Library Association, 1980), pp. 220-231.
g. Jassim Muhammed Jirjees, "The Accuracy of Selected Northeastern College Library Reference/Information Telephone Services in Responding to Factual Inquiries," Ph.D. dissertation, Rutgers University, 1981.
h. Terry L. Weech and Herbert Goldhor, "Obtrusive versus Unobtrusive Evaluation of Reference Service in Five Illinois Public Libraries," Library Quarterly, 52 (1982): 305-324.
i. Charles R. McClure and Peter Hernon, Improving the Quality of Reference Service for Government Publications (Chicago: American Library Association, 1983).

SOURCE: Charles R. McClure and Peter Hernon, Improving the Quality of Reference Service for Government Publications (Chicago: American Library Association, 1983), pp. 14-15.

age, only 37% of the questions were answered correctly; quick fact questions were more likely to be answered correctly via the telephone than in-person; 33% of all questions were given a response of "don't know," and of these, 24% were *not* referred to another person or source; 21% of the answers provided wrong data; and a positive relationship was identified between the duration of the question negotiation process and ability to provide a correct answer (McClure and Hernon, 1983, pp. 54-57).

Perhaps more important for purposes of this paper, is that unobtrusive assessment has applications to a broader spectrum of reference services other than answering questions. For instance, unobtrusive investigation can also assess:

—accuracy of telephone versus in-person answers
—duration and quality of the reference negotiation process
—selection and use of reference tools to answer questions
—non-verbal communication skills
—interpersonal skills
—comparative quality of different types of staff or staff with different levels of educational background or training
—impact of selected institutional variables on ability of staff to answer questions correctly

These and other aspects of providing correct answers have been assessed via the use of unobtrusive testing methodologies and examples of how such assessment can be done have been described elsewhere (McClure and Hernon, 1983).

However, the application of unobtrusive evaluation methodologies in the area of reference services has not yet reached its potential. Activities such as referral services, outreach programs, bibliographic instruction, information delivery services, selective dissemination of information, online data base searching, etc. have great potential for unobtrusive study. Unobtrusive assessment is essential if librarians are to better understand the *quality* of services provided, the factors that add to or detract from *quality* services, and programs that improve the *quality* of reference services.

Some librarians have voiced reservations about the appropriateness of the use of unobtrusive testing and are concerned about the possible uses of data resulting from such investigations. While it is possible that inappropriate uses of such data have, in fact, occurred, safeguards can be easily established to protect the privacy of individuals, to insure the use and dissemination of summary data only (data that cannot be linked to specific individuals), and to have as the PRIMARY reason for such evaluation the development of training programs and self-improvement.

Unobtrusive evaluation of reference services should be done primarily to assist both the library and individual staff members identify areas where improved reference services are possible, and to suggest specific strategies and techniques by which such improvements can be made. Use of unobtrusive testing specifically for personnel evaluation may be both destructive to the individual as well as dysfunctional for improving the overall quality of reference services. As a methodology, unobtrusive testing is best employed as a "cooperative venture" among the librarians as a self-diagnostic tool. The primary factor that currently limits the quality of reference services is an attitude of complacency—one which assumes that (1) the vast majority of answers given to questions are accurate and timely, (2) the reference services currently provided are, in fact, accomplishing service objectives and resolving the information needs of the library's clientele, and (3) existing reference staff competencies and skills are "adequate" and are not likely to need improvement. These attitudes are based on assumptions which can be best tested by the use of unobtrusive evaluation techniques. Once they have been tested, specific strategies can be taken to improve existing levels of services and staff skills.

IMPLEMENTING OUTPUT MEASURES AND UNOBTRUSIVE EVALUATION

The effective use of output measures and unobtrusive evaluation is linked to the development of a formal planning process. Planning can best be defined as the process of assessing needs, establishing goals and objectives, developing programs to accomplish those objectives, and then evaluating those programs (or services) in terms of the stated objectives. While such planning is likely to be most effective when instituted throughout the library organization, it can also be used effectively on a departmental or individual basis.

For example, if the reference department in a medium-sized academic library wants to improve the quality of its reference services in the areas of provision of correct answers, referrals, and delivery time for selected services, the first step is to establish objectives which are measureable, time limited, challenging, concise, and single purpose. Examples of objectives for each of the above activities might be:

—increase the percentage of correct answers given to telephone requests from 35% to 50% by June, 1985.
—establish a referral file of specific sources, individuals, or agencies outside the immediate reference area by June, 1985.
—reduce the delivery time for the production of class bibliographies by 50% by June, 1985.

These are illustrative only, but serve to demonstrate the types of *departmental* objectives that might be developed—regardless of whether the library has stated goals or not. Further, similar objectives could be established by an individual as well.

Once clear objectives are established, the next step is to make certain that measures are available to determine the degree to which the objectives are, or are not, accomplished. For the first objective, the previously described output measure "correct answer fill rate" can be used. The second objective, related to referral, can be measured by "inspection," that is, at the appointed time (June, 1985) one simply looks to see if in fact the referral file was established and if it meets certain predetermined criteria such as number of entries, format, content, and up-to-datedness. The third objective can be measured by the previously mentioned output measure "reference services delivery rate."

These examples deal, specifically, with objectives for reference services and are illustrative of ones that suggest (or include) performance measures. A scheme of reference goals and objectives dealing with evaluation, in general, has been suggested by Olson (1984). However, some of the objectives in Olson's model are not time limited nor do not suggest specific measures to determine when they are accomplished. Nonetheless, they are useful as examples of areas where reference services evaluation goals and objectives can be established.

OBJECTIVES

At this point, it is important to note that the objectives and the measures to assess the degree to which the objectives are accomplished should be in writing. Further, if the objectives are to be used for the reference staff as a whole, the staff should be involved in their identification and agreement of which objectives are to be used for the forthcoming assessment period.

After identification or creation of the performance measures, the data collection process is begun. In some instances it will be necessary to first collect "benchmark" data, that is, data that describes the current level of performance. For instance, to know if the objective of increasing correct answer fill rate by 20% is going to be accomplished, one must first know the *current* fill rate. Thus, data will have to be collected at the beginning *and* at the end of the assessment period to determine if, in fact, a 20% improvement was accomplished.

In most cases the use of sampling techniques will be necessary to assess reference services. There is no need to study *all* questions, or *all* referral transactions; a well-developed sample of questions or other specific services can be done economically and effectively without injuring the reliability or validity of the data (Swisher and McClure, 1984). Further, most library staff simply do not have the time or staff-power to collect data without sampling.

The data collection process is based on (1) identifying the specific data elements that will be needed to compute the performance measures, (2) developing a research design and methodology that will insure the reliable and valid collection of that data, (3) administering the data collection process, and (4) analyzing/reporting the data to determine if the objectives were accomplished, to identify the factors which contributed to or detracted from objective accomplishment, and to assist in the establishment of new objectives for the next assessment period (Palmour, et al., 1980; Zweizig and Rodger, 1982; and Oklahoma Department of Libraries, 1982).

Once an assessment of the data has been made and the degree to which the objectives were accomplished is known, it is essential then, to develop a program of in-house training and continuing education. Indeed, developing objectives, establishing measures, collecting data, and analyzing the results serves little practical utility if specific programs are not developed to improve reference services and staff skills. Numerous training programs and continuing education techniques can be developed or are available and should be exploited (Conroy, 1978).

For example, reference staff members can attend formal courses or workshops on reference skills and sources; staff can have some of their reference transactions video-taped for analysis and discussion at a later time—perhaps with other members of the reference staff; staff members can provide in-house training sessions on selected reference skills or sources; and regular discussion sessions can be established where staff can assess selected questions they have had in recent weeks and ask for comments and suggestions on their strategies from other staff members. These are but a few of the possible ways in which a regular *program* of continuing education related to reference skills can be instituted in the library (McClure and Hernon, 1983, pp. 111-160).

As suggested earlier, the primary purpose for the use of output measures and unobtrusive testing of reference services is to improve the *quality* of reference services. Thus, it is critical that once the results of the measures are known, specific treatments are developed to improve services and staff competencies. In addition, those services or staff skills which have the greatest impact on the quality of services, that have the greatest chance for improvement, or cost the least to improve should be attacked first. The overriding emphasis, however, should be on improving the service *outputs* delivered to the library's clientele.

IMPORTANCE OF UNOBTRUSIVE REFERENCE ASSESSMENT AND USE OF OUTPUT MEASURES

For most libraries, resources are tight, justifying the need for additional resources is becoming increasingly more difficult, and the ability of the larger institution to support various library/information services is decreasing. Within this context, increased demands are being made on libraries to provide "better," "more accurate," or "more timely" information services to their clientele. Services cannot be improved until they are assessed and decision support systems (e.g. information systems which assist staff in decision making by providing specially structured and easily accessible data) are established to assist in decision making (Heindel and Napier, 1981).

As pointed out by Bommer and Chorba in the context of establishing such decision support systems, "critical to any evaluation of a program is the availability of measures of performance by which the output of a system can be assessed according to some stated criterion" (1982, p. 23). Thus, for the immediate foreseeable future, a primary objective for many libraries will be to demonstrate accountability and increase organizational productivity, i.e. increase the services or outputs and keep the costs from increasing, or maintain current levels of services and decrease the costs.

Thus, key areas of library services to which significant resources are allocated, and from which key services result, are especially likely to come under review as to their overall effectiveness (degree to which they accomplish goals and objectives) and efficiency (degree to which they allocate resources appropriately). Reference services surely are an area which demands attention, review, and possible changes. Librarians would be better advised to initiate a careful assessment of reference services *themselves,* first, rather than wait for external pressures either from institutional administration or clientele.

The development of a program instituting unobtrusive assessment of reference with the use of output measures will require staff time and effort. Such efforts include planning, developing policies related to how the evaluation is to be done and how resulting data will be used, and developing procedures for the actual evaluation process. Further, there will be a considerable time-lag between the point at which the decision is made to initiate such a program and the point at which there are available data and results from which decisions can be made as to the quality of existing services and what actions, if any, should be taken.

One of the most important uses of output measures is to develop trend data that compares the results of those output measures over time. Having the results of the output measures takes on increased significance when they (1) can be compared over time, and (2) when different output measures are considered in conjunction with each other. Figure 1 is an example chart of trend data that compares correct answer fill rate, cost per correct reference answer, and reference services delivery rate.

The chart given in Figure 1 is hypothetical and is offered only to suggest the importance of looking at the performance of a service over time and in conjunction with other performance measures. This chart suggests that over a two year period, the degree to which the reference staff has increased its accuracy of answering questions has improved somewhat; that the delivery rate for selected reference services has increased (with some variation at month 12); that the cost per correct reference answer increased through month 12 and then decreased until month 24; and that correct answers per reference staff hour has continually improved over this two year period.

Combining the information provided on a chart such as this with traditional data regarding reference services, such as the budget, the number of staff, and the number of questions asked etc., is essential. Such information can significantly enhance librarians' ability to understand the current operations of the reference area, improve the effectiveness by which specific activities are accomplished, assist in speculation about ''why'' certain measures improved or decreased over time, and thus, improve the basis by which decisions can be made to insure that the reference services accomplish the stated objectives of the organization and department.

Recent studies suggest systematic relationships among various

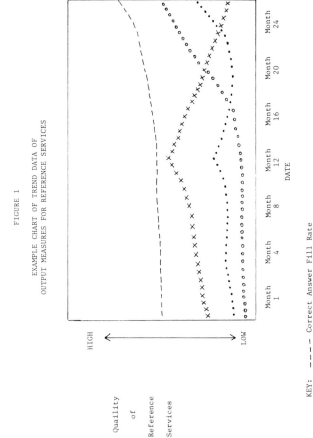

FIGURE 1

EXAMPLE CHART OF TREND DATA OF
OUTPUT MEASURES FOR REFERENCE SERVICES

KEY: ---- Correct Answer Fill Rate

        x x x x Cost Per Correct Reference Answer

        • • • • Reference Services Delivery Rate

        o o o o Correct Answers Per Reference Staff Hour

performance measures and although such relationships are not completely understood, it is essential to examine library performance in terms of *various* measures (Brooks, 1982). Therefore, one must be careful about making false conclusions, such as "there must be a relationship between cost per correct reference answer, and correct answers per reference staff hour," (see Figure 1) without additional statistical analysis and testing. Although trend data *can* identify time periods, services, and costs that may warrant additional attention, such charts *cannot* be assumed to show cause and effect relationships.

Thus, the use of unobtrusive testing and output measures provides a mechanism by which the reference area can *assess itself,* develop programs to *improve* its services, justify the *quality* of its services when necessary, and demonstrate *accountability* to appropriate administrative units when called upon to do so. In this sense, then, the emphasis on the use of unobtrusive testing and output measures is "self-diagnostic."

As suggested previously, specific output measures are available for assessing the quality of reference services, procedures and data collection instruments have been developed whereby librarians can model appropriate applications in their specific setting, and methods for reporting results that will improve the quality of services also are available. Apparently, the principal ingredient lacking before such assessment techniques are initiated is a commitment on the part of some reference librarians, a belief that such assessment is, in fact, necessary, and the acceptance of ongoing planning and evaluation as both desirable and appropriate activities for the library to pursue.

RESEARCH

Recent research studies which have unobtrusively evaluated the quality of reference services suggest that librarians cannot continue a Pollyanna view of how well services are provided. Nor can librarians continue to assume that just because user surveys indicate "satisfied" clientele that librarians have, in fact, provided accurate, timely, and relevant reference services. Until such assessments are done and incorporated into the regular activities of reference departments, librarians will not know the quality of services provided, and perhaps worse, they will be open to the charge of not caring how well such services are provided and if they are resolving clientele information needs.

Although clearly, unobtrusive testing and use of output measures are but one approach to the evaluation of reference services, they certainly are a critically essential component. Reference librarians must determine for themselves what type of assessment program is appropriate for their institution, setting, and services. And thus, assessment programs will vary from one library to another because each operates under unique constraints and operating conditions. The key, however, is less *which* evaluation assessment methodology is used than that *some* regular assessment technique is employed and that there is constant attention given to improving the quality of library and information center reference services.

REFERENCES

Bommer, Michael R. W., and Chorba, Ronald W. *Decision Making for Library Management.* White Plains, NY: Knowledge Industry Publications, Inc., 1982.

Brooks, Terrence A. "The Systematic Nature of Library Output Statistics," *Library Research* 4 (Winter 1982): 341-353.

Carmines, Edward G., and Zeller, Richard A. *Reliability and Validity Assessment.* Beverly Hills: Sage Publications, 1981.

Conroy, Barbara. *Library Staff Development and Continuing Education: Principles and Practices.* Littleton, CO: Libraries Unlimited, 1978.

Heindel, A. J., and Napier, H. A. "Decision Support Systems in Libraries," *Special Libraries* 72 (1981): 319-327.

Illinois Library Association. "Avenues to Excellence: Standards for Illinois Public Libraries," *Illinois Libraries* 65 (1983): 95-136.

Kantor, Paul. *Objective Performance Measures for Academic and Research Libraries.* Washington, D.C.: Association of Research Libraries, 1984.

Katz, William A. *Introduction to Reference Work Volume II: Reference Service and Reference Process,* Fourth Edition. New York: McGraw Hill, 1982.

Lancaster, F. W. *The Measurement and Evaluation of Library Services.* Washington, D.C.: Information Resources Press, 1977.

McClure, Charles R., and Hernon, Peter. *Improving the Quality of Reference Service for Government Publications.* Chicago: American Library Association, 1983.

McClure, Charles R., editor. *Planning for Library Services: A Guide to Utilizing Planning Methods for Library Management.* New York: The Haworth Press, 1982.

Myers, Marcia Jean, and Jirjees, Jassim Muhammed. *Testing the Quality of Reference Services.* Metuchen, NJ: Scarecrow Press, 1983.

Oklahoma Department of Libraries. *Performance Measures for Oklahoma Public Libraries.* Chicago: American Library Association, 1982.

Olson, Linda M. "Reference Service Evaluation in Medium-Sized Academic Libraries: A Model," *Journal of Academic Librarianship* 9 (January 1984): 322-329.

Palmour, Vernon E., Bellassai, Marcia C., and DeWath, Nancy. *A Planning Process for Public Libraries.* Chicago: American Library Association, 1980.

Swisher, Robert R. and McClure, Charles R. *Introduction to Action Research for Library Decision Making.* Chicago: American Library Association, 1984.

Weech, Terry L. and Goldhor, Herbert. "Obtrusive versus Unobtrusive Evaluation of Reference Service in Five Illinois Public Libraries: A Pilot Study," *Library Quarterly* 52 (1982): 305-324.

Zweizig, Douglas L., and Rodger, Eleanor. *Output Measures for Public Libraries.* Chicago: American Library Association, 1982.

Qualitative Evaluation of Reference Service

David Shavit

Recent years have seen a significant change in the methodologies used to study social phenomena, a change that has been called "welcome," "bewildering," and "profound" at the same time. While quantitative methods continue to play an important role, there has been an enormous increase in the use of, and reliance on qualitative methods. Researchers have come to accept the fact that no one method can answer all questions. Fieldwork and qualitative methods were in common use in the past in disciplines such as anthropology and sociology. Today, these methods have spread into, and become acceptable by, other disciplines, including education, adult education, mass communication, police and criminal justice, among others.[1] Qualitative methods also became an important tool in the evaluation of public policies and programs, and particularly their impacts and outcomes.[2]

Van Maanen sees several sources for the disenchantment with the results of quantitative studies, among which are the relatively trivial amounts of explained variance, and the high level of technical sophistication which makes quantitative research incomprehensible to all but the highly trained few.[3]

Library service has lagged behind. Librarians have been measuring and evaluating inputs and outputs, but have been reluctant to measure and evaluate outcomes and impacts. Various reasons have been set forth for not conducting evaluations of library service outcomes, including reference service. In his comprehensive study of measurement and evaluation of library service, Lancaster states that

Professor Shavit is with the Department of Library Science, Northern Illinois University, DeKalb, IL 60115.

235

" . . . in many situations, the benefits of library service cannot be measured in any objective way."[4] As a result almost all studies of reference service (as of other areas of library service), have refrained from dealing with the benefits of reference service. Many dismiss this problem altogether, as does Mary Jo Lynch in the *Library Data Collection Handbook:* "From a practical standpoint, however, the measurement of impact continues to be elusive, if not impossible."[5] However, even Lynch thinks that the measurement of outcomes remains "an important part of the information libraries would like to be recording and reporting."[6] As a result, most studies of reference service have been concerned only with the measurement and evaluation of various variables, many of which seem to be of little importance. The response to many of the studies measuring and evaluating reference service should be, as Helen Altman has asked: "So what?"[7]

A few studies of library service have used qualitative methods but, unfortunately, they are not all readily available. The following are some useful examples: Robert Taylor conducted open-ended and unstructured interviews with special librarians and information specialists to open up new ways of looking at libraries and to "allow reference and searching process to be seen from a point closer to actual fact."[8] Murfin observed reference service at a university library for a period of 45 hours and then asked the librarians for their assessment of their success in answering the questions and readers as to whether their needs were satisfied or not.[9] Perry Morrison has been a participant observer at Monash University Library in Clayton, Victoria, Australia for a period of nine months.[10] (Morrison conducted a literature search for the use of participant observation in libraries and turned up only one reference, although he suggests that this method could have been used without being called by that name).

SCHOOL MEDIA

For a study of school media specialists, Dodge systematically observed and collected data over a period of 20 weeks "to study the social relationships revolving about the job position of the school audio-visual media specialists" in two high schools within a large, suburban school district. Dodge obtained the school media specialists' perspective on their jobs and on their work setting and the perspectives of other members of the school organization relative to the school media specialist.[11] This researcher has used unstructured interviews and document analysis to study the impact of federal funding on state library agencies in five midwestern states.[12] These studies represent a different way of knowing. They often provide new evidence which runs contrary to the conventional wisdom of librarianship.

Almost all evaluators of reference services have relied on quantitative methods, using traditional close-ended interviews and questionnaires, even when using unobtrusive (or nonreactive) measures. These methods are not sufficient to answer many of the questions regarding reference service. A similar point has been made by Katz that some aspects of reference service, such as the reference interview and even the search can not be measured quantitatively. Katz states further: ''The recognition that statistical data are not the be-all and end-all of evaluation should be obvious . . . Evaluation measures of reference service need to develop models that reflect the social and the human behaviour.''[13]

In their study of the quality of reference service for government publications, McClure and Hernon review ten studies of reference service which have used unobtrusive evaluation of the accuracy and completeness of reference service. All these studies show a low percentage of accurate and complete answers to reference questions.[14] The ten studies, as well as many other studies of reference service, all answer the question: ''How many?'' But none of the studies answers what is surely a much more important question: ''Why?'' Why is the accuracy of answers to reference questions so low?

The question is not only how accurate is the reference librarian's response to the question, but also why is the answer inaccurate? What kind of questions were not answered or were answered incorrectly, and why could not they be answered? How does the reference librarian react to the question and to the person asking the question? How does he answer the question, and how does he conduct the interview? What are the interactions between the librarian and the user? It is interesting to note that McClure and Hernon found that of all the variables studied, only the method of question delivery (telephone vs. in person) was significantly related to quality of reference service provided.[15] This correlation shows clearly the importance of the human interaction aspect in the reference process, an aspect seldom dealt with in evaluation studies in the depth it requires.

SPECULATION

Jahoda and Braunagel speculated that some of the possible errors for incorrect or incomplete answers to reference questions were caused by misinformation, failure to fully circumscribe an answer, and failure to locate the most current answer available.[16] But there are other possible reasons which will surface only during a detailed observation of the reference process.

Evaluation of reference service cannot be only output oriented. It can not just deal with the service the users receive, but must also deal with service which users do not receive. Why do certain users of the library not use the reference service at all? Other questions are as important: What are users' perspectives of the reference service? How do users read the reference staff? What are the reference staff's perspectives of their role, and how do users perceive this role? What are the dynamics of the reference process?

It is not only that we have no answer to many questions regarding reference service, it is also that we often do not know what questions should be asked. It is for this reason that Wolcott suggests that the observer of social phenomena should observe and record everything but look for nothing in particular. The observer should, however, pay particular attention to contradictions and paradoxes.[17]

New strategies in dealing with reference service can be developed only when we have some answers to the "Why?" question. If the art of evaluating the benefits of reference service on users is not well developed, it should be. Evaluation of library service, including reference service, must become outcome oriented. Other disciplines have developed such methods, there is no reason why library service can not do the same. Evaluation of reference service should not only be an assessment of its effectiveness or worth, it should also be an analysis of its impact.

A review of the general literature on social science methodology reveals only a few references to the use of qualitative methods in the study of library service. The most interesting comment is made by Arnold:

> if you are interested in how people behave in public libraries, you might get some hints from Cavan's study of how people behave in bars [S. Cavan, *Liquor License: An Ethnography of Bar* (Chicago: Aladine, 1966)]. In fact, in a recent research project, one of my students found some evidence that people in

library reading rooms use techniques to indicate willingness or lack of willingness to engage in interaction with other patrons that are strikingly similar to what Cavan found among bar patrons.[18]

Michael Patton defined the nature of qualitative methods as follows:

> Qualitative data consists of detailed descriptions of situations, events, people, interactions, and observed behaviors; direct quotations from people about their experiences, attitudes, beliefs, and thoughts; and excerpts or entire passages from documents, correspondence, records, and case documentation obtained by qualitative methods are raw data from the empirical world. The data are collected as open-ended narrative. There are no attempts to fit institutional activities or peoples' experiences into predetermined, standardized categories, as the response choices that comprise typical questionnaires or tests do.[19]

Qualitative methodologies permit the researcher to record and understand in depth and in detail peoples' experiences and interactions in their own terms.

TECHNIQUES

Qualitative research techniques are amazingly versatile. The researcher has a whole arsenal of useful techniques. Smith and Manning suggest a typology of qualitative methods based on two dimensions of the investigator: whether or not the investigator identity is known by the subjects of the study and whether or not the investigator participates in the setting being studied.[20] The more useful techniques are participant observation, unobtrusive observation, in depth interviewing (also termed unstructured interviewing, open-ended interviewing, elite interviewing, etc), and document analysis.[21] Qualitative research has five characteristics:

1. Qualitative research has the natural setting as the direct source of data and the researcher is the key instrument. Since human behavior is influenced by the setting in which it occurs, the re-

searcher will have to spend a considerable amount of time in the reference area. He will also have to follow librarians and users in the library and in other areas in which they gather, such as offices, meeting rooms, staff room, etc.

2. Qualitative research is descriptive.
3. Qualitative researchers are concerned with process rather than simply with outcomes or products.
4. Qualitative researchers tend to analyze their data inductively. Researchers do not search out data or evidence to prove or disprove hypotheses they hold before entering the study.
5. Researchers are concerned in capturing perspectives. How do reference librarians make sense out of their work and experiences?[22]

Reference service can best be understood when it is observed in the setting in which it occurs. The researcher should be an outsider and should not be a member of the reference staff being observed. However, the researcher should be knowledgeable of reference service. The researcher should combine participant observation with in depth interviewing of the reference staff, users of the reference service and non-users of the reference service. The researcher should record all he sees, even the most trivial details. He should keep detailed field notes of what he has seen and what he has heard. He does not have to reduce all the observational data into numerical symbols.

There has been a concern about the fact that the observer of reference service does not have exact ways of measuring and recording what is seen.[23] This is a misplaced concern. There are certainly problems in observing reference service and in in depth interviewing, but measurement is not one of them. The qualitative researcher should be able to control the effects of his own biases. He must also be concerned with certain other issues involved in any fieldwork: the validity and reliability of the data, questions of ethics and maintenance of confidentiality, and the need to minimize the researcher's involvement in, and influence on, the setting he is observing. However,

> We have been encouraged to believe that quantification is impersonal and objective and, therefore, more reliable than quantitative methodology which takes into consideration such relatively intangible factors as values. But while qualitative analysis has been dismissed as too difficult, too intangible, and

too subjective, few have questioned the inherent subjectivity of quantification which requires "selection" of parameters and base line data, the interpretation of findings, and their selection of facts and evidence. There is much to be gained by destroying the myth of objectivity since subjectivity is already integrally involved—but disavowed.[24]

Data collection and data analysis are a simultaneous and integrated process. As the data is collected by the researcher, he begins looking for patterns. The theory will emerge as the study progresses.

MISCONCEPTION

Another misconception is that qualitative studies are necessarily long-term and costly projects. It is, however, possible to conduct short-term qualitative studies which will provide important and valuable information.[25]

The need to use qualitative methods to study reference service has been suggested before,[26] but Bunge did not go far enough. There is a need for a detailed and comprehensive field study of reference service.

A librarian, knowledgeable in reference service, who is not a member of the reference staff being observed, should observe the reference service for a period of several months. All aspects of the reference service should be observed and recorded in detail. All questions asked by users and all answers given by the reference staff should be recorded and later analyzed. The analysis of the answers, as well of the questions not answered at all, will assist the researcher in explaining why some answers were correct and others were incorrect, and why some questions were not answered.

What factors influenced the reference librarian in the search process, and in which way did the reference librarians and the users react to one another? How was the reference interview conducted and what factors effected the librarian in his handling of the user and his question? The in depth, unstructured, interviews will be conducted with both staff members and users, in order to analyze their perceptions of each other and of the reference process. What were the users' needs, and how, if at all, were they satisfied? What caused users to be satisfied or dissatisfied, and what caused reference staff to provide wrong answers to reference questions and their search to fail? A useful way to present the information gleaned from participant observation and the in depth interviews would be "storytelling." A journalistic documentation, this method of presentation will describe the environment and will communicate to the reader a general understanding of the situation.[27]

The major concern of the new Evaluation of Reference and Adult Services Committee of the Reference and Adult Services Division continues to be the translation of reference and adult service goals into measurable indicators of goal achievement.[28] Their concern continues to be focused on quantitative methods, such as statistical data and other output measures. While such data will be useful to some extent, they will not provide answers to the major questions raised regarding reference service. Evaluation of reference service must be concerned with more than "measurable indicators."

It will be a mistake to ignore quantitative techniques. Both quantitative and qualitative are necessary. When certain methods are more appropriate, they should be employed.

> It may be true that the knowledge gained by the qualitative researcher may be skewed by the biases of the investigation, but at the same time it may reveal a richness and depth of understanding of complex situations that is simply beyond the capacity of quantitative research, no matter how rigorously and artfully applied. . . . [It] must be recognized that many facets of social phenomena do not lend themselves to quantitative study. With all their limitations?, qualitative investigations may often have greater payoff in usable knowledge.[29]

REFERENCES

1. See, for example, Robert C. Bogdan and Sari Knopp Biklen, *Qualitative Research in Education: An Introduction to Theory and Methods* (Boston: Allyn and Bacon, 1981); Katheleen Rockhill, "Researching Participation in Adult Education: The Potential of the Qualitative Perspective," *Adult Education* 33 (Fall 1982): 3-19; Guido H. Stempel III and Bruce H. Westley, eds., *Research Methods in Mass Communication* (Englewood Cliffs, N.J.: Prentice-Hall, 1981); George J. McCall, *Observing the Law: Field Methods in the Study of Crime and the Criminal Justice System* (New York: Free Press, 1978).

2. Jerome T. Murphy, *Getting the Facts: A Fieldwork Guide for Evaluators and Policy Analysts* (Santa Monica, Calif.: Goodyear, 1980), and Michael Quinn Patton, *Qualitative Evaluation Methods* (Beverly Hills, Calif.: Sage Publications, 1980).

3. John Van Maanen, "Introduction," in *Varieties of Qualitative Research,* ed. by John Van Maanen et al. (Beverly Hills, Calif.: Sage Publications, 1982), p. 13.

4. F.W. Lancaster, *The Measurement and Evaluation of Library Services* (Washington, D.C.: Information Resources Press, 1977), p. 372.

5. Mary Jo Lynch, Library Data Collection Handbook (Chicago: American Library Association, 1981), p. 36.

6. Ibid.

7. Ellen Altman, "Assessment of Reference Services," in *The Service Imperative for Libraries: Essays in Honor of Margaret E. Monroe,* ed. by Gail A. Schlacter (Littleton, Colo.: Libraries Unlimited, 1982), p. 173.

8. Robert S. Taylor, "Question negotiation and information seeking in libraries," *College and Research Libraries* 29 (May 1968): 178-194.

9. M.E. Murfin, "A Study of the Reference Process in a University Library," Master thesis, Kent State University, 1970.

10. Perry D. Morrison, "Participant Observation as a Method of Studying Libraries," *PNLA Quarterly* 42 (Summer 1978): 4-11.

11. Martin Watson Dodge, "Selling Audio-visual: A Participant Observation Study of the School Media Specialist," Ph.D. dissertation, Syracuse University, 1973.

12. David Shavit, "The Impact of Federal Aid on State Library Agencies: Selected Case Studies," D.L.S. Dissertation, Columbia University, 1983.

13. William A. Katz, *Introduction to Reference Work, Vol. II, Reference Services and Reference Process,* 3rd ed. (New York: McGraw-Hill, 1978), pp. 252, 254.

14. Charles R. McClure and Peter Hernon, *Improving the Quality of Reference Service for Government Publications* (Chicago: American Library Association, 1983), pp. 11-16.

15. Ibid, p. 84.

16. Gerald Jahoda and Judith Schiek Braunagel, *The Librarian and Reference Queries: A Systematic Approach* (New York: Academic Press, 1980).

17. Harry F. Wolcott, "Confessions of a 'Trained Observer,' " in *The Study of Schooling: Field Based Methodologies Educational Research and Evaluation,* ed. by Thomas S. Popkewitz and B. Robert Tabachnick (New York: Praeger, 1981), pp. 254-256.

18. David O. Arnold, "Qualitative Field Methods," in *Handbook of Social Science Methods, Vol. II* Qualitative Methods, ed. by Robert B. Smith and Peter K. Manning (Cambridge, Mass.: Ballinger, 1982), p. 59.

19. Michael Quinn Patton, "Qualitative Methods and Approaches: What are they?" in *New Directions for Institutional Research: Qualitative Methods for Institutional Research,* ed. by Eileen Kuhuns and S.V. Martorana (San Francisco: Jossey-Bass, 1982), p. 5.

20. Robert B. Smith and Peter K. Manning, "Preface," in *Handbook of Social Science Methods, Vol. II: Qualitative Methods,* p. xix.

21. For practical guide to these techniques see, in addition to the books mentioned in notes 1 and 2, Robert Bogdan and Steven J. Taylor, *Introduction to Qualitative Research Methods: A Phenomenological Approach to the Social Sciences* (New York: John Wiley, 1975).

22. Bogdan and Biklen, *Qualitative Research in Education: An Introduction to Theory and Method,* pp. 27-30.

23. William Katz, *Introduction to Reference Work, Vol. II* Reference Services and Reference Process, 4th ed. (New York: McGraw-Hill, 1982), p. 260.

24. Eileen Siedman, "Why not *Qualitative* Analysis?" *Public Administration Review* (July/August 1977): 415.

25. See Arthur Levine, "Qualitative Research in Academic Decision Making," in *Varieties for Qualitative Research,* pp. 73-79.

26. Charles A. Bunge, "Approaches to the Evaluation of Library Reference Services," in *Evaluation and Scientific Management of Libraries and Information Centers,"* ed. by F. W. Lancaster and C. W. Cleverdon (Leyden: Noordhoff, 1977), p. 58.

27. Terry Denny, *Story Telling and Educational Understanding.* Kalamazoo, Mich.: Western Michigan University, School of Education, 1978.

28. Charles A. Bunge, "Measurement and Evaluation of Reference and Adult Services," *RQ* 22 (Spring 1983): 251-253.

29. William J. Reid and Audrey D. Smith, *Research in Social Work* (New York: Columbia University Press, 1981), pp. 90-91.

EVALUATING
REFERENCE SOURCES

Developing Criteria
for Database Evaluation:
The Example of Women's Studies

Sarah M. Pritchard

Since the advent of computerized databases as major sources of information, the evaluation of these tools has been a significant area of investigation by librarians and information specialists. The proliferation of both individual databases and search systems and the high costs associated with utilizing these services have necessitated careful review and comparison to ensure the best use of one's resources. Such studies have typically followed two directions: the evaluation of information retrieval systems as a whole and the detailed comparison of individual databases within a subject field. In the former case explicit criteria and methods have been devised and consistently applied, whereas in the latter there is greater variation in methodology and narrower use of formal criteria. This paper will review the literature addressing the second problem, the evaluation of database content. Using broad principles identified in that literature, the paper describes the development and application of specific criteria for determining the usefulness of various bibliographic databases for searches in the field of women's studies.

The need for criteria development became apparent during discussions among women's studies librarians and educators interested in creating an automated file of women's studies materials. A series of approaches to improve access to these materials were being considered in special libraries and research centers. Gaps in coverage of the field and inadequacies in the indexing of existing print and automated sources were the focus of librarians within the American Library Association (ALA), while the need for a coordinated listing of curricular materials was the impetus for proposals from universi-

Ms. Pritchard is Reference Specialist in Women's Studies, General Reading Room Division, Library of Congress.

247

ty-based educators. At the same time, the libraries of the Business & Professional Women's Foundation and of Catalyst, Inc., were taking steps to automate their catalogs, which in both cases provide access to collections in the area of women and work and women's economic issues. These diverse groups are now working on several fronts with the support of the National Council for Research on Women (NCRW), an umbrella organization of both independent and academically-based institutions devoted to research and programming in the field of women's studies.[1]

The basic assumptions underlying these proposals are that traditional reference tools do not provide adequate access to information in the growing interdisciplinary domain commonly called women's studies, and that specialized tools are at a scattered and early stage of formation. An excellent analysis of the problems encountered in women's studies and feminist research is given by Detlefsen.[2] She elaborates on five aspects: first, the conceptual differences between materials on women, feminist materials, and women's studies materials; second, the need for highly interdisciplinary approaches to the topic; third, the serious terminology and language biases and barriers; fourth, the lack of computer access to the indexes of choice for women's and feminist information; fifth, the hoped-for advent of new projects in this area, as alluded to above.

To understand the nature of current gaps in coverage and to establish a framework for developing new systems of access, an ad-hoc task force within ALA decided to evaluate existing bibliographic databases for their indexing of topics related to women's studies. Reviewers needed a uniform set of guidelines to be able to synthesize and compare the reports. At issue was not only coverage of core literature, but indexing language and certain policies of database producers. This paper represents the author's effort to prepare appropriate guidelines for evaluation, drawing upon her previous research and committee work in the evaluation of reference services and sources. Individual database critiques written in accordance with these guidelines could then be used to support grant proposals for new computerized services in this field.

DATABASE REVIEW LITERATURE

References to content evaluation of databases are found throughout the information science literature, but there have been few codifications of the principles. System-level studies usually consider factors like indexing but are not as concerned with individual files, and descriptions of the files rely on implicit evaluation standards which themselves are rarely examined. Conventional guidelines for reviewing reference books are also useful but need to be supplemented to address features unique to automated sources. A brief survey of this literature shows the varied approaches to content evaluation, leading to a group of documents that define certain core areas. Generally communicated as a series of questions or considerations, these core areas are what is meant by this author's use of the words "guidelines" or "criteria." Rarely couched in a quantitative fashion, such considerations cannot really be used as standards but rather as categories to assess the value of a file.

From the outset, librarians must be aware of the service issues raised by automated reference sources. Nichol identifies a number of concerns, for example standardization, vendor contracts, training, and duplication.[3] She discusses criteria for selecting a retrieval system, some of which apply to databases: data reliability, currency, form of displays. Although the responsibility of the librarian to apply subject knowledge from choosing files is stressed, no specific guidelines are given. A logical companion to Nichol is a bibliography by Shroder listing basic citations in areas such as finance, equipment, training, and outreach.[4] The section on comparing and rating databases includes references demonstrating the two trends described at the outset of this paper but does not cite a basic source for content evaluation methods or criteria.

From these overviews of automated reference services one moves to the specific study of database products. Stern's lengthy summary partially approaches content evaluation, but tends to focus on narrow technical issues or direct database comparisons, skirting the problem of developing common guidelines.[5] He concentrates on citation analysis in a broad sense and technical design factors for database creators, highlighting methods such as overlap studies or the use of test documents. Stern deplores the lack of reliable experimental design for database evaluation but doesn't discuss the existence of guidelines or criteria for content evaluation. Of more practical use is Pugh and John's listing of the many overlap studies and system comparisons.[6] These apply various evaluation techniques but do not critically define them. Most of the studies look at journals covered and type of indexing, but none attempts to generalize the underlying criteria.

Not only are there choices among databases in the same discipline, but interdisciplinary research such as that done in women's studies may require using several files to provide a complete response. Goodyear and Gardner searched the topic of abortion in four print and computerized indexes to see if journals outside the primary field of the index were being covered.[7] The results show very poor cross-discipline coverage for this topic which encompasses medicine, psychology, sociology, politics, law, and philosophy. Yerkey used the cross-file capabilities of the BRS system to identify clusters of databases relevant to particular topics, but remained within the scope of traditional disciplines.[8] Both articles are based on coverage as a single criterion of evaluation, as determined by noting which journals are cited or which files produce the most "hits." More detailed definitions of coverage are explored by Lancaster, who outlines a systematic way to compare databases using review articles as a source of sample citations.[9] This technique can be applied to a single subject or to an interdisciplinary field across several files. Tenopir compares Lancaster's "bibliography" approach with the use of a term-oriented search profile to see which method of evaluation is more effective.[10] Finding that both generate similar results, she recommends the profile method as easier and cheaper to use.

The tendency to focus on coverage as a criterion may be due to the difficulty of comparing other factors. The lack of standardization among databases makes it awkward to devise a set of evaluation guidelines while at the same time making their use even more important. However, an overall approach to content evaluation has been suggested by several principal authorities in the development of automated library services.

SOURCES

In looking at these sources chronologically, Williams' 1975 article is the first to give a general basis for establishing a series of comparable database reviews.[11] She discusses retrieval systems, individual databases, and service centers. Although our concern is database content, it is clear that system features and auxiliary services affect the usefulness of those contents. Williams outlines the following areas of evaluation: 1) general subject scope and orientation of the database, types of materials covered, completeness of coverage; 2) time lapse before citations appear in the database as compared to the hard-copy sources; 3) indexing and coding practices, such as key word searching, controlled vocabulary, enhanced titles or other special codes; 4) size and growth rate of the database and its corresponding print version (if any). In addition, Williams questions the services provided by database producers/vendors: document delivery, availability of manuals and thesauri, form of print-outs or displays, number and types of access points, and forms of search logic. These services are central to effective searching but may not always be under the control of the database producer. If the retrieval system (e.g., BRS, DIALOG) determines certain capabilities, these must be noted when making pure "content" comparisons.

F.W. Lancaster has thoroughly treated the evaluation of library systems and services in a number of works. In the latest edition of his book on information retrieval systems, he devotes chapters to criteria for evaluating information services, techniques for conducting evaluations, and the evaluation of machine-readable databases.[12] Lancaster places database quality in the context of service effectiveness criteria, as opposed to cost or time (i.e., time involved in using the service) criteria. Quality-related considerations include coverage, completeness, relevance, novelty, and accuracy. Completeness and relevance are often referred to as "recall" and "precision" and are in that intermediate area which may result from the interaction of the system with the individual database. Lancaster shows a table of major qualitative criteria, grouping factors in three areas similar to those of Williams: 1) coverage, including number and type of sources, time span, uniqueness and overlap; 2) time factors such as the frequency of update and the time lag between first publication and appearance in the database; 3) indexing and vocabulary factors, including the degree of vocabulary control, specificity and exhaustivity of indexing, search aids provided, and observable errors in accuracy and consistency.[13] In his section on the major steps of an evaluation, Lancaster prints a specimen statement of questions incorporating these factors and demonstrating their application to a specific database review.

EVALUATION

The evaluation of computerized indexes is a logical outgrowth of the librarian's traditional concern with the selection of printed abstracting and indexing services. Katz's basic text on reference work underlines the applicability to database review of such typical book evaluation principles as the purpose of the work, the reputation and authority of the publisher, the scope and originality of the work, the materials included and the reasons for their selection, and the currency of the work.[14] In the second volume of the text, Katz develops explicit guidelines for evaluating databases. Although initially one may use a bibliography of databases or a cross-file search to identify appropriate files, more detailed consideration is necessary to fully assess their usefulness. Katz presents a list of twelve questions which are formatted more clearly than those of Williams and are easier to use than Lancaster's which appear in several locations in his work. Once the basic areas noted above for printed sources have been explored, Katz recommends the following tests:[15]

1. How complete is the coverage in the database?
2. Does the distributor/publisher clearly specify which journals are indexed in depth and which are indexed selectively?
3. Are the journals indexed listed with their abbreviations, publishers' addresses, ISSN's?
4. How much does one database overlap another in its coverage?
5. How up-to-date is the database?
6. What are the retrospective capacities of the database?
7. Does the database provide only citations, or does it include abstracts?
8. Where a database indexes more than journals, is there a clear indication of the source of non-journal materials?
9. What methods are used for indexing or other types of subject analysis?
10. Is there a specialized thesaurus for the database?
11. How effective are the access points which are provided?
12. Does the publisher/vendor supply guides and manuals to assist the user? Does the publisher provide training courses, updates, "hotlines," etc.?

These questions are directed at the database itself and do not address either technical retrieval and hardware factors, or broad user satisfaction and reference effectiveness criteria, as Katz observes.

Williams, Lancaster, and Katz have provided a consistent body of guidelines within the context of acquiring and using machine-readable bibliographic databases. Professional journals in this field (for example *Online, Online Review, Database,* etc.) are beginning to adopt prescribed forms of review, at least for the more quantitative and factual characteristics of the database. Guidelines from the database review editor of *RQ* specify the elements to cover when writing brief reviews. In common with Katz and others, these mention subject coverage, indexing quality and depth, display formats, currency, record types, costs, manuals and training, and document delivery.[16] The Reference and Adult Services Division of ALA, which publishes *RQ*, has also demonstrated its interest in a standard of comparison through some of its committee work. The Database Products and Search Service Vendors Committee has proposed a draft matrix for the description and evaluation of databases.[17] The matrix is designed to facilitate comparison of databases to each other, and of the same database in different search systems. Within the broad categories commonly defined as criteria or guidelines, the matrix lists specific examples, record content fields, and the like. Under "coverage of document types," the matrix allows one to check off such formats as books, chapters in books, theses, journal articles, newspaper articles, research in progress, audiovisual media, laws, patents, people. For subject access, the matrix indicates abstracts, descriptor words, descriptor phrases, identifier words and phrases, major/minor term distinctions, coded access by classification numbers or other numeric codes. The RASD review guidelines and draft matrix are steps toward ensuring broad comparability in database evaluations.

CRITERIA FOR WOMEN'S STUDIES

Concern with evaluating database content has been shown throughout both general and specific articles related to automated information services, and certain factors have been repeatedly identified as necessary for a meaningful evaluation. The subject-oriented librarian must further adapt these criteria to conform to the particular requirements of the field. As explained earlier, the work in this paper was done to develop guidelines for evaluating databases in women's studies.

Feminist research and the study of women encompass a wide variety of sources, reflect a rapidly growing body of theory and applications, and occur within the context of definite political and ethical values. In addition to mainstream academic and popular literature in all subjects (a problem in itself), it is important for the researcher or activist in women's issues to have access to political and legal documents, the alternative and underground press, local community information, ephemeral organizational materials, and other non-traditional and multi-media sources. The feminist educator needs access to curriculum development resources for all educational levels, which can be found as separate units or as aspects of an integrated program. The increased awareness of sexism and other biases in language has led to the use of many new terms and phrases; if these are not found in database thesauri, the very point of the research may be obscured. Although the study of women and feminist studies are two distinct concepts, reference tools must be able to accommodate both and thus must ideally meet several philosophical and theoretical stances evolved by the contemporary feminist movement. These include a heightened concern with language and with the exclusion of women's ideas from many traditional sources; an obligation to represent the experience of all women, especially those who have often been marginalized: lesbians, poor and working-class women, women of color, physically or mentally disabled women; a resistance to treating some subjects as intrinsically of less value than others; a desire to support women-owned businesses and to increase the role of women in the use and control of new technology; and an insistence on breaking down barriers between academic studies and "real-life" social and political action by providing equal access to information for poor women, under-educated women, and others outside formal institutions of learning or policy-making. It is clear that these values are also close to long-standing values of librarianship.

GUIDELINES

Taking these information needs and movement values into account, the general database evaluation criteria found in the sources reviewed above were tailored for this application to women's studies. The main areas of analysis are the same: coverage and completeness, record and display formats, vocabulary and indexing, and retrieval and availability factors. As will be seen, some criteria are more affected by the feminist context than others. Parts IV and V of the criteria include those characteristics which may depend heavily on which retrieval system is used to access the database. These criteria also provide for a final overall assessment which may be rather subjective.

GUIDELINES FOR EVALUATING DATABASES IN WOMEN'S STUDIES

I. Database Coverage: Subject Scope, Completeness, Timeliness

A. Does the vendor/supplier clearly define the scope of the database? Are women's issues specifically cited as a strength?

B. What types of items and sources are included (books, journals, dissertations, government documents, newspapers, photographs, films, braille, phonorecords, maps, directory entries, laws, numeric data, microforms, etc.)?

C. Do the sources represent: the core items in the field, mainstream trade and academic work, small press, community information, ephemera, alternative and radical press, foreign language sources, Third World coverage, lesbian media, minority and disadvantaged groups? How well-represented are women's issues, women's media, women writers?

D. Who selects items for inclusion? Is there a refereeing process, are the criteria for inclusion made known, how are items solicited and submitted? Is the process likely to eliminate or overlook women's issues or materials from feminist sources?

E. If a journal or other source is covered, how much of it is indexed? As well as main articles, are book reviews, letters, columns, news notes, secondary subjects indexed?

F. What is the degree of overlap with other databases or printed sources? How many citations are new to the user, i.e., the degree of novelty in the search results?

G. What is the total number of items in the database? The number added each year or month (growth rate)? If the database has a print counterpart, are there more or fewer records online than in the print source?

H. What dates does the database cover? Is the full file available online? What is the publisher's update frequency (may differ from system's updates)? What is the time lag from appearance of the primary source until appearance in the database? How fast are new women's issues and concepts included?

II. Content of Individual Records

A. Is the record a brief citation only? Is there an abstract? Is there full-text or numeric data content?
B. What fields are included (full author names, brief names, organizational names, titles, sources, distributors, dates, abstracts, descriptors, codes and identifiers)?
C. In what order do the fields appear? Is it easy to identify and interpret them (for the librarians and the end-users)? Are (too) many abbreviations and symbols used?
D. Who prepares the citations and/or abstracts: editors, authors, subject specialists, librarians? Are the titles of the items "enhanced" with additional words to clarify their content? How full is the abstract or other information?
E. If the online version has a print counterpart, is the online version enhanced or supplemented?

III. Vocabulary and Indexing

A. Does the database have a controlled vocabulary? Is there a thesaurus? Who writes it, and what are the update/revision procedures? Is it easy to use, are there good definitions, a lot of cross-references? How many terms are there representing women's experiences and issues? How well are these terms cross-referenced from general terms?
B. What kinds of actual words are used?
   1. How do they relate to terms used in current women's literature, in politics, health, the women's movement, etc? How relevant are they to new topics, how free from bias?
   2. Are terms assigned to proper nouns not in other fields, project names, etc.?
   3. Are any format terms used, for example to categorize types of studies, review articles, bibliographies, educational level, methodology, statistics, etc.?
   4. Is there any way to determine an explicitly feminist perspective on a more general topic, e.g., philosophy of science, historiography?
C. How exhaustive is the indexing? How many terms are applied to each item? Are they divided into major/minor, or other groupings? Are both broad and specific terms given to each

item? Are terms used consistently and logically? Are terms used to bring out all the aspects of the original item, including novel perspectives, secondary subjects, detailed contents?

D. How are terms structured? Are they: unconnected, in strings, with built-in relator words, with subdivisions, inverted headings, phrases? Can they be truncated for searching? Does it seem that headings are too much or too little connected, which could cause too tight or too loose retrieval profiles? Is specifying word order a problem in searching?

E. Can you search across whole trees or hierarchical groups of terms at once? Do you *have* to search using existing structures or can you create new intersections? Can you move easily "up" or "down" in specificity of terms used?

F. What is the success of using Boolean combinations? This depends on the number and specificity of index terms assigned and the extent of pre- or post-coordination; you can only verify this absolutely when using a test database where you know exact contents and what you should be getting.

IV. Database Structure

A. What is the update frequency of the database?

B. Which fields are searchable? Is there truncation, free-text searching?

C. Which fields are limitable (by date, special codes, geographic area, language, etc.)?

D. Are any indexes browsable online? Are there cross-references online?

E. In what order are the citations displayed? Can the order be varied?

F. What are the various formats available for display? Can abstracts be printed online?

V. Availability Issues

A. Through which vendors is the database available: direct from producer, BRS, ORBIT, DIALOG, The Source, others?

B. What is the amount and nature of supporting documentation: manuals, thesauri, user aids, training courses? Is there a printed version of the online index?

C. What are the charges for the database (on top of charges for computer and telephone access)? Do royalty fees vary with time of use, amount of use, printing? What are the costs of documentation, of the printed version?

D. Document delivery: Is it easy to locate and acquire items? Is there an accompanying set of microfiche, or a document order service?

E. Are any of the phases of production or distribution of the information women-controlled? Does the producer/distributor's advertising or other literature demonstrate sexist attitudes? Are disadvantaged, minority, or non-privileged women likely to have a difficult time gaining access to the primary or secondary sources of information?

VI. General Subjective Assessment

A. "User effort": a combination of all of the above, i.e., how hard is it to use the source and what do you get out of it? Take into account:
   1. Flexibility in searching, multiple access points, manipulations;
   2. Vocabulary appropriate for women's studies, good thesaurus structure, capacity for free-text searching;
   3. Complexity of strategies needed to get at subjects related to women's and feminist issues, types of search strategies available;
   4. Time involved to prepare and execute search, effort to develop a successful strategy, and
   5. Ease of comprehension of system and results.

B. "Recall" and "precision": traditional measure of the performance of an information retrieval system; how much do you get and how appropriate is it to the original need?

C. Assessment of how useful the file is for women's issues: health, politics, history, literature, legislation, communication, social issues, technology, international concerns?

Using these criteria, an ad-hoc group of librarians connected with ALA and indirectly with NCRW performed sample searches on databases such as ERIC, SOCIAL SCISEARCH, *National Newspaper Index, Sociological Abstracts,* and *Economic Abstracts International.* The guidelines were also applied to a major print source, *Women Studies Abstracts.* Reviewers followed the categories of the guidelines when preparing their reports, which were two to three pages in length. However, there was a tendency to skip some of the detailed questions and focus on whatever characteristics were easily identifiable. Not mentioning some factors leads one to wonder whether the information wasn't there at all, was too difficult to find, or was considered unimportant by the reviewer. Reviewers generally avoided making overt negative analyses, but by following the guidelines objectively they made implicit criticisms in demonstrating gaps and inadequacies. The database summaries gave immediate impressions as to the usefulness of each file for women's studies or feminist research. A query letter sent to some reviewers elicited favorable comments about the guidelines: sections I to IV were considered the most crucial. The guidelines were found to be equally valuable for assessing print sources, disregarding the obvious factors pertaining only to computerized retrieval. The reports were drawn together as one portion of the justification in a grant proposal, and despite minor variations in style they formed a cohesive body underlining the need for improved access to resources for women's issues. Taken as a whole, the major drawbacks in existing databases are the lack of coverage by both primary and secondary sources of the relevant subjects, the very problematic language barriers, and the inconsistencies in citation formats and search strategies.

The reports are not only comparable to each other, but are also condensations of the kind of information now appearing with regularity in women's studies journals and other documents. Databases related to women and politics are highlighted in a series of articles examining bibliographic and numeric files.[18] Written by subject specialists, these describe content in detail but give little analysis of indexing practices or file structure. Falk's recent survey of databases for the history of European women gives much more of this latter information, including sample search strategies, but is primarily directed at the end user rather than the librarian.[19] Falk discusses ways to get around limitations in vocabulary and to identify sources not before viewed in the context of women's history. Wheeler has compiled a comprehensive guide to print and online periodical indexes and abstracting services relevant to feminist research.[20] Speaking to the student or research user, she cites the general scope of each tool, any special features, sample subject headings and examples of which journals are covered. In this large bibliography our detailed criteria would be excessive but could provide a broad framework for description. A notable event for librarians, educators, and researchers in women's studies is the appearance of the first public bibliographic file focusing exclusively on this topic, *Catalyst Resources for Women.* Available through BRS, the file has been thoroughly documented by Dadlez.[21] She does not measure the database against any external models or criteria, but her article furnishes answers to many of the questions in our evaluation guidelines, listing types of sources, time span, indexing terms, citation formats, access points, search strategies, and the like.

CONCLUSIONS

Evaluating the content of databases is an essential part of providing high-quality information retrieval services. As the review of the literature has shown, the problem is widely acknowledged but only examined in depth by a few writers. Three or four categories of criteria form the foundation for content evaluation but must be modified to answer the requirements of a particular subject. Developing criteria forces the information specialist to critically define the goals, sources, and structure of the field in question. The process leads one to identify gaps in the actual source materials as well as deficiencies in the access tools. One must recognize the interaction of the system and the database, and test the guidelines to see if the resulting evaluations are meaningful. As a dynamic interdisciplinary subject drawing on both contemporary and historical sources, women's studies can be a pattern for this development process in other emerging multi-dimensional fields. Widespread application of similar guidelines may eventually lead to a commonly-accepted evaluation format, and may ultimately serve to overcome the lack of standardization among databases and the proliferation of redundant indexes.

REFERENCES

1. For a summary of the database project in women's studies, see *Feminist Collections* vol. 4 (Summer, 1983), published by the Office of the Women's Studies Librarian-at-Large of the University of Wisconsin System.

2. Detlefsen, Ellen Gay. "Issues of Access to Information About Women," *Special Collections* vol. 3 no. 1 (Spr., 1984). This issue is also forthcoming as a monograph, *Women in Special Collections,* eds. Suzanne Hildenbrand and Lee Ash (New York: The Haworth Press, 1984).

3. Nichol, Kathleen M. "Database Proliferation: Implications for Libraries," *Special Libraries* vol. 74:110-118 (April 1983).

4. Shroder, Emelie, ed. "Online Reference Service—How to Begin: A Selected Bibliography," *RQ* vol. 22:70-75 (Fall, 1982).

5. Stern, Barrie T. "Evaluation and Design of Bibliographic Data Bases," in Martha E. Williams, ed., *Annual Review of Information Science and Technology* (vol. 12). White Plains, NY: Knowledge Industry Publications, 1977.

6. Pugh, W. Jean, and John, Stephanie C. "A Bibliography of Database and Search System Comparisons," *Online* vol. 6:41-44 (September, 1982).

7. Goodyear, Mary Lou, and Gardner, Tracy. "The Inadequacy of Interdisciplinary Subject Retrieval," *Special Libraries* vol. 68:193-197 (May-June 1977).

8. Yerkey, A. Neil. "A Cluster Analysis of Retrieval Patterns Among Bibliographic Databases," *Journal of the American Society for Information Science* vol. 34:350-355 (September, 1983).

9. Lancaster, F. Wilfrid. *Information Retrieval Systems: Characteristics, Testing, and Evaluation.* 2nd edition. New York: John Wiley, 1979. p. 208-209.

10. Tenopir, Carol. "Evaluation of Database Coverage: A Comparison of Two Methodologies," *Online Review* vol. 6:423-441 (October, 1982).

11. Williams, Martha E. "Criteria for Evaluation and Selection of Data Bases and Data Base Services," *Special Libraries* vol. 66:561-569 (December, 1975).

12. Lancaster, *op. cit.*, chapters 8, 9, and 15.

13. *Ibid.*, p. 207.

14. Katz, William A. *Introduction to Reference Work.* 4th edition. New York: McGraw-Hill, 1982. vol. 1, *Basic Information Sources*, p. 21-25.

15. Katz, *op. cit.*, vol. 2, *Reference Services and Reference Processes*, p. 151-153.

16. Nitecki, Danuta. Undated memorandum, personal communication from the author.

17. *RASD Update* vol. 3 (Jan.-Feb., 1982), p. 3.

18. See the following issues of *Women & Politics:* vol. 1, no. 4 (Winter, 1980/81); vol. 2, no. 1/2 (Spring-Summer 1982); vol. 2, no. 3 (Fall, 1982).

19. Falk, Joyce Duncan. "The New Technology for Research in European Women's History: 'Online' Bibliographies," *Signs: Journal of Women in Culture and Society,* vol. 9:120-133 (Autumn, 1983).

20. Wheeler, Helen Rippier. "A Feminist Researcher's Guide to Periodical Indexes, Abstracting Services, Citation Indexes and Online Databases," *Collection Building* (forthcoming).

21. Dadlez, Eva M. "Catalyst Resources for Women on BRS," *Database,* vol. 6:32-43 (December, 1983).

Evaluation of Legal Database Systems by Law Librarians in Private Law Firms

E. Leslie Kanter, Esq.

The continued growth and expansion in the field of on-line legal information retrieval has raised questions as to how and to what extent these systems are currently being used. Additionally, questions have arisen as to the impact this use may have had on the role of the law librarian and on the general character of the law library. Earlier studies on this topic have suggested that in this rapidly changing field continued research is necessary in order to keep abreast of developments.[1] In response to this need, a survey was devised in which these issues would be examined.

The reference librarian in today's law library is faced with an onslaught of computer technology. These changes have permitted the skilled reference librarian to access legal information without having to rely fully on the more traditional paper based information resources. Automated information retrieval has similarly impacted on other reference librarians. It is assumed that the findings of this study will have relevance to professionals throughout the field.

The two commercial legal database systems most often found in the law firm library are LEXIS and WESTLAW. First marketed in 1973 by Mead Data Corporation, the LEXIS system is a full text interactive computer system capable of retrieving federal and state court decisions, statutes, administrative rules, regulations and a variety of other special legal documents.[2] In LEXIS these documents are separated into categories named libraries and then divided into more specific files enabling the user to confine a search to a particular legal point in a specific area.[3] In 1980, the LEXIS system underwent extensive modification making it considerably

263

faster and more comprehensive.[4] In addition, the LEXIS system can be utilized to access various nonlegal research database systems such as Dialog.[5]

WESTLAW, the major competitor of LEXIS, has entered the information retrieval market somewhat more recently. The WESTLAW system is produced by West Publishing Company and bases its indexing structure upon West's key number system.[6] In addition to offering full text information, the WESTLAW system includes West's summary and headnote structure for all case opinions.[7] Recently, WESTLAW underwent dramatic modifications. In March 1983, a major restructuring enabled WESTLAW to have increased capabilities.[8] Theoretically, under this new design, WESTLAW and LEXIS should now be comparable in speed.[9] Over the past year, additional features have been added to the system which have expanded WESTLAW's coverage.[10] This coverage, however, still appears to be somewhat less comprehensive than that of LEXIS.[11]

PROCEDURE/METHODOLOGY

A fifteen part, eight page questionnaire was devised for use by law librarians in private law firms. By design, this questionnaire comprised three distinct parts. The first section was created to identify the pertinent demographics of the firms responding. The second section examined the nature of the firm's use of and experiences with on-line legal database system(s). The final section was designed to ascertain the impact such use had on the law librarian and on the law library.

Participants in this study were selected from firms employing fifty or more attorneys in the cities of New York, Chicago and Cleveland. A minimum firm size requirement was imposed on the assumption that firms under fifty would be less likely to have an on-line database system. The survey sample was obtained by counting the number of attorneys listed by individual law firms in the 1983 edition of the Martindale Hubbell Law Directory. An attempt was also made to include approximately equal numbers of firms in three categories: 50-100 attorneys, 101-150 attorneys, and over 150 attorneys, in order to determine the possible effect of firm size on the issue to be studied. After the survey sample was compiled, it was cross-referenced with the 1983 edition of the AALL-Directory of

Law Libraries in order to obtain the name of each firm's law librarian and the appropriate mailing address.

Questionnaires were then sent to law librarians in one hundred private law firms located in the three cities previously cited. Enclosed along with the questionnaire was a self-addressed, stamped envelope and a cover letter informing participants of the purpose and nature of the survey. Recipients were requested to return the questionnaire within a four week period but not later than March 16, 1984. The questionnaire was designed to provide the respondent with a cloak of anonymity. This decision was based upon studies which indicated that a higher percentage of returns would occur when identification was not required.[12] While respondents remained anonymous, the postmark on the return envelope, however, did allow for identification of the city of origin.

RESULTS/DISCUSSION

To ensure that the study only included law firms with fifty or more attorneys, question one asked respondents to report the number of attorneys employed by their firm. The ranges listed were: under 50, 50-100, 101-150, and over 150. Of the sixty responses received to the 100 questionnaires sent out (60% yield), four were from firms which reported having fewer than fifty attorneys, nineteen had 50-100 attorneys, twenty had 101-150 attorneys, and seventeen had over 150 attorneys. The attempt to survey approximately equal numbers of firms in the 50-100 range (designated "medium" size), 101-150 range (designated "large" size), and over 150 range (designated "very large" size) appeared to have succeeded. The fact that four firms reported employing fewer than 50 attorneys, in spite of the author's original count of over 50 attorneys, was puzzling but was accepted at face value and those responses were eliminated from the study. Thus, the study was based on questionnaires returned from 56 private law firms in New York, Chicago, and Cleveland.

In question two, respondents were asked to designate the size of their library collections. Seven percent (4) of the firms reported holdings of less than 10,000 volumes. Seventy-seven percent (43) of the firms reported holdings of 10,000 to 50,000 volumes. Sixteen percent (9) of the firms reported holdings of 50,000 to 100,000 volumes. As perhaps expected, firms with fewer than 10,000 volumes were in the "medium" size range while firms with 50,000 to 100,000 volumes were either "very large" (5) or "large" firms (4).

In question three, law librarians were asked if their firm had an on-line legal database system and if so, the date it was first acquired. All fifty-six of the firms reported having an on-line legal database system. Eighty-nine percent (50) of the firms reported that the systems were installed in the 1970's while eleven percent (6) of the firms reported acquisition of the systems in 1980 or later. Of the fifty systems installed in the 1970's, five were acquired in 1979 while twenty-six were reported installed in 1978 or earlier. Nineteen did not respond to the question concerning date of acquisition, some indicating uncertainty due to the time elapsed.

Question four asked respondents to identify the on-line system(s) employed by their firms. Ninety-eight percent (55) of the firms in the study reported employing the LEXIS system. One firm reported employing the WESTLAW system alone. Twenty-two percent (12) of the fifty-five firms with LEXIS also employed WESTLAW. Forty-five percent (25) of the firms with LEXIS, reported having one or more non-legal database systems with Dialog being cited twenty-three times.

In question five, the law librarian was asked to indicate how frequently the on-line legal database system(s) was used for research. Ninety-five percent (53) of the firms reported that they used their systems daily. The remaining three firms, all in the medium size category, reported use of the system(s) on less than a daily basis, ranging from three to four times a week. Of those firms using their systems on a daily basis, forty-seven percent (25) reported conducting ten or more searches per day. Within this group of twenty-five firms, ten reported more than twenty searches per day, while two reported fifty or more searches per day. Several firms reported their number of searches per day in terms of ranges while eight others did not respond to this portion of the question. In general, it would appear that law firms with on-line legal database systems utilize them extensively.

In question six, respondents were asked to identify who carried out on-line legal searching in their firms. The data set forth in Table 1 indicate that these searches are carried out by a variety of individuals. Paralegals' use of the on-line legal database system(s) tended to vary depending on the particular firm. In sixty percent of the

Table 1:   Who Carries Out On-Line Legal Database Searches in Private
           Law Firms

	Never	Sometimes	Frequently	Routinely
Partners	11	39	0	0
Associates	0	1	22	33
Law Librarians	1	4	22	27
Paralegals	7	26	11	9

The numbers represent individual law firms reporting in each instance.
Not all firms responded to the question or all parts of the question.

firms responding, paralegals either "never" or "only sometimes" carried out on-line searching. In twenty percent of the cases they searched frequently while in seventeen percent of the firms they searched routinely. The data also indicate that partners conduct searches far less frequently than associates. Indeed, no firm reported that partners used the system frequently or routinely. The results of the current study would appear to indicate that law librarians share an equal role with associates in conducting legal searches. In fact, many law librarians indicated in their comments that they were considered the in-house database specialists in their firms. This finding contrasts markedly with the results of a study conducted in the fall of 1976 which reported that it was primarily attorneys who carried out these searches.[13]

Question seven asked law librarians to evaluate the training package provided by their on-line research system(s). Eighty-eight percent (45) of the fifty-one firms responding to this question reported that LEXIS was "easy" to learn, while twelve percent (6) reported it "somewhat difficult" to learn. None reported LEXIS "difficult" to learn. Of the twelve firms reporting on WESTLAW, sixty-seven percent (8) indicated that it was "easy" to learn while twenty-five percent (3) reported it "somewhat difficult" to learn. One firm reported WESTLAW "difficult" to learn.

It would appear, on the whole, that the on-line legal database systems have been sufficiently well prepared to enable most users to learn to operate them without difficulty. A few respondents did indicate, however, that they were not informed when new features and improvements were to be added to the LEXIS system. They felt this lack of information prevented them from providing the best research services possible. They further suggested that LEXIS could alleviate this difficulty by issuing newsletters on a regular basis to keep users abreast of changes.

In question eight, respondents indicated the extent to which they considered the on-line legal database system employed by their firm to be "user friendly". Ninety-three percent (51) of the firms employing LEXIS reported the system "easy" to use while only seven percent (4) reported it "somewhat difficult" to use. Out of the thirteen firms which reported using WESTLAW, the responses were equally divided between those which found the system "easy" to use and those which found it "somewhat difficult". One respondent found WESTLAW "difficult" to use. In addition, one firm which had formerly used WESTLAW reported discontinuing the system because of difficulties encountered in its use.

Analysis of the above responses appears to indicate that the overwhelming majority of LEXIS users perceive it to be easy to use while only half of the WESTLAW users have a similar perception of that system. Whether these differences in perception may be ascribed to differences in the systems themselves or to the fact that WESTLAW use has become more common only in recent years is not known. Additionally, this pool of WESTLAW users may be too small a sample from which to draw a conclusion.

Question nine asked respondents to indicate both the extent to which they encountered problems with response and down time in their legal database systems and to evaluate the assistance provided to remediate these problems. Of the fifty-four firms reporting LEXIS use, thirty-one percent (17) "seldom encountered" problems with response time while sixty-five percent (35) "sometimes encountered" problems. The experience with WESTLAW was similar.

The firms employing LEXIS indicated somewhat fewer problems with down time. Forty-one percent (22) of the firms reported that they "seldom encountered" problems, while fifty-seven percent (31) reported that they "sometimes encountered" problems. The experience reported by the small WESTLAW sample (11 firms) was even more positive with fifty-five percent (6) of the firms reporting problems "seldom encountered".

Experience with "Assistance to Problem Calls" in firms using LEXIS showed that seventy-two percent (39) of the firms "seldom encountered" problems in this category. Only twenty-six percent (14) of the firms "sometimes encountered" problems. Similarly, the firms employing WESTLAW found service to be satisfactory; with sixty percent (6) of the firms reporting that problems were "seldom encountered".

The responses appear to indicate that the experience of firms employing LEXIS and WESTLAW ranged from problems "seldom encountered" to problems "sometimes encountered". Few firms cited "frequent problems" in any category. On the basis of these responses, it may be concluded that both the LEXIS and WESTLAW systems provide acceptable technical services.

Question ten sought to ascertain the frequency of use of individual WESTLAW databases and the degree of satisfaction experienced in their use. Although thirteen law firms in the survey had the WEST-LAW system, only eleven responded to this question. The responses appear to indicate that most WESTLAW databases, with only two exceptions, were not used frequently. Indeed, seven of the fifteen databases listed were never cited as being "frequently used" while four additional databases were cited as being "frequently used" by only one firm. The two library files cited as "frequently used" were the Federal Law Library's General Database (5 firms) and the Regional and State Database (7 firms). It would appear, however, that despite the relative infrequency of their use, most respondents regarded all WESTLAW databases as satisfactory.

Question eleven queried librarians on the frequency of use of individual LEXIS databases and on the degree of satisfaction experienced in their use. Not all firms reported in all categories. The results indicate that of the twenty-one databases listed in this question, seven were cited as being "frequently used" by an overwhelming majority of firms reporting. The databases thus cited were the General (46), the Tax (46), and the Securities (43) databases, within the Federal Law Library, as well as, Nexis (46), Auto-Cite (44), Shepard's Citations (44), and State Law Libraries (38). Seven databases were cited by a majority of firms as "never" or "rarely used". These included Energy (40) and Public Contracts (34) within the Federal Law Library as well as English Law (44), French Law (43), Matthew Bender Publications (44), Lexpat (43), and American Bar Association (30). The remaining databases were utilized "sometimes" and "frequently" by a majority of firms. Presumably, variable use of these databases may be attributed to the nature of the law practice of each firm.

The overwhelming majority of firms found all LEXIS databases "satisfactory". Most LEXIS library files did not receive a single "unsatisfactory" citation. Of interest, however, is the fact that although some firms reported "never or rarely" using certain databases, they nevertheless rated them as "satisfactory". This result would perhaps indicate that these respondents found a given database satisfactory but did not need to employ it on a regular basis.

A comparison of the data on LEXIS and WESTLAW appears to indicate that LEXIS is used extensively and frequently by nearly all the law firms surveyed, while WESTLAW, with the exception of two databases, is not used as frequently. It would appear therefore, that, at the present time, WESTLAW is being retained more as a secondary or auxiliary system.

Question twelve asked the law librarian to evaluate the impact of the on-line database system on the firm's printed holdings. As shown in Table 2, seventy-one percent of the firms responding indicated that use of an on-line system had not affected the size of their printed holdings. Only fourteen percent found any increase due to the system and five percent cited a decrease. Nine percent of the firms were unable to make any correlation.

In evaluating the rate of acquisition, approximately sixty-six percent of the firms cited no change due to on-line usage. However, twenty-nine percent of the respondents did cite an increase indicating a possibly significant change in law firm acquisition policies.

Finally, while sixty-one percent of the respondents indicated no

Table 2:   Effect of Use of On-Line Legal Database System on Firm's Printed Holdings

	Decreased	Increased	Remained Substantially the Same	Unknown
Size of Printed Holdings	3	8	40	5
Rate of Acquisition of Printed Holdings	1	16	37	2
	Changed Substantially	Changed Somewhat		
Nature and Variety of Printed Holdings	0	20	34	2

Numbers represent individual law firms reporting in each instance.

change in the nature of their printed holdings, thirty-six percent, a possibly significant number, reported some change had occurred due to their on-line system(s). For example, some firms reported that newspapers which could be accessed through NEXIS were not ordered on microfiche. Additionally, some respondents indicated they would now consult the contents of the on-line library files before purchasing printed materials and were thus more judicious in making acquisitions. A few librarians also indicated that if they could obtain the full text of a periodical on-line, they would not purchase the paper copy. Finally, some respondents indicated that they would not purchase duplicate copies of items that could be accessed on-line. Thus, it would appear that the nature of printed holdings is undergoing some change as the use of on-line systems expands.

Question thirteen asked law librarians to evaluate the impact of on-line legal database systems on the space requirements of their firms. Sixty-five percent (35) of the firms reported that their space requirements had remained substantially the same while thirty-three percent (18) of the firms cited an increase. One firm reported that its space requirements had decreased. A number of respondents offered comments relating to this issue. Three reported that their libraries did not require increased space because this need had been anticipated and planned for earlier. Several others pointed to the need for space to accommodate terminals, printers and sound barriers. It must be assumed that the majority of librarians who reported that their space requirements had not increased, had accommodated the hardware and any additional users and staff within existing space.

In question fourteen, respondents were asked to evaluate the impact of on-line use on the duties and perceptions of library staff and on staffing requirements. The results, as set forth in Table 3, indicate that on-line information retrieval has indeed affected library staff. Fifty-three percent of the respondents (28) reported an increase in research responsibilities attributable to the use of on-line system(s), while forty percent (21) reported that their responsibilities had remained substantially the same. The remainder of the respondents indicated that use of these systems freed them to fulfill other tasks and responsibilities. In this connection, a number of librarians commented that additional research responsibilities were welcomed by the professional staff. Indeed, some took exception to the use of the word ''burdened'' in the phrase ''burdened by increased research responsibilities'' as used in the survey.

Table 3: Impact Use of On-Line System Had on Duties and Perceptions of
Library Staff and Staffing Requirements

Professional Library Staff Has Been:	4 freed to fulfill other tasks/responsibilities
	28 burdened by increased research responsibilities
	21 functioning in approximately the same manner as before
Professional Library Staff Has Experienced:	0 a decreased perception of professionalism
	39 an increased perception of professionalism
	17 no difference in their perception
Staffing Requirements Have:	0 decreased
	25 increased
	29 remained substantially the same

The numbers represent individual firms responding in each instance. Not all firms responded to each part of the question.

Fully seventy percent (39) of the librarians reported that professional staff had experienced an increased perception of professionalism as a result of the use of on-line system(s). This finding would appear to be related to the increased research responsibilities reportedly engendered by these systems. Indeed several respondents reported that they were now viewed as in-house experts in LEXIS and WESTLAW.

It is of interest to note that the results of an earlier study contrasted markedly with these findings. In a 1976 study on the impact of on-line systems, M. Myers reported that some LEXIS users were of the opinion that it created more work for librarians and therefore constituted a poor morale factor.[14] This perception appears to be quite different from that of the law librarians sampled in the current survey.

When librarians were asked to assess the impact of on-line information retrieval on staffing requirements, they appeared to be almost evenly divided with forty-six percent of respondents (25) reporting an increase in staffing requirements. Even among the fifty-four percent (29) who viewed staffing requirements as substantially unchanged, there were several responses which cited the need for additional people trained and skilled in on-line searching. Again, in comparing these results with Myers' earlier study, it would appear that significant change has occurred in this area as well. According to the Myers' study, "responses received overwhelmingly indicate that staff size has not changed since the introduction of LEXIS".[15] This study went on to state that "most responses indicated that attorneys being the primary LEXIS users, are quite self-sufficient and do not demand time from the librarians other duties".[16] The current data would indicate that law librarians have now come to share with associates the chief responsibility for on-line searches.

In question fifteen, librarians were asked to evaluate whether on-line legal database systems had affected the services they provided. The results, as set forth in Table 4, indicate certain changes have indeed taken place. In examining the amount of time needed to deliver services, fifty-eight percent of the respondents (32) held that the time needed to complete these tasks had decreased while thirty-one percent of respondents (17) claimed the amount of time had remained the same. Interestingly, eleven percent indicated that the amount of time necessary to complete a search had actually increased. Some librarians attributed this increase in time to the greater thoroughness of research made possible by the new technology while others blamed lack of familiarity with appropriate search techniques.

In examining the thoroughness of reference work, eighty percent

Table 4: Effect of Use of On-Line Legal Database System on Services Provided by Library

	Decreased	Increased	Remained Substantially the Same
Service Time	32	6	17
Reference Work Thoroughness	0	45	11
Range of Services	0	49	7
Research Output	0	46	10

Numbers represent individual law firms reporting in each instance. One firm did not respond to the first section of this question.

of the respondents (45) indicated that thoroughness had increased, while twenty percent (11) indicated it had remained the same. A few respondents reported that thoroughness had increased to such an extent that librarians could now locate decisions with only scraps of information.

Eighty-eight percent of the respondents (49) reported that the range of services they provided had increased with the installation of on-line systems. Some respondents indicated that due to their increased ability to access information more was now required of them in a wider variety of areas.

Finally, eight-two percent of the respondents (46) indicated that research output had increased. This finding was perhaps due in large part to the shortening of time needed to access information.

SUMMARY AND CONCLUSION

A few conclusions may be drawn from the data gathered in this survey. It appears that marked changes have occurred in the decade since on-line legal information retrieval became a reality. These systems have now become greatly accepted and are used extensively by law firms. Every firm which responded to the survey reported that it had at least one database system and many indicated two or more systems at their disposal. The results of this survey have tended to indicate, however, that the LEXIS system is used far more frequently than its competitor, WESTLAW. Perhaps this is due to the fact that WESTLAW is a somewhat newer system and only became full text in recent years.

More important, however, is the fact that on-line systems have affected the role of the law librarian. As cited in an earlier study, the law librarian was initially responsible for few on-line searches. The primary responsibility for this activity lay with attorneys. Today, however, the situation has entirely changed. The law librarian now shares an equal role with associates in carrying out computer searches. In fact, many librarians regard themselves as the in-house experts in on-line information retrieval.

A large percentage of the librarians indicated that due to the legal database systems, they were given added research responsibilities which significantly heightened their perception of their own professionalism. Approximately one-half of the respondents went on to state that increased library staffing was now necessary to keep up with these added research responsibilities. Even those librarians who believed additional staffing was unnecessary, concurred that the need existed for librarians highly skilled in on-line techniques. Additionally, it appears that these computer systems have affected the services provided by law librarians. Most respondents to the survey indicated that the amount of time necessary to deliver services had decreased. At the same time, respondents reported that the thoroughness of the reference services they provided had increased.

There is little doubt that on-line legal database systems have had a significant impact on the role of the law librarian and on the character and function of the law library.

REFERENCES

1. Mindy J. Myers, "The Impact of LEXIS on the Law Firm Library: A Survey." *Law Library Journal,* 71, February 1978, p. 167.

2. Myers. p. 158.

3. Kate Marek, "Automation in the Private Law Library." *Law Library Journal,* 73, Winter 1980, pp. 138-39.

4. James A. Sprowl, "The Latest on Westlaw, Lexis and Dialog." *American Bar Association Journal,* 70, March 1984, p. 88.

5. Marek. p. 139.

6. M.A. Voges, "LEXIS and WESTLAW in Legal Education." *Bulletin of the American Society for Information Science,* 6, No. 3, February 1980, p. 17.

7. Sprowl. p. 90.

8. Sprowl. p. 87.

9. Ibid.

10. Ibid.

11. William W. Wells, "LEXIS and WESTLAW: The Strengths and Weaknesses." *Legal Reference Services Quarterly,* 2, No. 2, Summer 1982, p. 55.

12. Robin, "A Procedure for Securing Returns to Mail Questionnaires." *Soc. and Soc. Research,* 50, 1965, p. 24.

13. Myers. p. 161.

14. Myers. p. 164.

15. Myers. p. 161.

16. Myers. p. 162.

BIBLIOGRAPHY

Andrews, D., "Legal Information Retrieval—have they got it right." *American Bar Association Journal,* 69, pp. 1865-7, December 1983.

Bull, Gillian, "Technical Developments in Legal Information Retrieval." *Law Librarian,* 11, No. 2, p. 36, August 1980.

Childress, S.A., "Warning Label for LEXIS: The Hazards of Computer-Assisted Research to the Legal Profession." *Lincoln Law Review,* 13, pp. 91-9, 1982.

Day, Elizabeth, "Application of Computers in the Legal Profession: A Selected Bibliography." *Legal Reference Services Quarterly,* 2, No. 3, p. 101, Fall 1982.

Galvin, F.J., "Computer-aided research for the law firm." *Res Gestae,* 27, pp. 78-82, August 1983.

Green, Lynn, "Computers Gain Prominence as Tools for Libraries in Private Law Firms." *The National Law Journal,* p. 22, July 9, 1979.

Harrowes, D., "Computer Assisted Legal Information Retrieval." *New Law Journal,* 130, pp. 575-7, July 3, 1980.

Herrity, C. and E. McGrath, "Use of Computer Technology by Major Boston Law Firms." *Massachusetts Law Review,* 67, pp. 194-9, Winter 1982.

Jessup, Libby F., "The Possibilities of Information and Dissemination in Private Law Libraries." *Law Library Journal,* 59, pp. 30-36, 1966.

Kent, Allen, "The Online Revolution in Libraries 1969- ." *American Libraries,* 10, pp. 339-342, 1979.

Kouo, Lily, "A Survey to Investigate the Feasibility of On-Line Legal Research at the New York State Department of Law's Six Regional Offices." State University of New York at Albany, School of Library and Information Science, LIB 680 paper, Spring 1983.

Lockwood, B.B., "Electric Shock: The Impact of Computer Technology on the Practice of Law." *Dalhousie Law Journal,* 7, pp. 743-61, October 1983.

Marek, Kate, "Automation in the Private Law Library." *Law Library Journal,* 73, pp. 134-142, Winter 1980.

Menanteaux, A. Robert, "A User's Comparison of WESTLAW and LEXIS." *Legal Reference Services Quarterly,* 2, No. 2, pp. 19-23, Summer 1982.

Menanteaux, A. Robert and Mary M. Schmidtke, "LEXIS and WESTLAW: A Table of Equivalent Operators." *Legal Reference Services Quarterly,* 2, No. 2, pp. 25-31, Summer 1982.

Munroe, Robert, "LEXIS vs. WESTLAW: An Analysis of Automated Education." *Law Library Journal,* 71, pp. 471-76, May 1978.

Myers, Mindy J., "The Impact of LEXIS on the Law Firm Library: A Survey." *Law Library Journal,* 71, pp. 158-169, February 1978.

"Online Information Retrieval for the Legal Profession." *Law Library Journal,* 70, pp. 532-49, November 1977.

Robin, "A Procedure for Securing Returns to Mail Questionnaires." *Soc. and Soc. Research,* 50, p. 24, 1965.

Rubin, S., "LEXIS has Made Computer Assisted Legal Research in the United States a Practical Reality." *Law and Computer Technology,* 7, p. 34, 1974.

Soma, J.T. and A.R. Stern, "A Survey of Computer Information for Lawyers—LEXIS, JURIS, WESTLAW and FLITE." *Rutgers Computer and Technology Law Journal,* 9, pp. 295-314, 1983.

Sprowl, James A., "Computer-Assisted Legal Research: WESTLAW and LEXIS." *American Bar Association Journal,* 62, pp. 320-3, March 1976.

Sprowl, James A., "New Age of Computers in the Law Office." *Illinois Bar Journal,* 71, pp. 478-85, April 1983.

Sprowl, James A., "The Latest on Westlaw, Lexis and Dialog." *American Bar Association Journal,* 70, pp. 85-90, March 1984.

Voges, M.A., "LEXIS and WESTLAW in Legal Education." *Bulletin of the American Society for Information Science,* 6, No. 3, p. 17, February 1980.

Wells, William W., "LEXIS and WESTLAW: The Strengths and Weaknesses," *Legal Reference Services Quarterly,* 2, No. 2, pp. 51-57, Summer 1982.

Quality Assurance in Computer Searching

Diane L. Glunz

Computer bibliographic searching has become a prominent feature of most libraries today. Portable terminals, VDU's (video display units), high speed printers and microcomputers represent an established and important access point for our information consuming society. To help satisfy this craving, databases and databanks with which the hardware interfaces have proliferated to an all time high. Yet, ease of access to the great variety databases does not truly alleviate the information access problems which have plagued individuals in most every field. Unfortunately, the mere availability of database information does not ensure the quality of the ultimate product.

Assurance of quality is dependent on the human factor—the search analyst. From the beginning of the search process to its conclusion, the search analyst provides the key to quality. And with the increased sophistication of many of our users, especially those having their own microcomputers, the maintenance of excellence is a constant concern.

Evaluation of any sort must have a purpose—not be a haphazard affair. In the appraisal of computer search services we should consider the purpose to examine the effectiveness and efficiency of the process in order to identify deficiencies and strengths. The examination should be designed to reveal the pluses and minuses of the system as well as the personnel involved.

GOALS AND OBJECTIVES

In its truest form, an evaluation is designed to compare the goals and ideals of the search process with the reality of service. The goal of most search service programs could be stated as follows: the user

The author is Reference Librarian, Norris Medical Library, University of Southern California, Los Angeles, CA 90033.

277

of the service is provided with an accurate and adequate information product based on the specific requirement supplied by the user. Factors of time and cost are usually included into the considerations of review. The most significant error encountered in search services is that these goals and objectives are left unstated. Generally, these goals are usually implied and may even be well understood by all involved in the process. It is good practice, however, to state any goals and all objectives in a statement of service.

The basic goal of user satisfaction is unquestionably the ultimate goal to which all search analysts aspire. To attain this goal, objectives defining the measureable aspects of the goal(s) should be put into place. Some objectives could be stated concerning the accuracy of the information retrieved, a sufficient quantity of items located, a suitable turn around time for the product and the costs involved.

Goals and objectives form one of the two basic components necessary to an evaluation. The other component is forms and records. This documentation is the mainstay of any evaluative function. Forms usually pervade all aspects of the process, from the initial search request to the delivery of the search results. The initial request form must be so designed as to guide the requestor to provide adequate information and also to provide a record of information about the overall search process. As the example of the MEDLINE request in Figure 1 illustrates, there are also items which can later be used for an evaluation of the services as it impacts the users and potential users as a total community. A worksheet form for the recording of search process information is also helpful.

Other aspects of documentation necessary to the operation of search services have been detailed by Fenichel.[1] These items can be kept by support staff in a manual format or in a microcomputer system. If a microcomputer is used to access the databases, it might be useful to develop a program to automatically record information about searching during the logon or logoff process.

With goals and objectives defined, the search process can operate with the prospect of judging success. Reliable documentation expressed by specific forms and clear record keeping allows for a smooth evaluation.

THE SEARCH PROCESS

For the purpose of this discussion, the computer based search process will be defined to incorporate all aspects involved in the request of information from a computerized database—from the initia-

FIGURE 1

MEDLINE (MEDLARS ONLINE) DATE: request _____
REQUEST FORM payment _____

PLEASE CHECK ONE OR MORE:

REFERENCE OFFICE
NORRIS MEDICAL LIBRARY
USC HEALTH SCIENCES CAMPUS
2025 Zonal Avenue
Los Angeles, California 90033
Tel: (213) 224-7234

___ MEDLINE (1982-present)
___ 1980-81
___ 1977-79
___ 1975-76
___ 1971-74
___ 1966-70

92°8

___ Monthly Current Alerting Service

___ RUSH PROCESSING OF BACKFILES
(Additional Fees Required)

1. Individual Who Will Actually Use This Bibliography First Middle Last Name	TELEPHONE:
2. Department 3. Institution	IN A HURRY Pick up a few recent refs? ___
4. Street Address and/or Bldg., Rm. No. 5. City, State, Zip Code	COMPLETE RESULTS ___ Pick up ___ Mail

6. Please Check One:

USC School of Medicine
___faculty (A)
___med student (-)
___grad student/post doc/fellow (B)
___other health occupations (C)
___admin/clerical/other staff (M)

USC School of Pharmacy
___faculty (AP)
___pharmacy student (PS)
___grad student (BP)
___other health occupations (CP)
___admin/clerical/other staff (MP)

LAC/USC Medical Center
___USC faculty (AU)
___Intern/resident/fellow (DU)
___other health occupations (CU)
___admin/clerical/other staff (MU)
___student (BU)

Other USC Affiliated Institution
(specify): _____
___USC faculty (A_)
___intern/resident/fellow (D_)
___other health occupations (C_)
___admin/clerical/other staff (M_)
___student (B_)

USC Main Campus
___faculty (AN)
___grad & undergrad (BN)
___other (CN)

Courtesy
___Community Hospital
    Network (CHN)
___health professional (KP)
___business & industry (KQ)
___UCLA/Cal Tech faculty (KA)
___UCLA/Cal Tech grad
    student (KB)
___other (KT)

7. INFORMATION REQUIREMENTS: Describe your search request in narrative form. Be specific:
define terms that may have special meaning, and describe any aspects not to be included.

Purpose of search:

8. KNOWN RELEVANT PAPERS: Please list articles published in the LAST THREE YEARS that
are relevant to your request.

a.

b.

c.

9. SEARCH REQUIREMENTS:

Broad or Narrow: Please check one of the boxes below to indicate the type of search
you would prefer:

☐ Broad Search: retrieves as many articles as possible, but may include many
       irrelevant ones.

☐ Narrow Search: retrieves relevant articles with very few irrelevant ones.

Number of Citations Published: Please estimate the number of relevant articles published
within the last three years:

☐ 0 ☐ 1-9 ☐ 10-25 ☐ 26-50 ☐ 51-100 ☐ 101-200 ☐ 201-300 ☐ over 300

Maximum Number of Citations Desired: ____

FIGURE 1 continued

10. <u>SEARCH LIMITATIONS</u>: Please check all boxes that are appropriate to the scope of your request.

☐ Human Subjects ☐ Male ☐ Female ☐ In Vitro Studies

☐ Animal Experiments: If only certain animals or animal groups are of interest, please list these:

<u>Geographic Restrictions</u>: If only certain regions are of interest, please list these:

Language Restrictions:

☐ English only ☐ English or foreign language with English summary

☐ All languages ☐ Certain languages only (please specify): _____

Age Groups: If only certain age groups are of interest, please indicate:

___ to 1 month ___ 2-5 years ___ 13-18 years ___ 45-64 years
___ 1-23 months ___ 6-12 years ___ 19-44 years ___ 65- years

11. <u>PRINT FORMAT</u>: Please check desired print format (cost varies):

___ cits only ___ cits with MeSH ___ cits with abstracts ___ cits with abstracts and/or MeSH

12.

☐ sorting by_____

tion of the search with a specific request to the delivery of the final information product to the requestor. The search process with respect to bibliographic databases will be emphasized.

This discussion will focus on the "delegated" search as described by Lancaster.[4] The delegated search is one in which the individual requiring the information delegates or transfers the responsibility for locating the information to an intermediary. This intermediary may be a librarian, a search analyst or possibly some other information specialist.

The end result of a computer bibliographic search request is a package of information covering the topic(s) which have been specified by the requestor. The process involved in reaching this goal—herein designated as the search process—includes several elements which have a significant impact on the quality of the end result. there are four general sections included in the process: a) submission of the search request, b) the search interview, c) interpretation and formulation of the search and d) running the search. These area facets are based on the concepts discussed by Fenichel.[1]

Beginnings

This initiation of the search process begins with the submission of a request for information. The requestor may already have decided that a computer search is a preferred approach for reasons of topic complexity or simply for the ease. Or an individual may arrive needing assistance with an inquiry which ultimately would best be handled by a computer bibliographic search. Despite the form of the presentation, the requestor is the initiator of the process. And as such it can serve as an indicator of the requestor's perceptions of computer retrieved information and the process involved in obtaining that information.

The Search Interview

Following the submission of a computer search request, an interview of the requestor takes place. Termed the search interview, it can take place either on-site (in person) or off-site (transacted via the telephone or a remote computer terminal). The interview can occur when the initial request is submitted, but it is not uncommon for a delegated search to be submitted at one point and the interview to take place at a later point in time. This situation occurs more frequently in an institution with high search volume or where a searcher may not be available full time.

The purpose of the interview is to clarify the requirements of the information request. This being a pivotal point in the searching process, much interest has been taken in it. The topic has generated discussions of the psychological and informational aspects, body language and more. Yet, the primary goal of the interview remains that the request is critically assessed for the true nature of the information needed. The interview time also furnishes the opportunity to guide the requestor to the proper expectations of what a search will provide. Some of the analysis utilize the searcher's own knowledge and experience of the databases or subject matter. In many cases it is the searcher's background which will alert him/her to a potential problem in the search request.

Searchers also play a role in providing counsel on cost effectiveness and the appropriateness of accessing a computer database. There are situations where a computer search may not be indicated to satisfy the request. A search for information on the adverse effects of beta-carotene in the MEDLINE system could be just as easily accomplished by a manual search in the printed counterpart INDEX MEDICUS. Under the heading of Carotene/adverse effects you would find pertinent articles just as those retrieved in a computer search. The area of suitability of computer searches is of particular concern when the requestor is responsible for the costs incurred in searching.

Interpretation of the Search

The search interview is followed by the interpretation of the request. At this point the information requirements of the search are analyzed and an appropriate search strategy is developed. This process can take different forms in different information settings. Basically, the search analyst will assess the type and depth of the required bibliography and then prepare a search strategy to accomplish the search. The basic components of the search analysis are based on tenents from the discussion by Glunz and Wakiji.[2]

With the written requirements of a search and input from a search interview, the mechanism of translating the request into the optimum search strategy is the objective. This part of the process calls on the analytical abilities of the searcher. The depth and time involved at this point will vary greatly from search to search, and for that matter, from institution to institution.

This process can take different forms in varying instances. In a clinical medical setting, the analysis and formulation may be a relatively short process to produce a bibliography containing a few recent articles relating to the care of a patient. While a research request will require more time and analysis to compile a comprehensive bibliography which contains all related aspects of the topic requested.

The topical vocabulary chosen by the searcher in some databases relies entirely on a controlled vocabulary list. In other systems it is based on a list of free-text terms gathered on the subject. The optimum search strategy could be a combination of these two. The choice of which approach to use will be decided based on the topic and database being accessed. Indexing policies employed by the producer of the database and the manifestation of these policies in the vendor systems also impact this phase of the process. The capabilities and limitations of the individual vendor systems likewise will reflect on the formulation of the search.

Running the Search

The next aspect is the actual running of the computer search. There are several factors which can influence the search process in this area. Running the search may be a relatively simple case of the input of selected terms and retrieval of the desired items, or it may be a more complex interaction of the searcher and database, sometimes with the searcher making instant adjustments to the original formulation if it proved unsuccessful. The searchers capabilities in running the search is a function of the searcher's ability to interact with the vendor system and manipulating the specific database. Another factor of varying influence is the presence or absence of the requestor when the search is being performed. This has been the subject of considerable debate. The requestor being present may provide useful information for refining the search, especially for a particularly abstruse topic. Conversely, the individual may simply be a distraction and actually impair the searcher in preparing a quality information end-product.

Completion

The completion of the search process occurs with the delivery of the search results. The end product may consist of a computer generated bibliography printed online or the search may be delivered at a later point if the results were requested in an offline format. In some vendor systems, such as the National Library of Medicine's MEDLARS and SDC's ORBIT, there exist several options for the delivery for an offline printout, including having it sent directly to the requestor's address. This convenience for the requestor detaches the search analyst from the final aspect of the search process.

Evaluation of the Process

Each of the four sections just discussed contain checkpoints for assessing the searching process. These checkpoints can serve as the basis for evaluating the quality and success of the searching process in any institution. A closer look at each aspect checkpoints reveals the means to conduct an effective evaluation.

Evaluation of the checkpoints in the search process can be done on the individual level or for the assessment of a group or institution. The assessment may be designed as a one time review or it can be set up as an on-going process. Each institution must decide the reason for the evaluation (goals and objectives) and then determine what style of evaluation is appropriate. A review done at regular intervals provides a clear picture of the process with the searchers involved receiving feedback in a timely fashion.

Consider also whether these principles will be applied to a group or large body of information or whether to apply some aspects to evaluating the individual approach to the search process. Some aspects of the search process can be judged as strictly correct or incorrect. Yet there are many items which must be considered in sliding scale terms based on the requirements of the institution.

Perception of Searching

A computer bibliographic search utilizes current information technology to address the requestor's inquiry. The initiation of a search therefore becomes an interplay of the requestor's conceptual understanding of computer searching and their ability to describe their needs. These constitute the first two checkpoints—the first impacting the initiation process; the second influencing both the initiation and search interview fields.

The requestor holds the key to an important facet of this area. Whatever perceptions the individual holds about computer searching—the type of information available for the search, the speed and/or accuracy of the retrieval—they will all shade the request for information and the remainder of the search process. This may become apparent as soon as the search is submitted. However, it may not become known until late in the search process.

A related aspect of requestor perceptions deals with whether searches are being requested at all. To get an adequate view of users of the service, an analysis of the user community would pinpoint groups underutilizing services. Direction for promotion programs to maximize computer search use is brought out in this type of analysis.

The ability of the requestor to describe their needs in information potentially impacts in several areas in the search process. Consistently inadequately prepared request forms indicates either a lack of understanding for the subject matter and/or the information technology or the requestor was in too much of a hurry. A review of search request forms that shows this pattern should prompt a look into the abilities of the user population and the possibilities for educational programs on the institutions' computer search services. Sometimes the best instruction is on an individual level at the initiation of the search.

Educational programs, such as the ones employed at the Norris Medical Library, approach this education function based on which user groups such as researchers, graduate students or support personnel. Many entering students receive an introduction to computerized searching as part of their regular instruction. Surveys of a group prior to instruction can access the type and scope of instruction needed.

Question Negotiation

On first glance a request may seem legitimate, such as the request submitted with the terms "Immunology and Cancer". This is, however, a case where a search interview would be critical. The literature dealing with cancer and any aspect of immunology is voluminous. The alert searcher can, through the interview, find the true focus of interest. In this request it turned out to be the development of immunodeficiency symptoms in lung cancer patients.

At the heart of the search interview is a question negotiation process which is based on interactive communication between the search analyst and the requestor. Question negotiation relies on the skills of both the requestor and the searcher to bring out the exact nature of the request. As defined by Taylor,[6] question negotiation consists of five "filters":

a. determination of subject
b. objectives and motivation
c. personal characteristics of inquirer
d. relationship of inquiry to the files
e. anticipated or acceptable answers

A word to clarify each filter. The first is straightforward; What are the limits of the inquiry? The second also is easily understood; Why does the requestor need the information? The third item relates to the requestor's subject background and level of experience with information services. With the search analyst as the intermediary, s/he is able to match the question to the appropriate file or database. The format in which the information is required or expected is the final filter in the definition of the question.

In a search interview, these "filters" are closely linked and are often covered simultaneously. Within these are found the clues to a successful search interview. A search analyst may already be using the "filters", having developed the characteristics through experience. A conscious consideration of each will aid in the definition of the interview. To assist in correcting deficiencies identified during a review, role playing using scenarios developed to elucidate each filter will serve to enhance the abilities of the searcher's techniques.

Aspects of question negotiation and other influencing factors are noted in a review of the MEDLARS search interview by Kolner.[3] This discussion includes an excellent checklist for analysis of the interview. Each of the steps illustrates specific facets of the question negotiation process. This checklist is highly recommended for review as is the step by step guide prepared by Somerville.[5] The study reviews the total search interaction from the initiation of the search through the interview. The final listing of do's and don't further elucidates the communication aspects of question negotiation. Both these lists can prove valuable in developing criteria to fit a specific setting.

FORMULATION REVIEW

To increase and maintain the quality of the content of computerized bibliographic searches, a system of regular review is advisable. Glunz and Wakiji[2] discuss the use of a regular weekly meeting to evaluate the search formulation to maximize the quality of the computer searching done at their institution.

On a rotating basis, searches which have been completed are reviewed by different search analysts and evaluated on the basis of specific criteria. These being 1) the correct interpretation and use of stated information requirements, 2) the topical vocabulary, 3) indexing policies, and 4) vendor system mechanics. The priority of this peer evaluation is to sharpen the searching techniques of all involved.

This aspect of the evaluation of the search process is most dependent on the written record of the computer search. The computer search request form establishes the topics to be searched. A computer search worksheet which is designed to contain the proper information to identify and process the search allows an analysis of the progression of the search. On a worksheet, such as the example in

Figure 2, the concepts of the request are grouped including the vocabulary choices to be used.

A review of all the factors involved in the formulation and running of a search may be seen as an inordinate consumer of time. To adequately inspect a number of searches and consider aspects of terminology, indexing specifications, the vendor system options and the actual execution of the strategy at the terminal does require a time investment. The use of this style of review not only enhances the capabilities of the search analysts; it also allows for correction of errors, possibly before the requestor receives the search.

Peer evaluation of searches uses one of the best resources available to search analysts—that of other analysts. In this way, the abilities and experience of others can benefit the pool of searchers. This technique of evaluation is not isolated to the larger institutions with multiple search analysts. Smaller institutions and individuals can organize this search evaluation to their mutual benefit. The diversity of information settings can indicate the various approaches to setting up these meetings. Telephone conferencing, regular mail, electronic mail, online user groups and even remote computer interaction are just a few of the possibilities.

FIGURE 2

REQUESTER _____

TITLE _____

TIME PERIOD COVERED _____

DATE(S) PROCESSED: _____ SEARCH ANALYST: _____ COMPUTER: _____

TIME: Formulation _____ Terminal _____ Edit _____ Rush Processing _____

	Med.	80	77	75	71	66		
ONLINE	___	___	___	___	___	___	Mailed ___	Phoned ___
OFFLINE	___	___	___	___	___	___	Mailed ___	Phoned ___

MAILED DIRECT ____   MAILED HERE ____   DATE REC'D _____

*** ____ CHECK IF RERUN (see over)   rev. 12/83

DATE RERUN: _____ SEARCH ANALYST: _____ COMPUTER: _____

TIME: Reformulation _____ Terminal _____ Edit _____ Rush Processing _____

	Med.	80	77	75	71	66		
ONLINE	___	___	___	___	___	___	Mailed ___	Phoned ___
OFFLINE	___	___	___	___	___	___	Mailed ___	Phoned ___

MAILED DIRECT _____   MAILED HERE _____   DATE REC'D _____

The Follow-up

In information retrieval there are two defined types of evaluation: 1) retrieval effectiveness and 2) relevance. These factors are the basis of how the user will evaluate his bibliography. The retrieval effectiveness is usually determined in terms of precision . . . the correct articles retrieved with no irrelevance, or recall . . . the total body of literature available to be accessed. These concepts as presented by Lancaster[4] can be utilized by the search analyst to approximate the quality of the results. In the final assessment, it is the requestor's specifications which determine the products overall usefulness.

To put the requestor's assessments to work, an evaluation form should be available for possible comments. Not only does this provide relatively immediate feedback on effectiveness and relevance for the search analyst, the information on these forms can be instrumental in assessing if the objectives of the service are being accomplished. An evaluation form can include aspects of user satisfaction and also background on the perceptions of the requestor about the service. Figure 3 is an example which could serve as an example for the form. Of course, the form should include a means to identify the search and searcher and also allow for easy return. Even the most aggressive attempts to get requestor to return evaluation forms will probably be under 50%, so they cannot provide an ultimate determination on whether the individual search or the service as a whole is accomplishing its purpose. It is merely one factor to assess the quality of the search process.

Statistics in Evaluation

Statistics are a valuable tool in any type of evaluation—search services are no exception. The nature of computer searching actually lends itself to a form of quantitative analysis. The information which results from a numeric assessment of the service will reflect on a particular element within the process, while other data will be an indicator of the sum total of the process or service. Table 1 lists various numeric items which can be considered.

These items are best compiled monthly. The data can then be evaluated for trends, such as seasonal fluctuations in requests. Annual reports are dependent on this type of information. As the quantitative compilations continue, larger trends and variations from year to year are easily noted.

A check of statistics will indicate who is and who is not requesting the computer services. This can form the basis of the user population survey. Formal or otherwise, an analysis of the user community will supply important data which when combined with the use statistics will disclose the nature of computer search users and the potential users. Based on this data, plans can be formulated for a promotional program to inform about computer literature services.

The Search Environment

The environment of the information setting will impact the quality of the end product and should therefore be reviewed for optimization. Under the broad concept of search environment are topics like

FIGURE 3

Reference Section
Norris Medical Library

COMPUTER SEARCH EVALUATION

NAME: _____   DATE: _____

SEARCH TITLE: _____

DATABASE: _____   TIME PERIOD COVERED: _____

Dear Patron:

☐ Your search is complete.

☐ Your search is incomplete. Some references are attached. The balance will be mailed to you direct from the computer center and should arrive in about one week.

AFTER YOU HAVE REVIEWED YOUR COMPLETED SEARCH, please take a few moments to answer the following questions concerning your printout. Your feedback is needed to help us monitor the effectiveness of your search. This pre-addressed form may be returned by campus mail. Thank you.

1. Was the information and assistance you received when submitting the search adequate? Yes _____   No _____   If NO please explain:

2. Please check the percentage of references which were useful:

   0-20% ____   20-40% ____   40-60% ____   60-80% ____   80-100% ____

3. In summary, how well did this search meet your information needs?

Excellent		Satisfactory		Poor
1	2	3	4	5

4. Would you like information concerning monthly updates on your topic(s)?

              Yes _____   No _____

5. Please feel free to call _____ at 224-7234 to discuss the search strategy used.

6. Additional comments or suggestions:

FIGURE 3 continued

Staple Here

Campus Mail

or

Stamp

Reference Section
Norris Medical Library
USC Health Sciences Campus
2025 Zonal Avenue
Los Angeles, California 90033

_____

Fold on Line

_____

Fold on Line

ambiance of the search interview, the surroundings of the terminals, the condition of the searching equipment, and the accessibility of searching aids.

The interview is unmistakingly impacted by the surroundings during the interview. A hurried and noisy background is only a distraction for the searcher and the requestor. A relatively quiet atmosphere will maximize the interaction. Similarly, a subdued area is beneficial for the running of the search formulation. The concentration of the search analyst is therefore less impaired, which is especially useful if a quick online reformulation of a search is necessary.

A critical look at the search equipment and searching aids will assist to optimize the operation of the search process. Properly functioning equipment reduces frustration levels. The availability of the various thesauri, manuals, newsletters and updates assist in both the formulation of searches and the peer evaluation as well.

A Word About Databanks

A computer bibliographic search is not the sole format in which information is available from a terminal. Databanks make up another part of the information available in a computer readable format. A databank is a computerized file which contains specific points of information, much like a handbooks online. Databanks are a common part of the scientific fields such as chemistry, engineering and biology. Examples of these are files containing spectral properties of elements or toxicity information of environmental compounds of the DNA sequences of genomes.

The search process is streamlined in this style of search. The search interview becomes the most critical factor in the whole process. Determining the particular compound under study and the verification of the data point(s) required are the items on which the search strategy rests. A clear picture of this will dictate databank choice, vendor choice and form of output necessary to the requestor.

```
   TABLE 1  STATISTICAL ELEMENTS

Number of searches
Turn around time for the search
Which database(s) used
Cost per search by database
Type of search (research, ready reference, etc.)
Number of references retrieved by type of search
Time involved to complete search:
     1. pre-search - interview, formulation
     2. terminal time to run search
     3. follow-up

Also consider:

How search was submitted (in-person or by phone)
Support staff time requirments
Additional institutional costs
     1. supplies
     2. search aids, thesauri, etc.
     3. searcher training
```

The measure of quality for a search of these systems is the speedy retrieval of the correct data the requestor needs. Cost effectiveness is thus assured in this manner.

CONCLUSION

From the submission of the request to the follow-up questionnaire, the search process is a series of complex and intertwined elements. Not unlike the game of chess, the elements build successively the previous ones. An alteration in one factor will influence the rest of the process. Evaluation serves to consider and optimize each factor in the progression to maximize the quality of the final product.

For computer information services, evaluation is not simply a technical activity. It is in reality a form of study to aid in program management. Close examination of the multi-faceted operation including all the levels, individual and group, moves the institution to higher quality. On the individual level, the capabilities of the search analyst are enhanced and for the totality of the search service, definition of goals and objectives is facilitated.

Evaluation not only identifies deficiencies for correction, it also serves as a challenge the abilities the search analysts. The human factor—the search analyst—is thereby better prepared to serve the intelligence-seeking public as an effective intermediary to the great quantity of information available.

BIBLIOGRAPHY

1. Fenichel, Carol H. and Thomas H. Hogan. *Online Searching: A Primer.* New Jersey: Learned Information. 1980.

2. Glunz, Diane and Eileen Wakiji, Maximizing search Quality Through a Program of Peer Review. *Online,* 1983 September, 7(5):100-110.

3. Kolner, Stuart J. Improving the MEDLARS Search Interview: A Checklist Approach *Bulletin of the Medical Library Association,* 1981 January; 69(1):26-33.

4. Lancaster, F.W. *The Measurement and Evaluation of Library Services.* Washington: Information Resources Press. 1977.

5. Somerville, Arlene N. The Pre-Search Interview: A Step by Step Guide, *Database,* 1982 February; 5(1):32-38.

6. Taylor, Robert S. Question-Negotiation and Information Seeking in Libraries. *College and Research Libraries,* 1968 May; 29(3):179-194.

One in a Hundred:
Choosing the Year's
Outstanding Reference Sources

K. M. Rosswurm

Reference sources are tools and reference librarians are crafts-men. As any good craftsman knows, each task requires its own im-plement. But with so many tools at hand, which one is the right one for the job?

Helping librarians select the correct tool is one of the objectives of the ALA/RASD Reference Sources Committee. Through its an-nual list of notable sources and the quadrennial *Reference Sources for Small and Medium-sized Libraries,* the committee tries to call the attention of librarians to the best reference tools available.

The first annual list, "Reference Books of 1958—a Selection," was published in the March 1, 1959 issue of *Library Journal.*[1] Each of the five years previous to that Louis Shores had selected a group of notable reference books for *LJ.* When the work became too much for one person, an RASD committee was formed for the purpose and continues to this day. The yearly lists appeared in *Library Jour-nal* for twenty-five years. This year, and in the future, however, "Outstanding Reference Sources" will be published in the May issue of *American Libraries.* In the past quarter century over 200 librarians have served on the Reference Sources Committee (RSC) and have named 1,739 Outstanding Reference Sources.[2]

The other duty of the RSC is less frequent, but just as important and time consuming. Since 1981 the committee has assumed the responsibility of compiling *Reference Sources for Small and Medium-Sized Libraries.* The fourth edition, edited by Fr. Jovian P. Lang and Deborah C. Masters, will be available from the American

---

The author is Head of Adult Services at the Mt. Vernon (NY) Public Library; and has served on the RASD Reference Sources Committee since 1980, from 1982-83 as Chair.

293

Library Association in May, 1984. By evaluating thousands of reference sources each year, and publishing its results, the committee attempts to meet its ultimate objective—giving guidance to reference collection development librarians.

In twenty-five years there have been some changes in the committee's objectives and procedures, but those changes have been gradual and unsubstantial. The RSC's audience has remained the same—small and medium-sized public and college libraries. This orientation circumscribes the committee's work, making the list both general and specific at the same time. We serve general public and academic libraries, but more specifically small and medium-sized libraries. This is not to say that high school or university libraries will not find the selections useful, it simply means that we do exclude many worthwhile sources because they are not appropriate for our audience.

While many excellent works are excluded from the list because they are too specialized, a good many other sources fall outside the purview of the committee for different reasons. The RSC "Policy and Procedure Manual" clearly states that "annuals, yearbooks, new printings of encyclopedias, etc. will be omitted unless the first issues appear during the year, or unless they have truly important revisions or changes in editorial and publication policy."[3] Also excluded are pamphlets, works of purely local scope, foreign publications, and "how to" materials. Spin-offs from other publications are considered only if they are of unique value and convenience.

EXCLUSIONS

While a large number of sources are excluded because of their *content,* no sources are excluded because of their *format.* Prior to 1980 the committee selected only books. Since then the committee has given equal consideration to all forms of reference information. The criteria for the inclusion of microforms and databases, however, differs from those of books. Microforms must be "uniquely available in nonprint format. . .or. . .shall in some way provide access to or present the information in a form unavailable in print."[4] Databases must be publicly available on a " 'per use' basis, i.e., costs for connect time used and printout charges for amount used only. There should be no substantial start-up costs that would preclude use by a small to medium-sized library."[5] The fact that the list is geared to smaller libraries and that we give priority to print formats, has precluded the inclusion of a large number of nonbook sources.[6] The committee eagerly examines all types of reference sources, however, and will no doubt select more databases and microforms in the future.

Even with these exceptions and qualifications, there are literally thousands of sources for the committee to evaluate each year. And because the committee must critique so many different subjects in such a wide range of formats, its membership must be both large and diverse. Fully staffed the RSC consists of eight members and a chair, ideally all front-line reference librarians from different sections of the country, equally divided between small and medium-sized public and college libraries, having some subject expertise as well as general experience, and having access to extensive reference holdings. The ideal is not often met, but an effort is made. Working on the RSC is literally a year round, part-time job, requiring a great deal of diligence and endurance.

The Dewey decimal centuries (000s, 100s, 200s, etc.) are divided among the committee members, with each person having a major area of responsibility, as well as a minor area. Throughout the year each member carefully monitors her major area and divides all of the sources into those that are recommended for the annual list, those not recommended, and those that she is not able to examine. All of these lists are exchanged twice during the year, prior to the RSC meeting at Midwinter.[7] Each person also keeps an eye out for additional sources that should be considered for the next edition of *Reference Sources for Small and Medium-sized Libraries.*

REJECTIONS

While most of the sources on the "not recommended" list have been examined personally, some are rejected on the basis of one or more negative reviews. Any source that is named to the annual list, however, must be examined by at least two committee members. In actuality, almost all of the sources that are named outstanding are evaluated by the majority of the committee.

With the initial examination of the sources and their assignment to categories, the first phase of the committee's work is completed. The second facet begins at the Midwinter meeting. At Midwinter it is the responsibility of each member to convince the remainder of the committee that a particular source is truly outstanding and deserves to be named to the list. In their presentations some of the members are demonstrative and effusive, others low-keyed and to the point. They are all objective, however, and clearly present the merits, or demerits, of each source. They attempt to persuade the committee that a particular source is well crafted, but at the same time freely point out whatever limitations it may have. There is a great deal of discussion, as each member voices her opinion or asks pertinent questions. While some personal battles may be won or lost, each member is aware that the committee's objective is the best possible list. A majority vote determines whether a work is included on the list or not.

In evaluating these sources the committee uses the critical skills and methods of any good reference librarian. Mudge's outline of "How to Study Reference Books" offers basic guidance; specific reviews offer additional evaluations.[8] But what the committee is really looking for are those things that make a work *more* than just adequate, things that make it stand out.

GUIDELINES

First of all, will it be used? Is it appropriate for the collection of a medium-sized library? The committee tries not to be swayed by publishing pyrotechnics and superficial gloss. Because we are working reference librarians we tend to focus on the practicality of each source. Many works are rejected immediately because, although they appear to be excellent, the committee feels that they will be of little use in a medium-sized library. This is obviously not an easy decision to make. What exactly is a medium-sized library? And what about the difference between public and college libraries? As many of the committee members work, or have worked, in what they consider small or medium-sized libraries, their experience tells them what types of sources are useful in that size library. There are obvious, and many, disagreements on this issue, however. There is simply no archetypical medium-sized library to which all of the RSC members can refer. The best we can do is educate one another on the kind of work we do and the types of sources we use.

At the same time, personal experience is of no help in reconciling the major differences between public and college library reference work. This difference is most apparent in the use of bibliographies. Generally, public libraries have little use for bibliographies—even the best of them. Small and medium-sized public libraries serve elementary and secondary students and out-of-school adults. These people do not want, or in many cases need, a large list of items published on a given subject. They want something recent and they want it *now*. They want to leave the library with something. In almost all cases the card catalog and a periodical index will suffice. In medium-sized public libraries bibliographies sit and offend those allergic to dust.

In college libraries, however, this is not the case. Because of the type of patron and the level of research, bibliographies are heavily used reference works. The best of them offer guidance and save the patron's time. Taking all of this into consideration, and because the list is intended for use by both public and college libraries, the committee makes compromises. While we consider all of the sources on the list outstanding, some of them are clearly intended for use in public libraries, others for use in their academic counterparts.

THREE CATEGORIES

During the committee's deliberations the sources tend to fall into three categories of very uneven proportions: most of the sources are obviously not notable, a much smaller group are borderline, and a miniscule number of them really shine. The latter group are obvious to any clear thinking librarian, especially librarians who have waded through hundreds of sources just to find that one gem. Not only do these works treat important and useful subjects, but they are easy to use (by librarians and laypeople alike), authoritative, accurate, up-to-date, objective, and clearly state their scope and limitations. The outstanding source must be this and more. It must be the kind of work that a small library will acquire if it only wants one or two sources on the subject. It must have lasting value. It must compare favorably with the other sources already on the list. It must be the kind of work that we, as professional reference librarians, admire. And it must have the amenities and demonstrate the attention to detail that cause it to be not merely good, but excellent. If the RSC is positive on all of these counts, the work is named an Outstanding Reference Source.

Clearly, with nine different librarians, the committee will not be of one mind, and just as clearly, the committee's selections are not perfect. If the RSC tends to err, it is when its initial excitement over a source on a timely subject overrides its usually acute critical sense or when a particularly vociferous or persuasive member wears down the rest of the committee. Once in a while there will be a serious disagreement over the worth of a source, but most frequently the question is not whether a work is outstanding, but whether it is suitable for a medium-sized library. In the end, a majority vote determines the outcome.

No effort is made to give the list "balance." That is, there are no set number of sources to be named, nor does the committee try to include a variety of subjects. Over the years the number of sources included on the list has varied considerably. There were 97 books on the 1958 list, while only 37 sources were named to the 1983 list. The norm for the past ten years has been 35 to 45 sources. Over the years the committee has obviously become much more selective.

Within reason the committee does not consider price when selecting a source.[9] Simply put, the RSC attempts to choose what it considers the year's notable sources, leaving it up to individual librarians to select from those the ones that they consider the most useful. The entire list is not for every library.

Over the years the RSC has "made a significant contribution to reference service in public and college libraries," according to Sheets and Masters, "by selecting the outstanding reference books and compiling an annotated bibliography."[10] One indication of this is the fact that the RASD membership, in a 1977 survey, ranked the RSC highest in relevance to member interests.[11] Thomas S. Shaw, in his ten-year evaluation of the committee, stated that "it is obvious that the [RSC annual] list is fulfilling its purpose of bringing to the attention of librarians the notable reference books for small and medium-sized public and college libraries."[12] And that the committee "deserves the highest commendation" for its competent selection of sources, for its honesty, and for its hard work.[13]

The committee takes its role seriously. It tries its best to select the year's notable sources. The RSC's most difficult task is the same one confronting collection development in general: How do you best integrate new technology into a print oriented institution? The committee answers this question, in the words of Sheets and Masters, by recognizing the fact that our first concern should be to give the "technical aspects of format and medium due consideration without overlooking our primary focus, i.e., whether the work provides a unique or outstanding reference source fitting the same basic criteria that we apply in examining any printed reference work."[14]

While future lists of outstanding reference sources will no doubt be dominated by books, the committee will examine reference information in all of its various packages and evaluate those sources based on content, not format.

REFERENCES

1. Helen M. Focke, ''Reference Books of 1958—a Selection,'' *Library Journal,* 84: 687-97 (March 1, 1959).

2. Originally named the *Library Journal* List of Reference Books Committee, the committee's name was changed to the Outstanding Reference Books Committee (1976), the Outstanding Reference Sources Committee (1979), and finally the Reference Sources Committee (1981). See ''Policy and Procedure Manual for the Reference Sources Committee,'' (revised edition; Chicago: American Library Association, 1981), unpaged.

3. Ibid.

4. Ibid.

5. Ibid.

6. For a retrospective list of nonbook sources selected by the committee, see Janet Sheets and Deborah C. Masters, ''The RASD Outstanding Reference Sources Committee: Retrospect and Prospect,'' *RQ* 20: 363-65 (Summer 1981).

7. For a full treatment of the work schedule of the committee, see Ibid. and the ''Policy and Procedure Manual.''

8. Isadore Gilbert Mudge, ''Reference Books and Reference Work,'' *Guide to Reference Books,* compiled by Eugene Sheehy, 19th ed., (Chicago: American Library Association, 1976), pp. xiv-xv.

9. The only exception to the committee's price-blind philosophy is if a source were to cost many hundreds or thousands of dollars, or if a database were to have excessive start-up costs.

10. Sheets and Masters, p. 359.

11. Ruth Katz, ''Results From RASD Membership Survey 1977,'' *RQ* 17:202 (Spring 1978).

12. Thomas S. Shaw, ''Ten Years of Reference Books,'' *Library Journal* 93: 1586 (April 15, 1968)

13. Shaw, p. 1590.

14. Sheets and Masters, p. 362.

Apparatus:
A Mnemonic for the Evaluation
of Reference Resources

Janine Betty Schmidt

What is a reference resource? The A.L.A. glossary now defines a reference resource as:

> Any source used to obtain authoritative information in a reference transaction. Reference sources include printed materials, machine-readable databases, library bibliographic records, other libraries and institutions and persons both inside and outside the library.[1]

This definition is much wider in its ambit than earlier treatments which emphasized sources of concise factual, and occasionally evaluative, information (dictionaries, encyclopaedias, handbooks, manuals, directories, yearbooks, atlases) and bibliographical sources (catalogues, bibliographies, indexing and abstracting services). The change in the nature of reference resources has occurred with information technology making available different formats of audiovisual and machine readable resources and also with a recognition of a greater need for an active maximum reference service, the provision of information rather than instruction in how to find it. Any information resource becomes a reference resource—books, serial and audiovisual materials, people, and organizations, internal or external to a library's environment.

Students being prepared for the practice of a profession must acquire knowledge, skills, and attitudes which will enable them to cope with the many changes they are likely to encounter in a career

Janine Schmidt is Senior Lecturer, Department of Information Studies, Kuring-gai College of Advanced Education, Eton Road, Lindfield, Australia.

301

spanning many years. In reference work, the nature of reference resources and the nature of the service provided will inevitably change. In meeting the challenge of preparation for a rapidly changing future, the teaching of reference work has focused in recent years on the activities of the reference process, including question negotiation and search strategies. The reference resources which provide the information are a vital component of the reference equation, but are viewed as an integral part of the entire search process. The effective use of reference resources in this context stresses their functions and uses. Passing nodding acquaintance with a host of reference resources currently extant will not provide a satisfactory basis for the provision of effective information services in the future.

Teaching the effective use of reference resources at Kuring-gai College of Advanced Education[2] has concentrated on three areas:

— identification of categories of resources available and their characteristics
— understanding strategies for the effective location and use of a range of resources to satisfy information requirements
— evaluation of resources against standard criteria.

It is this latter aspect of evaluation which will now be addressed.

APPLICATIONS

Evaluation, with its origins in the educational area, has been applied in various ways in library and information science, its meaning varying with that which is being evaluated. The evaluation of a reference resource is determining its value or worth. One evaluates resources for purchase, selection for a particular enquiry, or effective utilization. Evaluating a resource involves an examination of its component parts, uses, stated purpose, and a comparison with others available. The description of reference resources is a well established activity. Any catalogue provides an objective and non-judgemental description of a work. Evaluation results from a critical and analytical judgement of the characteristics and functions of a resource.

A list of criteria to be used in evaluation must first be developed. The following list, represented by the mnemonic APPARATUS has been found to be a most useful device for students to use in evaluating reference resources, and also for practising librarians in determining the value of an item with a view to purchase or use.

A—AUTHORITY

The *authority,* reputation or standing of both the author(s) and the publisher should be examined. The author may be one individual, several individuals, an organization or an editorial board. The qualifications and experience of the author and their appropriateness to the subject covered should be established. Read the introduction, and check biographical sources if the qualifications are not listed. Where many individuals are involved in the production of sources, for example, an atlas, the publisher's authority will be more important. Publishing firms gain good reputations, for example John G. Batholomew for atlases, Oxford University Press for dictionaries, and these may be of help in checking the authority. Indexing and abstracting services are produced by libraries, professional associations, or commercial publishers. Different organizations have different levels of authority.

Articles in encyclopaedias should be signed. The sources of data in directories, and the means of verification, should be specified in the introductory materials. Any reference resource inevitably selects material to be included involving extensive editorial responsibility, and a subsequent need for checking authority. Handbooks and manuals produced by one person reflect the value judgements and opinions of that person. Evaluating the authority of online databases is particularly difficult, as the origin of information included is rarely given.

P—PURPOSE, PRICE

The *purpose,* or WHY a work has been written and WHAT it is trying to achieve, must be determined. A quick reading of the introduction or preface should reveal this information. The publisher's notice or the book jacket may be helpful also. The evaluative question must be posed: ''Has the author fulfilled the purpose?'' Scan the text, trying to determine if the work does all it purports to do. Determine the type of person for whom the work is intended, and the level at which it is written. For dictionaries, one should establish whether the approach is a prescriptive or descriptive view of language.

The element of *price* in evaluation involves assessing whether the resource is worth the money. Purchasers of information resources must consider not only the excellence or usefulness of the resource, but also whether it represents good value for money and what proportion of the available funds it will consume. In evaluating the physical appearance and attractiveness of resources, remember that improvements might increase the price and reduce the market. The high price of an item does not necessarily guarantee its usefulness. An inexpensive pamphlet may be more useful than an expensive encyclopaedia.

Any particular plans for advance or installment purchase should be investigated. The pricing of future updating of looseleaf services should be investigated. It may be cheaper to access online an expensive reference service which is infrequently used.

P—PHYSICAL FORMAT, PICTURES

The *Physical format* of all resources must be appropriate to the type and level of information required. Background information may be best supplied by a printed resource. Introductory material may be most effectively contained in a film. Up-to-date information may be best provided by a computerized database. Opinions may be best supplied by personal sources.

Each format of resource has its own specific evaluation criteria. For printed resources, binding and paper should be examined for colour, quality and durability. Materials which encounter heavy use require durable bindings and covers. Print size, typeface, page-layout, style of headings and size of margins should be checked for legibility, attractiveness, and suitability for intended use and user. Books intended for children and older people require a larger type size, and generous margins. Evaluating audiovisual resources like audio and video discs, cassettes and films involves an examination of such areas as the clarity, intelligibility and fidelity of sound, durability of packaging, and compatibility with existing hardware.

In certain resources, *pictures* or illustrations are important. When included, they should be up-to-date, clear, well-captioned, suitably located, preferably in colour, and of an appropriate size to complement the textual material. Ask the question, 'Do they enhance the text?' Similar evaluation criteria apply to diagrams, tables, maps and charts. Illustrations are vital in manuals containing "how-to" information, a picture or a diagram may convey meaning in a way words cannot. Graphic details are particularly important in atlases. How effectively does the colouring indicate contour lines, country divisions and topographic details? Does the colour provide good contrast with lettering and symbols? Is a colour key provided? Where is it located? These are some of the questions which must be put. With audiovisual resources, effective focus and exposure, picture/frame composition and clarity of visual images must be examined.

A—ARRANGEMENT

Reference resources should be arranged in a way which facilitates quick access to the details they contain. Some possible *arrangements* are alphabetical, by author or topic, chronological, or some other systematic arrangement, depending on the type of resource. Clear and succinct explanations of the arrangement should be included. As well as the arrangement of the entire work, arrangement within sections or entries should also be examined. The arrangement of an encyclopaedia article may be general to specific or chronological.

The position and sequence of various parts of a resource are important. A good table of contents or an index are central to the effective use of a resource. Cross references should link related or alternative headings. Ideally, any arrangement should be supplemented by alternative means of access to the contents through an index. The lack of an index or the provision of an inadequate index may prevent the retrieval of the contents of a work. To judge the effectiveness of the index, read a section of the text, and then try to locate the appropriate entries in the index. Check the index for errors in page references and for blind or circular references. Check how easy it is to locate a specific item through, for example, the use of page divisions.

The positioning of instructions for symbols and abbreviations should be such that it facilitates their use at the same time as the body of the work—some appear on each page in a dictionary.

The arrangement of online databases is less important, as free text searching enables multiple access points. Evaluating the arrangement of audiovisual resources involves examining sequencing of material. Some audio dictionaries have indexes superimposed on the tape to facilitate easy access. Microform sources should have clear descriptions readable to the naked eye.

Sources containing bibliographic information may be arranged alphabetically by author, title and subject in one or more sequences, or in a classified subject sequence. An alphabetical subject index to any source may use keywords from entries, or use subject headings from a standard list of descriptors. It may be arranged by broad general subject headings or narrow specific ones. The method of indexing used in an indexing service determines its arrangement. One approach is the listing of title pages of a number of sources. The depth of indexing and the terminology used should be appropriate to the subject area covered, and the user for whom the work is intended.

R—RECENCY, REVISION

The *up-to-dateness* and *currency* of reference resources are vital. The data of publication should always be examined, and the actual contents of the work compared with this date. The dates of material included in bibliographies can be useful for checking how up-to-date a particular work is. Be careful in evaluating on this basis, however. For a particular topic a work produced in 1960 may still in 1984 be the most recent authoritative work. Sometimes indirect evidence, such as style of dress in illustrations, provides a clue. The up-to-dateness of audiovisual resources is relatively easy to establish from the visual imagery. Information on topics like science and politics increases and changes so rapidly that a resource must be as up-to-date as possible. However, resources dealing with other subjects like history may not date as rapidly. There is frequently a delay of at least six months and possibly two years, between collection and organization of material and publication or production. Check the introduction for information on how the resource will be updated. This might be by the publication of new editions, by continuous revision (each reprint contains a percentage of new material), by the issue of inserts, cumulations, yearbooks or supplements.

A dictionary should be responsive to contemporary language usage, especially with a descriptive approach. Check works like encyclopaedias for their inclusion of current events and recent changes in political leadership. Many publishers are well aware that librarians check items concerning libraries and related topics, and these are consequently frequently updated. Check another topic. The date of a yearbook may be the year it is issued and not the year it covers. Atlases and other locational directories often use maps from many sources, so the copyright date of each map included and should be compared with the date of publication of the whole work. Some so-called new editions of works are occasionally reprints. The precise changes in different editions should be noted.

Since the purpose of an indexing or abstracting service is to provide access to the contents of materials as they are published, the up-to-dateness or recency is vital. Most indexing services are published àt regular intervals and the frequency (weekly, monthly, etc.) of publication reflects the urgency of need for recent information in that subject. Unfortunately many indexes are now being produced months after the materials being indexed have been published. These delays reduce the usefulness of the indexing service. The date of publication of the service and the date of the material covered should be compared and any time lag noted. Some services are used principally for current awareness and their recency is vital.

Another aspect of up-to-dateness which should be evaluated is the frequency of cumulation of many sources. Some resources, particularly indexing services, are issued monthly, with several monthly issues later combining into one issue, perhaps quarterly or annually. The more frequently published services should be cumulated as often as is economically possible so that instead of checking through several months of weekly or even monthly issues, one single volume can be checked.

Many of the problems associated with the up-to-dateness of indexing services are being solved by the use of computers in indexing and production, and different methods of indexing. Less intellectual input speeds up the whole process. Details of updating and loading of recent data should be established.

A—ACCURACY

Determining the *accuracy* of the content of information resources is often difficult. Checking the treatment of a familiar subject, seeking advice from specialists, or reading published reviews will all help. The authority of the author(s) or publisher will also be a reasonable guarantee of accuracy. Accuracy is related to up-to-dateness. Checking the accuracy of a particular source involves comparing its content with others. This is particularly important with directories.

Two additional factors to consider when examining a resource for accuracy are objectivity and bias. If a resource presents all viewpoints on a topic, it is considered to be an objective presentation. Even if a resource adopts certain cultural, geographic, ideological, intellectual, practical or moral viewpoints, it need not be thought of as biased IF these emphases are fully stated. For example, an encyclopaedia designed for the American market may devote considerable space to American affairs and history. Some sources even adopt a more obviously particular viewpoint—for example, the *Great Soviet encyclopedia* interprets events from a communist viewpoint, whereas *The new Catholic encyclopedia* gives a Catholic interpretation. Provided that such emphases are fully acknowledged, they do not constitute bias and are not legitimate grounds for condemning the resource. However, an acknowledged emphasis may make a resource unsuitable for a particular purpose, for example an American handbook of etiquette in an Australian library.

Bias, then, is *unacknowledged* emphasis on a particular viewpoint or culture. In addition, the silent suppression of alternative viewpoints or interpretations constitutes bias. An example of this would be an encyclopaedia which claimed to be universal but ignored third world countries, or claimed to be non-sectarian but did not mention alternative viewpoints on moral issues.

T—TREATMENT

An information resource may treat a subject at various levels. For example:

—At a *popular* or superficial level, aimed at the *general interest* user.
—At a *scholarly* or indepth level, aimed at the specialist user.
—At a *simplified* level, aimed at the *juvenile* or new user.

The level of treatment is indicated by language (the difficulty, diversity and length of words used and grammatical construction), style (popular, scholarly or technical), complexity of verbal concepts, complexity of visual images and use of technical terms or jargon. Some resources include glossaries explaining terminology used.

U—USE

This criterion is linked with the previous one, TREATMENT, in that the intended use will determine the level of treatment of the material. When examining a resource, ask the following questions:

— Who will use the resource? (e.g. professional, child, student, general reader, researcher)
— For what purpose will the resource be used? (e.g. job training, self improvement, leisure)
— What kinds of questions could it be used to answer? (e.g. biographical, geographical, bibliographical, historical)
— How easy is it to use? (e.g. provision of instructions, use of abbreviations, location of keys to abbreviations, use of headings, legibility, dependance on prior knowledge, comprehensiveness of index)

Each type of reference resource has its own specific uses. Dictionaries are used for checking spellings, uses, pronunciation, and meaning of words, either generally or in a specific subject or geographic area.

Encyclopaedias are used for locating facts like the cost of building the Sydney Opera House, background details on a topic where little is known, and further reading on a topic. Handbooks and manuals are used for "how to" information, for example recipes for pavlova, rules for cricket. Yearbooks are used for recent developments and rapidly changing details like statistics. Directories are used for finding addresses and details about people. Online services are increasingly being used for information which requires constant updating. Indexing and other bibliographical sources provide access to the world's output of published and recorded information resources. They help users identify materials relevant to particular topics. The evaluation of these sources is also related to the availability of the materials indexed or listed.

S—SCOPE

The *broad scope* of an information resource includes the subject(s), topic(s) or areas it covers and the completeness of subject coverage.

Narrow scope refers to the scope of individual entries within a resource. How much information does each entry include? Does each entry have the same inclusions and format?

In examining the scope of a dictionary, what types of words it covers must be considered—slang, place or personal names, scientific terms. The number of words included in a dictionary determines whether it is abridged or unabridged and frequently determines its use. For general works like encyclopaedias, the range and depth of subject coverage and the countries mentioned must be determined. Check subjects in the humanities, social sciences and sciences for inclusion and underdeveloped countries (particularly Australia!). The time period covered should also be checked. Bibliographical sources in particular must be examined for coverage of particular languages, countries, and formats of resources as well as subject areas. Introductory materials should state the scope quite clearly. Many bibliographical sources are selective, and the basis and extent of the selection must be given. Many resources contain supplementary information which is incidental to the main coverage e.g. a dictionary containing pictures of flags of the world. These are good for home use, but are often not suitable for libraries. It is difficult to locate the material when required, and other sources are usually more comprehensive and easier to use. The scope of each entry must also be evaluated. In a dictionary, are antonyms included? Are bibliographies given for articles in an encyclopaedia? Is the bibliographical citation in an indexing service complete?

Many of the criteria used in the mnemonic APPARATUS overlap. Scope cannot always be separated from purpose, treatment or use. When evaluating any given item, not all criteria may apply equally. One must ask, "Which criteria are relevant?" In other words, establishing priorities is necessary. Different criteria will assume priority for different categories. For example, "recency" is most important in a Year Book. Some criteria may need to be disregarded under special circumstances. This might be true of a book on local history even if it is of poor quality in physical format or arrangement. It may be the only item available on this subject.

Much of the skill of evaluation lies in deciding in a particular situation which criteria have the highest priority. This varies for particular formats of reference resources and in particular subject areas and contexts. In medicine, recency is a vital criterion. In history, authority is most important.

Evaluation of reference resources for purchase or effective use can be carried out using physical examination of the materials following the criteria indicated by the mnemonic APPARATUS. Advertising material for the resources can also be examined, and the advice of specialists sought. Reviews of new resources are useful, and the annotations in books about reference resources. Materials can also be obtained on approval for examination with a view to purchase. Evaluation is carried out on a continuing basis, comparing sources used in relation to particular types of use or information enquiries, and so establishing their value. Evaluation is also the spirit of enquiry.

REFERENCES

1. *A.L.A. Glossary of library and information science: ed.* by H. Young. Chicago: American Library Association, 1983. p.189.

2. Kuring-gai College of Advanced Education is a tertiary institution located in the leafy green suburb of Lindfield in Sydney, New South Wales, Australia. It is not located in woop-woop (Australian colloquialism for a long way away from anywhere) as its Aboriginal name referring to the tribes which frequented the area, might indicate. The College has been offering superlative courses in library and information studies since 1977.

BIBLIOGRAPHY

Cheney, F.N. and Williams, W.J. *Fundamental reference sources.* 2nd ed., Chicago: American Library Association, 1980.

Higgens, Gavin ed. *Printed reference material.* London: Library Association, 1980.

Katz, W.A. *Introduction to reference work.* 4th ed. 2 vols. New York: McGraw-Hill, 1982.

Schmidt, J.B. and Anderson, B.P. *Sources of brief factual information.* Lindfield, Sydney: Kuring-gai College of Advanced Education, 1982.

The Detailed Reference Collection Development Policy: Is It Worth the Effort?

Fred Batt

This summer Bill Katz asked me for an article for a compilation of reference collection policies.[1] In my response to Dr. Katz, my thinking was that elaborate collection development policies for reference (although impressive to display and a nice addition to the many policies which libraries produce) was not really that useful. I thought that the way reference collections typically evolved and were evaluated could be supported as well by only a concise conceptual statement or list (perhaps less than one page) without any damage to the collection. It was decided that I would pursue this concept for the "Evaluation of Reference Services" issue of *The Reference Librarian* rather than as part of the proposed book.

Detailed collection development policies and manuals can be found in many libraries and throughout the literature. What initially strikes me as I look through many of these policies (some extending to hundreds of pages detailing levels and specifics for every subject area) are the overall similarities. One could conceivably draft policies for small, medium and large libraries with a fill-in-the-blank final section labeled "exceptions" or even "local peccadilloes." This would save many librarians hours of unnecessary work. Simply add information about the development of local and emphasized collections as well as procedural variations. There aren't that many differences between libraries. Many libraries are built by similar approval plans and/or librarians reading the same review journals. For that matter, there aren't that many differences between reference collections either. Generally, reference collections have to support similar course listings, similar groups of students with similar needs, as well as provide a vehicle for answering predictable (and

---

Mr. Batt is Head of the Reference Department, Bizzell Memorial Library, University of Oklahoma, Norman, 73019.

313

often unpredictable) questions or locating places where these answers can be obtained.

More recently I've begun to realize potential needs for policies. I've noted naive entry level librarians as well as faculty (thrown into the library ordering business by their academic departments) who could benefit from the overview as well as subject specifics. With increasing dependency on approval programs for building large portions of many collections, profiles would be more accurately and easily developed and maintained if an up-to-date collection policy were on paper. Also, with cooperative ventures no longer a concept of the future, and networks beginning to mutually share information about collection strengths, weaknesses, and future directions (e.g. RLG Conspectus Project and online collection management and development programs), in-house collection development policies and an accurate gauge of collection levels are important. These and many other reasons support the vast efforts which go into constructing collection development policies for some libraries. Perkins amply discusses the benefits of both training manuals (information on materials selection environment) and reference manuals (compilations of internal policies and procedures).[2] Among his reasons for writing a collection development manual are procedural consistency, forcing its authors to consider the unspoken and unrecorded assumptions, forcing its authors to think more systematically about collection development, reducing the perceived complexity of collection development, and providing a basis for contact between the bibliographer and supervisor. I can't really argue with any of these points other than they seem a bit contrived. These things should occur without the need for a collection development policy to stimulate them. I also question whether the payoff is worth the effort in a busy library setting when it is a challenge just to provide basic public services and spend the ever shrinking dollar on essentials which are routinely ordered without consulting any kind of policy.

LIBRARY SURVIVAL

A library can survive without a detailed manual. Perkins does point out that the size and complexity of the institution is an important consideration. Effective library communication patterns can negate the major benefits of the invested time to write as well as maintain a manual. Another consideration is that a policy might really be more theoretical than practical; more of an ideal than what really occurs in library life, i.e. what is applied in the practice of collection development. Discussions with many respected collection builders corroborate my impression. When asked ''Do you (or would you) consult your collection development policy?'' a typical answer is ''no'' or ''rarely'' usually accompanied by a shrug and/or look of disinterest. Hours of time writing, rewriting, revising and updating these policies result in something which is nice to display, comforting to have, but rarely even thought about during our daily collection building, weeding, evaluation, etc. Baatz acknowledges a minority ''hard-core'' who do not believe in collection development policies.[3] I'm not so certain that it is a minority who question whether they are really practical. I've heard too many effective librarians say that they trust their own intuition and judgment rather than any written policy which may be out of date by the time it is on paper, or may not be flexible enough to actually treat the special cases which may arise.

This leads me to the main subject of this paper, the need for reference collection policies. Certainly if a library goes through all of the trials and tribulations of producing an extensive overall policy, then the reference collection should be part of it. Otherwise I am inclined to keep it simple. My feelings are partially a matter of priorities; a matter of time management. Throughout my library career I've avoided procrastination. Yet, as a reference head at two institutions, I've never been able to get the revision of an outdated reference collection development policy towards the top of my ''to-do'' list. There have always been more important projects to attack. It has never been an ''A Activity'' as I strive to gain control of my time and my life.[4] In fact, it doesn't even make it to my ''necessary evils'' group, i.e. items which must be done but contribute only marginally to my goals. Perhaps it isn't even a ''C Activity,'' but more appropriately a ''CZ,'' i.e. it can be deferred indefinitely without harm. Even the marvelous managerial method of delegation didn't work. Two assistant heads of reference treated this assignment with the enthusiasm that a librarian with a deep-rooted fear of computers treats my attempts to push database searching. I find that reference books get selected and deselected, the collection gets evaluated and the questions get answered without the consultation of a detailed collection development policy. With one (at most two) individuals ultimately responsible for coordinating the collection (even if many people order reference books and/or a reference committee exists for desiderata, expensive items, etc.), a massive treatise on the recommended contents of each aspect of the collection seems unnecessary.

REFERENCE COLLECTION

The reference collection is developed, used and depended on differently than other library collections. For the sake of this article, let me define the reference collection as a detached or distinct collection of materials used to answer questions and support the staff at reference and/or information desk(s). I will assume that anyone reading this article knows what a reference source is within this context (although some librarians term every resource, living or inert, as part of the reference collection, whether a book in the stacks or the local butcher—I can live with that definition too, e.g. I recently sent a library patron to consult a placemat at a local Chinese restaurant as part of the answer to a query). As I examine various reference collections, I see strengths and weaknesses which are a function of numerous factors:

1) The amount of money available during various time periods to set up standing orders and ongoing commitments influences collection building (strengths when each edition of a worthwhile source is guaranteed without worrying about submitting orders; weaknesses when money is laid out annually for sources that are not as useful as others not purchased, i.e. once a standing order is started, neglect can allow it to continue beyond its usefulness).

2) The same tools tend to end up in each library because librarians all tend to read the same blurbs and consult the same reviews. Also, publishers and sales people with effective types of pressuring techniques and advertising can shape collections more than we would like to admit.

3) End of FY funds contribute to the acquisition of larger sets when money is left over and smaller purchases are not feasible due to time constraints, e.g. "congratulations—we just found $10,000 that you have to spend by tomorrow." Sometimes this results in marvelous acquisitions. Other times expensive sets are purchased which are never touched. Money is wasted.

4) Periods of neglect when either coordination was not effective or money was not available are apparent. One could write a marvelous reference collection development policy and not effect the

power of these factors at all, i.e. the policy has little influence on what really happens.

EVALUATION

Evaluation of a reference collection is also somewhat different than the rest of the library. It is more constant, systematic and visable. Every reference query leads to some degree of reference collection evaluation. One doesn't need a policy to perceive this function. I believe that the most constructive building, evaluation and weeding of the reference collection simply comes from daily use. The reference tools are under constant surveillance and testing. Feedback concerning the performance of the reference collection is much more obvious than in the stacks. Patrons are more apt to consult the desk when looking for information in the reference area than when consulting the regular collection. When the reference collection fails, we know it. Obscure and useless items can be weeded or transferred as needed. New items can be ordered as a function of this daily feedback. Deficiencies can be corrected.

It is important that all individuals serving at the reference desk have the proper mental set to be able to vocalize collection weaknesses to the reference head as they occur. The response "we don't have the reference book to answer that question" not followed up by pursuit of the availability of a reference tool to satisfy future similar queries shortchanges both the patrons and the librarians. This daily building of a reference collection does not require a collection development policy. Of course a periodic (yearly?) systematic review of the collection should also be conducted.

Communication serves yet another important function in the scheme of reference collection development and evaluation. We must keep in mind that there are two important strains of reference collection use: 1) Use by the reference staff to provide reference service, and 2) Provision of a collection for users to consult themselves.

Not all library patrons consult reference librarians. Despite our wonderfully approachable reference personnel available to put every ounce of their energies into effective reference service, some patrons prefer to fend for themselves. We must not lose track of these individuals and should communicate via various means (memos to academic departments, short bibliographies, on shelf dummies, etc.) any changes that we make in the collection. We've all seen patrons who are accustomed to a particular source or location become frustrated and agitated if the collection is shifted, a source removed, etc. Let patrons know what is new or changed (e.g. a new source or access in *MLA Bibliography*), what is available online, etc. Also provide vehicles for patrons to suggest sources or types of sources (suggestion box?). These and other communication efforts may be worth more to patrons and overall service than spending time constructing a policy which attempts to cover each potential acquisition alternative.

LONG LIST-OUT

What would suffice as a reference collection policy? What I believe *isn't* really necessary is the common long list of the types of materials included in the collection (e.g. almanacs, annual reviews, bibliographies, biographies, concordances, dictionaries, directories, etc., etc., etc.) with a notation of the specific type of source, limitations, currency, etc. for each group. Some of this may be arbitrary, some based solely on historical reasons, some only the opinion of the author, some too limiting. It seems obvious when a particular tool has reference value. If it isn't obvious, it is usually the job of the reference head to make or delegate the decision. It is a judgment that I believe would rarely necessitate the need for a detailed written policy. If poor judgment occurs on occasion, big deal! Any decision can be reconsidered (as long as you remain friendly with your catalogers). The rare negative results are not traumatic. A book with marginal reference value ending up in the reference collection instead of the stacks will not create problems. Nor will the world end if a book with potential reference value ended up in the stacks and, God forbid, circulated. We don't need a policy to make these decisions. I realize that some people will take issue and feel uncomfortable if each potential alternative is not dealt with on paper. Yet I don't believe that a blow-by-blow descriptive reference collection policy would alter much reference collection building. Accountability is in reference and collection performance, not a written policy. Decent reference collections are molded without it.

All that is necessary are decent and short in-house procedural statements for weeding and inventory (modified prior to each major project); an understanding of in-house acquisitions procedures (written); and a verbal concept of the daily evaluation and building of the reference collection, a collection in a constant state of flux. A written collection scope analysis by both subject and format should concentrate on the exceptions, e.g. areas that are strong for particular reasons (a library might strive to maintain one of the best collections in the country on the works by and about a specific author), or areas which need to be developed (a library might need to beef up a specific reference collection because of a forthcoming doctoral program), or areas which need to be avoided (a reference department might not select specific items because they are all housed in another campus location). These and other exceptions should be noted and emphasized, perhaps in a page or less. Why bother writing down all of the obvious items?

We don't need definitions of reference tools. We don't need to write about how encyclopedias need to be updated. We don't need lists about how to evaluate books. We don't need reprints of Freedom to Read Statements. We don't need rehashings of policies which should be in succinctly written reference manuals or other communications, not collection development policies. We don't need a statement such as "Our aim is to acquire the most authoritative reference tools available in the fields within the college curriculum." What is the alternative? Why even say this? All of these types of things are virtually the same in libraries of like size and function. For these types of statements, we'd do as well consulting good reference textbooks and published lists of recommended reference tools.

Unlike general collection development policies which may serve as public relations tools, support profiles for approval plans, or go hand-in-hand with cooperative ventures, reference collections and their supporting policies serve a different need. Major strengths and weaknesses, areas to avoid, and areas which need particular attention are where emphasis should be directed. Anything else just fills up paper.

REFERENCES

1. Personal communication, July 26, 1983.
2. David L. Perkins, "Writing the Collection Development Manual," *Collection Management* 4:37-47 (Fall 1982).
3. Wilmer H. Baatz, *Collection Development in 19 Libraries of the Association of Research Libraries.* U. S. Educational Resources Information Center, ERIC Document ED153606, 1978.
4. Alan Lakein, *How to Get Control of Your Time and Your Life.* New York, Peter H. Wyden, 1973.

Evaluation of Library Workbooks in a Community College Setting

Joan S. Holt
Steven Falk

A review of recent literature on evaluation of bibliographic instruction shows two complementary trends. One is a strong interest in promoting evaluation and in describing proper techniques of evaluation, such as sampling, test validation, survey construction, and statistical methodology.[1] A second trend is the reporting of evaluation of specific bibliographic instruction tools and techniques used in individual libraries.[2] These trends are complementary because as practicing librarians become aware of the benefits of evaluation, they are more likely to apply evaluation techniques to their own instruction procedures and products. The more these applications (both the successful and unsuccessful) are reported, the more help will be available to librarians structuring their own evaluations. And even though it is difficult to determine whether the evaluation of a specific local instruction tool would hold true for the general case, the cumulative effect of similar, well-designed studies is such that one begins to assume the results may be generalized.

One commonly used bibliographic instruction tool which has not been widely evaluated is the library skills workbook. In a helpful overview of the use of library workbooks, Patricia Berge and Judith Pryor note that many such workbooks are based on one written in 1969 by Miriam Dudley at UCLA.[3] In fact, the Dudley workbook and a similar tool written by reference librarians at the University of Missouri-St. Louis served as models for the workbook evaluated in this paper. Two obvious questions to ask when one considers the workbook as a working tool are: (1) is it an effective teaching de-

---

Joan S. Holt is Reference Librarian at St. Louis Community College, 3400 Pershall Rd., St. Louis, MO 63135. Mr. Falk is Director of Library Services at the same institution.

321

vice; and (2) is it more effective than the other teaching tools one has available, and, if so, under what conditions and for which types of students. Berge and Pryor state that, notwithstanding its wide acceptance in education in general and in library instruction in particular, the workbook has not been proven conclusively to be any more effective than any other method of instruction.[4] While discussing the results of a University of Arizona study on the use of a library workbook,[5] they conclude that:

> the findings of this study are most useful for documenting the value of formal library instruction versus no formal instruction. However, because no other method of instruction was tested, the findings have little meaning when comparing workbooks with other teaching methods.[6]

Berge and Pryor also state that the study at Arizona was the only one to their knowledge which tried to measure "changes in student knowledge although there are studies which measure change in student attitudes" following use of a library workbook.[7]

A more recent report on the evaluation of a workbook as a library teaching tool was published by Maria Sugrañes and James Neal, who used a workbook as one component of a "self-paced bibliographic instruction course" at California State University, Long Beach.[8] Like the Arizona study, Sugrañes and Neal reported that California State students using the workbook showed significant improvement in library knowledge as measured by scores on criterion-referenced pre-tests and post-tests.[9] Also like the Arizona study, the California study did not try to compare use of a workbook to any other type of bibliographic instruction. These two studies do lead one to believe that the profession's intuitive faith in the value of workbooks as instruction tools is not misplaced.

When the reference staff at St. Louis Community College at Florissant Valley decided to explore the advantages of using a library workbook in our bibliographic instruction program, we felt it important to evaluate our product before making a major commitment to it. We wanted to convince ourselves that our workbook was at least as effective a teaching tool as the other programs of bibliographic instruction we provided. We also saw the evaluation process itself as an opportunity to work closely with the teaching faculty. Not many papers have mentioned that one of the potential benefits of a careful evaluation project is the opportunity to work with nonlibrary faculty in the institution.[10] We thought that if faculty were involved in the evaluation process, with the understanding that whenever possible their suggestions would be incorporated into the final version of the program, we would achieve a better product and one which might be more easily accepted. We also would strengthen our working relationship with those faculty members through the process.

I. DESCRIPTION OF THE PROJECT

Librarians at Florissant Valley have had a long tradition of providing bibliographic instruction to large numbers of students in a wide variety of courses of study. The primary method of formal library instruction has been the instruction tour—almost 200 per year. The basic tour consists of an explanation of the general arrangement, policies, and practices of the library; a demonstration of our microfilm catalog; an explanation of the purposes and content of the reference collection; and a demonstration of the use of one or more standard periodical indexes. Tours have been requested primarily by English instructors, but many other faculty also have brought their classes into the library for subject-related tours. We had no system to ensure that the majority of students enrolled on the campus in a given semester would get library instruction or to prevent some students from hearing the same information over and over. Due to this lack of organization, we covered the same basic information in almost all tours before we moved on to more course-specific information.

Unsatisfied with this arrangement, we decided to create a more organized and systematic program of library instruction. Our goal was to provide basic library instruction to as many students as possible and to do so as early as possible in their academic career at the College. We wanted the faculty to feel confident that their students possessed a basic library literacy. We also wanted to be able to move past basic literacy and provide specialized instruction which did not duplicate the basic instruction already provided.

Because of its wide acceptance as a teaching tool in a variety of libraries, we decided to try using a workbook as an alternative to our basic instruction tour. We felt the "active" learning a workbook promotes would be particularly valuable to our students. Our students come to us with a diversity of library experience and skills;

therefore the self-paced nature of a workbook seemed promising.[11] However, unlike some other institutions, we did not design our workbook to be entirely self-directed. We determined early on that we wanted to maintain some aspect of the human contact provided by the tour, so we proposed to introduce the workbook to a class with a short ''mini-tour'' around the main floor of the library. And since our intention was to bring students up to a level of basic library literacy, we decided to require students to review their graded workbooks with a reference librarian and either discuss or re-do the questions they had missed.

To reach as many students as possible, we solicited the help of the English Department.[12] Almost every program on campus requires at least one basic composition course (usually Composition I). In addition, we felt that the research papers required in composition courses would make library instruction particularly relevant. The English faculty suggested that the workbook might be more valuable in the Composition II course, the second course in the sequence, where a major research paper is required.[13] We were somewhat opposed to this because we wanted students to use the workbook early in their enrollment at the College, and many students postpone Composition II until their second year. Also, many more students are required to take Composition I than Composition II. However, because we felt that our pilot project would be self-defeating if it caused us to lose the support of the English faculty, we agreed to test the workbook in both classes. This decision complicated our evaluation but allowed us to gain some valuable information which we otherwise would not have had.

The first draft of our workbook was written in the summer and fall of 1982. It was a 25-page booklet, containing 11 sections, each of which consisted of a one or two page description of a library resource followed by a short exercise. With the cooperation of the English Department and the assistance of faculty trained in statistical methodology,[14] we designed an evaluation project to test the workbook in the spring, 1983. In particular we wanted to answer the following questions.

1. Was the workbook well-written?
2. Was the workbook an effective means of library instruction?
3. Was the workbook more effective than the tour?
4. Did it make any difference whether we used the workbook in Composition I or Composition II?

5. Would the English faculty consider the workbook useful enough to accept it into their curriculum?

II. EVALUATION STRATEGIES AND RESULTS

We designed the evaluation to contain four components: (1) an objective measure of student achievement; (2) a formal survey of student attitudes; (3) an informal survey of library staff attitudes; and (4) a formal survey of faculty attitudes.

Student Achievement

Richard Werking has described the common pre-test/post-test evaluation as the "agricultural-botany paradigm,"[15] i.e., measure something, treat it, and measure it again. Notwithstanding Werking's tongue-in-cheek description, we developed a project to objectively measure student achievement which involved a pre-test, a treatment (either use of the workbook or attendance at an instruction tour), and a post-test. We included in the project a control group which took the pre-test and post-test but received no library instruction.

With the cooperation of the English Department, we used eight classes of approximately 28 students each—four Composition I classes and four Composition II classes. Under the assumption that the instructor's attitude might affect student performance,[16] we worked with four faculty members each of whom taught two Composition I or two Composition II classes. We gave two Composition I classes with different instructors the workbook; the second class of each instructor received either an instruction tour or no formal library instruction. The arrangement was similar for the Composition II classes—two workbook groups, one tour group, and one control group. The best arrangement would have been to work with four faculty members, each of whom taught three sections of the same course (Composition I or Composition II). This would have given us sample groups of approximately equal size. Unfortunately, the faculty were not scheduled in that configuration that semester.

Each student was given a pre-test to measure his/her beginning level of knowledge. The pre-test (and the post-test, which was identical) consisted of 15 questions which were intended to measure our major objectives of library instruction. One week after the pre-test students either had a tour or were given the workbook. The control group students received no instruction. Three weeks after the pre-test each student was given a post-test.

In order to be included in the final sample, a student had to complete the pre-test, complete the workbook or be present for the tour, and complete the post-test. For various reasons, many students did not answer all the questions on the pre-test or post-test.[17] These students were withdrawn from the study. Absenteeism also was an unexpected, but important, factor. These problems resulted in a very high subject mortality rate, and even though we used classes which contained about 28 students each, we averaged only about half that number in our final sample groups.

For those students who completed all the components of the objective evaluation, the mean scores were calculated (see Table I). A repeated *t*-test was used to calculate the significance of the mean improvement for each group (see Table 2).[18]

For both Composition I and Composition II students who completed the workbook, we found a significant improvement with a 99% level of confidence. For both groups having the tour we also found a significant improvement with a 95% confidence level. The control group students in both courses also improved slightly on the post-test, perhaps due to test sensitivity, but their mean improvement was not found to be statistically significant.

An analysis of variance of the mean improvements was calculated to determine whether the improvement in the workbook group was significantly greater than the improvement of the tour or control

TABLE I

MEAN SCORES

Composition I

	Mean Pre-test	Mean Post-test	Mean Improvement
Workbook	7.04	9.31	2.27
Tour	7.54	9.08	1.54
Control	6.69	7.46	0.77

Composition II

	Mean Pre-test	Mean Post-test	Mean Improvement
Workbook	9.07	11.30	2.23
Tour	6.67	8.80	2.13
Control	8.62	9.77	1.16

```
                          TABLE  2

                       Composition  I


    Workbook         t (25) = 5.54, p <.01
    Tour             t (12) = 2.22, p <.05
    Control          t (12) = 1.16, p >.05



                       Composition II

    Workbook         t (26) = 4.83, p <.01
    Tour             t (14) = 2.45, p <.05
    Control          t (12) = 2.04, p >.05
```

groups. We found no statistical significance between the improvements of the three groups. The mean scores for the workbook students were higher than those for the tour students, and the tour students scored higher than the control group, but the degrees of differences in the mean improvements were not large enough to be statistically significant. In other words, by combining the results of the *t*-tests and the analysis of variance, we may conclude that both our workbook and instruction tour are effective methods of instruction but that, at least in this evaluation, neither proved to be conclusively superior to the other.

When we compared the Composition I scores to the Composition II scores, we found that the Composition II workbook student scores were higher on the pre-test and post-test than the Composition I workbook scores, but the mean improvement was very similar for both groups (2.27 and 2.23). Graphs 1 and 2 provide a comparison of the pre-test and post-test scores. Not only did the mean scores improve, but the mode, or most frequently attained score, was raised by three to four points for both workbook groups. The range of scores on the post-test was narrower than the range of scores on the pre-test for both workbook groups. We concluded that the workbook did increase the level of library knowledge and make it more uniform within the group.

Problems

After all the data was collected, certain problems with our testing procedure became apparent. The most obvious problem was the decline in the number of students in each sample group due to absen-

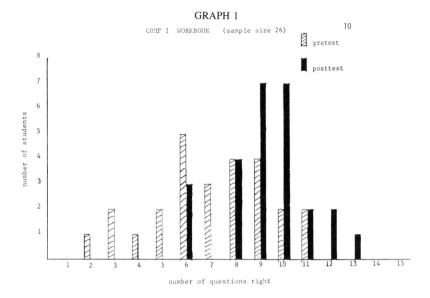

GRAPH 1

COMP I WORKBOOK (sample size 26)

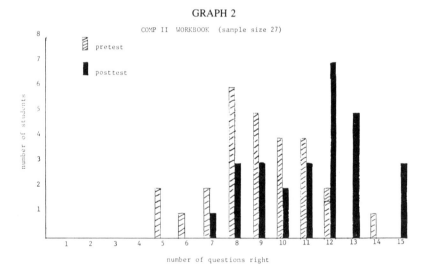

GRAPH 2

COMP II WORKBOOK (sample size 27)

teeism and other factors mentioned above. When the sample size falls below 15, individual differences have a disproportionate effect on the outcome, and it becomes more difficult to predict that the results would hold true for a large population. While we feel that our test questions were valid measures of our instructional objectives, we did not field test our questions to guarantee their reliability.[19] We also learned that a 15 question test did not provide enough sensitivity to sufficiently measure all the learning changes taking place. Some questions were so easy that almost everyone answered them correctly. Thus the actual variation (as opposed to the potential variation) turned out to be much less than 15.

Student Attitudes

At the time of the post-test each student was given a questionnaire on which he/she was asked to assess his/her change in attitude toward the library. In each category all or almost all students returned a completed survey. A numerical scale was used; answers were tabulated in percentages since the size of the groups varied.[20] Table 3 shows the results of Question 1, results which are typical of the other questions.

The attitude survey results differed somewhat between the Composition I and II students. Both the workbook and tour Composition I students expressed positive changes in attitude, with the tour group reporting the more positive change. The Composition II workbook and tour students expressed positive changes in attitude in nearly equal amounts.

```
                          TABLE  3

                    STUDENT ATTITUDE SURVEY

Question 1:  The (tour/workbook) helped me feel more confident about
             using the library.

For control group students, only:

Question 1:  I feel more confident about using the library.
```

Composition I

	Strongly disagree				Strongly agree		
	1	2	3	4	5	6	7
Workbook	0%	7%	12%	14%	26%	24%	17%
Tour	0%	0%	0%	19%	25%	38%	19%
Control	38%	6%	19%	31%	0%	6%	0%

Composition II

	1	2	3	4	5	6	7
Workbook	0%	3%	6%	21%	24%	29%	17%
Tour	0%	0%	15%	25%	20%	30%	10%
Control	0%	0%	5%	52%	19%	14%	10%

One surprising result seen in the responses to the questions on feeling more confident about using the library was that the Composition I control group expressed a very negative reaction while the Composition II control group reported feeling neutral or somewhat positive, even though they had received no formal library instruction. We assume that many Composition II students had begun their research papers and were learning about the library on their own. The Composition I students, on the other hand, probably had had minimal exposure to the library and may have learned from the pre-tests and post-tests just how little they knew about using the library.

Another unexpected result from the attitude survey was that on the statement "I am more likely to ask the library staff for help when I need it," the tour groups reported noticeably more agreement than did the workbook groups. In fact, even the control groups agreed more strongly with this statement than did the workbook groups. Evidently, it was difficult to communicate to the workbook students that although they were expected to do the workbook essentially on their own, they still should feel free to ask for help at other times.

Evaluation by Reference Staff

We did not create a formal survey for the reference staff. We did have a meeting late in the semester to analyze and discuss the workbook in comparison to the standard tour. Answering the questions of workbook students at the reference desk and grading 200 workbook answer sheets readily allowed us to become familiar with the workbook in operation. Since all members of the reference staff had long experience in leading instruction tours, each person was able to make thoughtful comparisons between the two instruction methods.

In general, the staff felt that the workbook offered some distinct advantages over the tour. Grading the answer sheets certainly took time, but some suggested that at least the same amount of time normally would be spent leading tours. Also, workbooks could be graded at non-peak times (such as late evenings), and tours tend to be scheduled at the busiest times of the day, the times when most classes are offered. The most substantive reservation about the workbook was the concern that students need the human connection that the tour provides, and the staff felt strongly that the workbook should not become a strictly self-directed enterprise.

We analyzed the completed workbook answer sheets to help discover weaknesses in the workbook itself. The majority of student errors were due to less than careful reading of the text of the workbook or of the questions in a given exercise. To help counter this, in the second edition of the workbook, we tried to get all key words of each question on the first line of the question. As always happens in library assignments, in a few cases a pattern of wrong answers helped uncover ambiguities or quirks in our library catalog. Such problem questions were eliminated or revised in the subsequent edition of the workbook.

Faculty Evaluation

The Spring 1983, evaluation project involved eight classes taught by four instructors. In the fall semester, the workbook was used by 14 instructors in 30 Composition I classes. At the end of the fall semester, a questionnaire was sent to the 14 faculty members.

The main thrust of the questionnaire was to learn what kind of responses the faculty were getting from their students and to see whether the instructors thought the workbook was worthwhile.[21]

Eleven faculty members returned the questionnaires. All said they felt the workbook was a successful way to teach library skills. Three instructors said they could not judge whether their students did better on their research projects, but the other eight responded affirmatively to this question.

Some of the comments made were that the students "made more effective use of the library" and "I saw a better variety of sources, and I had fewer 'dumb' questions thrown at me about material available in the library." As to whether the faculty were interested in using the workbook again, the answer was a unanimous "yes."

III. CONCLUSION

The study done at St. Louis Community College at Florissant Valley was an attempt (1) to validate our library skills workbook as an effective teaching tool; (2) to compare the workbook's effectiveness with that of our customary instruction tour; (3) to determine whether the workbook would be more effective in the first or second course in our English composition sequence; and (4) to reinforce the importance of formal library instruction in the minds of the English Department faculty. As we have explained in this paper, we were hampered somewhat by the fact that we did not field test the questions on our testing instrument and by a high subject mortality rate in our sample groups.

Even given these flaws, however, we were able to verify that our workbook is an effective teaching tool. We were able to use the project results to improve the quality and consistency of the workbook in a second edition. We were not able to show that the workbook is necessarily more effective than our standard instruction tour. We determined that while students react positively to the workbook, they seem to appreciate the human contact provided by the tour. Finally, we found that the English instructors involved strongly felt that use of the workbook resulted in more efficient library research by their students and should become a regular component of the Composition I curriculum.

This last factor should not be underestimated. A library instruction program which is proven effective but not adopted because of personal, political, or other reasons is unsuccessful. Evaluation projects which involve teaching faculty may increase their support for library instruction.

What questions remain regarding the use of library workbooks? First, of course, more studies should be reported which assess the merits of workbooks as teaching tools. More important, perhaps it is time to try to respond to the issue raised by Berge and Pryor[22] (and addressed in our own study): that is, to what extent is a workbook more or less effective than other methods of bibliographic instruction, such as lectures, tours, slide tape programs, video tapes, or computer-assisted instruction, such as lectures, tours, slide tape programs, video tapes, or computer-assisted instruction? What is the proper mixture of these methods under what types of conditions? How can reference librarians use these methods to respond to the needs of students who have different learning styles and personality types? Answering these questions presents a most interesting and valuable challenge to librarians concerned with library instruction.

REFERENCES

1. For example, see John Lubans, Jr., "Evaluating Library-User Programs," in John Lubans, Jr., ed., *Evaluating the Library User* (New York: R.R. Bowker, 1974), pp. 232-253; various papers in R. T. Beeler, ed., *Evaluating Library Use Instruction* (Ann Arbor, MI: Pierian, 1975); Carolyn A. Kirkendall, ed., *Improving Library Instruction: How to Teach and How to Evaluate* (Ann Arbor, MI: Pierian, 1979); Richard Hume Werking, "Evaluating Bibliographic Education: A Review and Critique," *Library Trends* 29 (1980):

153-172; James Rice, Jr., *Teaching Library Use: A Guide for Library Instruction* (Westport, CN: Greenwood, 1981), pp. 97-129; and Anne F. Roberts, *Library Instruction for Librarians* (Littleton, CO: Libraries Unlimited, 1982), pp. 84-89.

2. Some recent examples are Stuart Glogoff, "Using Statistical Tests to Evaluate Library Instruction Sessions," *Journal of Academic Librarianship* 4(1978):438-442; Larry Hardesty, Nicholas Lovrich, Jr., and James Mannon, "Evaluating Library-Use Instruction," *College and Research Libraries* 40(1979): 309-317; Julia F. Baldwin and Robert S. Rudolph, "The Comparative Effectiveness of a Slide/Tape show and a Library Tour," *College and Research Libraries* 40(1979):31-35; Larry Hardesty and John Wright, "Student Library Skills and Attitudes and Their Change: Relationships to Other Selected Variables," *Journal of Academic Librarianship* 8(1982):216-220; Penelope Pearson and Virginia Tiefel, "Evaluating Undergraduate Library Instruction at the Ohio State University." *Journal of Academic Librarianship* 7(1982):351-357; Timothy D. Jewell, "Student Reactions to a Self-Paced Library Skills Workbook Program: Survey Evidence," *College and Research Libraries* 43(1982): 371-378; and Gertrude N. Jacobson and Michael J. Albright, "Motivation Via Videotape: Key to Undergraduate Library Instruction in the Research Library," *Journal of Academic Librarianship* 9(1983): 270-275.

3. Patricia A. Berge and Judith Pryor, "Applying Educational Theory to Workbook Design," in Cerise Oberman and Kalina Strauch, ed., *Theories of Bibliographic Instruction: Design for Teaching* (New York: Bowker, 1982), p. 93.

4. *Ibid.*

5. For the original report of this study, see Shelley Phipps and Ruth Dickstein, "The Library Skills Program at the University of Arizona: Testing, Evaluation, and Critique," *Journal of Academic Librarianship* 5(1979):205-214.

6. Berge and Pryor, p. 94.

7. *Ibid.*

8. Maria R. Sugrañes and James A. Neal, "Evaluation of a Self-Paced Bibliographic Instruction Course," *College and Research Libraries* 44(1983):444-457.

9. *Ibid.*, p. 453.

10. One paper which discusses the reasons for cooperation between English teachers and librarians is James E. Ford, "The Natural Alliance between Librarians and English Teachers in Course-Related Library Use Instruction," *College and Research Libraries* 43(1982):379-384. This paper does not discuss the advantages of involving faculty in the *evaluation* of any specific bibliographic tool.

11. For an overview of the issues involved in teaching library skills to community college students, see John Lolley, "Instruction in Junior and Community Colleges," in Lubans, ed., *Educating the Library User,* pp. 57-69.

12. The chairperson of the English Department, Dr. Ann Dempsey, was an early and enthusiastic supporter.

13. In the Fall semester, 1983, the English Department included a short research paper in the Composition I curriculum. This decision was unrelated to our workbook project, but one result was to make the workbook even more appropriate for Composition I.

14. In particular, we wish to acknowledge Dr. Gerald Schaeffer, Associate Dean of Instruction at Florissant Valley, who helped us design the evaluation and interpret its data.

15. Werking, p. 157.

16. This problem is discussed in Jewell, pp. 376-377.

17. We discovered that we made a substantial error in having test questions on the back of the last page. Some students did not turn the page over and finish the test.

18. Dr. Linda Wickstra, Assistant Professor of Psychology at Florissant Valley greatly assisted us by running the *t* tests and analysis of variance on her department's microcomputer. She also helped us interpret the results of the tests and suggested areas where we could strengthen our evaluation process if we repeat it.

19. For a discussion of test validity and reliability, see Hardesty, Lovrich, and Mannon, pp. 311-312.

20. See Rice, p. 112, for an explanation of the use of numerical scales in attitude surveys.

21. A number of authors have emphasized the need to evaluate library instruction in terms of student products, such as term papers and bibliographies. See Thomas Kirk, "Bibliographic Instruction—A Review of Research," in Beeler, p. 3; and Werking, pp. 154-155.

22. Berge and Pryor, p. 94.